Prestwick House

Vocabulary, Reading, and Writing Exercises

SAT™

POWER PREP

SECOND EDITION

SUMMIT

Project Editor:
Daniel Reed

Production Editor:
Darlene Gilmore

Senior Editor:
Paul Moliken

Contributors:
Rachel Natbony
Lisa Tetrault
Leah Rodriguez
Sydney Palmer
Allison Billmire
Alana Domingo

Cover Design:
Chris Koniencki

ISBN: 978-1-62019-370-9

Prestwick House

Vocabulary, Reading, and Writing Exercises

SAT™
POWER PREP
SECOND EDITION

OVERVIEW:

2 Full-length **SAT** Reading and Writing and Language
practice tests with vocabulary instruction

2 Units divided into 20 lessons

54 Contextual vocabulary exercises based on
vocabulary used in the **SAT**-style practice passages

18 Grammar for writing exercises to prepare
for the **SAT** writing test

Writing prompts and scoring guides for
SAT essay practice

Table of Contents

Reading Test

Each passage or pair of passages, some of which are accompanied by graphics such as maps, charts, or graphs, is followed by a set of questions. Read the passage and then choose the best answer to each of the questions.

SUMMIT

UNIT ONE

Lesson 1

Questions 1–11 are based on the following passage.

This passage is adapted from Edgar Allan Poe's short story "The Imp of the Perverse," published 1845.

In the consideration of the **faculties** and **impulses**—of the *prima mobilia* of the human soul, the phrenologists have failed to make room for a **propensity** which, although obviously existing as a radical, primitive,
5 irreducible **sentiment**, has been equally overlooked by all the moralists who have preceded them. In the pure arrogance of the reason, we have all overlooked it. We have suffered its existence to escape our senses solely through want of belief—of faith;—whether it
10 be faith in Revelation, or faith in the Kabbalah. The idea of it has never occurred to us, simply because of its supererogation. We saw no need of impulse—for the propensity. We could not perceive its necessity. We could not understand, that is to say, we could not
15 have understood, had the notion of this *primum mobile* ever **obtruded** itself;—we could not have understood in what manner it might be made to further the objects of humanity, either temporal or eternal. It cannot be denied that phrenology and, in great measure, all
20 metaphysicianism have been **concocted** from theory. The intellectual or logical man, rather than the understanding or observant man, set himself to imagine designs—to dictate purposes to God. Having thus **fathomed**, to his satisfaction, the intentions of Jehovah, out of these
25 intentions he built his innumerable systems of mind.
Real evidence would have brought science to admit, as an **innate** and primitive principle of human action, a **paradoxical** something, which we may call perverseness, for want of a more characteristic term. In
30 the sense I intend, it is, in fact, a mobile without motive. Through its promptings we act without comprehensible object; or, if this shall be understood as a contradiction in terms, we may so far modify the proposition as to say, that through its promptings, we act, for the reason

35 that we should not. In theory, no reason can be more unreasonable; but, in fact, there is none more strong. With certain minds, under certain conditions it becomes absolutely irresistible. I am not more certain that I breathe, than that the assurance of the wrong or error of
40 any action is often the one unconquerable force which **impels** us, and alone impels us to its prosecution. Nor will this overwhelming tendency to do wrong for the wrong's sake, admit of analysis, or resolution into ulterior elements. It is radical, a primitive impulse—
45 elementary. It will be said, I am aware, that when we persist in acts because we feel we should not persist in them, our conduct is but a modification of that which ordinarily springs from a tendency to defend or resist. But a glance will show the fallacy of this idea.
50 Combativeness has, for its essence, the necessity of self-defense. It is our safeguard against injury. Its principle regards our well-being; and thus the desire to be well is excited simultaneously with its development. It follows, that the desire to be well must be excited simultaneously
55 with any principle which shall be merely a modification of combativeness, but in the case of that something which I term perverseness, the desire to be well is aroused, but a strongly **antagonistic** sentiment prevails.
An appeal to one's own heart is, after all, the best
60 reply to the **sophistry** just noticed. No one who trustingly consults and thoroughly questions his own soul, will be disposed to deny the entire radicalness of the propensity in question. It is not more incomprehensible than distinctive. There lives no
65 man who at some period has not been tormented, for example, by an earnest desire to tantalize a listener by **circumlocution**. The speaker is aware that he displeases, he has every intention to please; he is usually **curt**, precise, and clear; the most **laconic** and luminous
70 language is struggling for utterance upon his tongue; it is only with difficulty that he restrains himself from giving it flow; he dreads and **deprecates** the anger of him whom he addresses; yet, the thought strikes him, that by certain involutions and parentheses this anger may be
75 **engendered**. That single thought is enough. The impulse increases to a wish, the wish to a desire, the desire to an

Lesson 1 continued:

uncontrollable longing, and the longing (to the deep regret and **mortification** of the speaker, and in defiance of all consequences) is indulged.

80 　We stand upon the brink of a **precipice**. We peer into the abyss—we grow sick and dizzy. Our first impulse is to shrink from the danger. Unaccountably we remain. By slow degrees our sickness and dizziness and horror become merged in a cloud of unnamable feeling. By

85 **gradations**, still more imperceptible, this cloud assumes shape, as did the vapor from the bottle out of which arose the genie in the Arabian Nights. But out of this our cloud upon the precipice's edge, there grows into palpability, a shape, far more terrible than any genius or

90 any demon of a tale, and yet it is but a thought, although a fearful one, and one which chills the very marrow of our bones with the fierceness of the delight of its horror. It is merely the idea of what would be our sensations during the sweeping precipitancy of a fall from such

95 a height. And this fall—this rushing annihilation—for the very reason that it involves that one most ghastly and loathsome of all the most ghastly and loathsome images of death and suffering which have ever presented themselves to our imagination—for this very cause do

100 we now the most vividly desire it. And because our reason violently deters us from the brink, therefore do we the most **impetuously** approach it. There is no passion in nature so demoniacally impatient as that of him who, shuddering upon the edge of a precipice, thus

105 **meditates** a plunge. To indulge, for a moment, in any attempt at thought, is to be inevitably lost; for reflection but urges us to forbear, and therefore it is, I say, that we cannot. If there be no friendly arm to check us, or if we fail in a sudden effort to **prostrate** ourselves backward

110 from the abyss, we plunge, and are destroyed.

　Examine these and similar actions as we will, we shall find them resulting solely from the spirit of the Perverse. We perpetrate them merely because we feel that we should not. Beyond or behind this there is no

115 intelligible principle; and we might, indeed, deem this perverseness a direct instigation of the arch-fiend, were it not occasionally known to operate in furtherance of good.

　I have said thus much, that in some measure I may

120 answer your question—that I may explain to you why I am here—that I may assign to you something that shall have at least the faint aspect of a cause for my wearing these fetters, and for my tenanting this cell of the condemned. Had I not been thus prolix, you might either

125 have misunderstood me altogether, or, with the rabble, have fancied me mad. As it is, you will easily perceive that I am one of the many uncounted victims of the Imp of the Perverse.

　It is impossible that any deed could have been

130 wrought with a more thorough deliberation. For weeks, for months, I pondered upon the means of the murder. I rejected a thousand schemes, because their accomplishment involved a chance of detection. At length, in reading some French memoirs, I found an

135 account of a nearly fatal illness that occurred to Madame Pilau, through the agency of a candle accidentally poisoned. The idea struck my fancy at once. I knew my victim's habit of reading in bed. I knew, too, that his apartment was narrow and ill-ventilated. But I need not

140 vex you with impertinent details. I need not describe the easy artifices by which I substituted, in his bed-room candle stand, a wax-light of my own making for the one which I there found. The next morning he was discovered dead in his bed, and the coroner's verdict was—'Death

145 by the visitation of God.'

　Having inherited his estate, all went well with me for years. The idea of detection never once entered my brain. Of the remains of the fatal taper I had myself carefully disposed. I had left no shadow of a clue by

150 which it would be possible to convict, or even suspect, me of the crime. It is inconceivable how rich a sentiment of satisfaction arose in my bosom as I reflected upon my absolute security. For a very long period of time I was accustomed to revel in this sentiment. It afforded me

155 more real delight than all the mere worldly advantages accruing from my sin. But there arrived at length an epoch, from which the pleasurable feeling grew, by scarcely perceptible gradations, into a haunting and harassing thought. It harassed me because it haunted.

160 I could scarcely get rid of it for an instant. It is quite a common thing to be thus annoyed with the ringing in our ears, or rather in our memories, of the burthen of some ordinary song, or some unimpressive snatches from an opera. Nor will we be the less tormented if the

165 song in itself be good, or the opera air meritorious. In this manner, at last, I would perpetually catch myself pondering upon my security, and repeating, in a low under-tone, the phrase, 'I am safe.'

　One day, whilst sauntering along the streets, I arrested

170 myself in the act of murmuring, half aloud, these customary syllables. In a fit of **petulance** I remodeled them thus: "I am safe—I am safe—yes—if I be not fool

Lesson 1 continued:

enough to make open confession."

No sooner had I spoken these words, than I felt an
175 icy chill creep to my heart. I had had some experience
in these fits of perversity (whose nature I have been at
some trouble to explain), and I remembered well that in
no instance I had successfully resisted their attacks. And
now my own casual self-suggestion, that I might possibly
180 be fool enough to confess the murder of which I had been
guilty, confronted me, as if the very ghost of him whom I
had murdered—and beckoned me on to death.

At first, I made an effort to shake off this nightmare
of the soul. I walked vigorously—faster—still faster—at
185 length I ran. I felt a maddening desire to shriek aloud.
Every succeeding wave of thought overwhelmed me with
new terror, for, alas! I well, too well, understood that to
think, in my situation, was to be lost. I still quickened
my pace. I bounded like a madman through the crowded
190 **thoroughfares**. At length, the populace took the alarm
and pursued me. I felt then the **consummation** of my fate.
Could I have torn out my tongue, I would have done it—
but a rough voice resounded in my ears—a rougher grasp
seized me by the shoulder. I turned—I gasped for breath.
195 For a moment I experienced all the pangs of suffocation;
I became blind, and deaf, and giddy; and then some
invisible fiend, I thought, struck me with his broad palm
upon the back. The long-imprisoned secret burst forth
from my soul.

200 They say that I spoke with a distinct enunciation, but
with marked emphasis and passionate hurry, as if in dread
of interruption before concluding the brief but pregnant
sentences that assigned me to the hangman and to hell.

Having related all that was necessary for the fullest
205 judicial conviction, I fell prostrate in a **swoon**.

But why shall I say more? Today I wear these chains,
and am here! Tomorrow I shall be fetterless!—but where?

1

As it is used in line 2, the phrase *prima mobilia* most
nearly means
A) existence.
B) rights.
C) motives.
D) errors.

2

The specific human tendency, or propensity, at the
central focus of the passage is best described as
A) lying frequently.
B) living in the past.
C) inventing illnesses.
D) perverse behavior.

3

Choose the lines from the passage that provide the best
evidence for your answer to the previous question.
A) lines 2-3 ("phrenologists have...propensity")
B) lines 6-8 ("In the...it")
C) lines 13-16 ("We could...itself")
D) lines 26-30 ("Real evidence...motive")

4

According to the author, the type of people who claim
to understand the workings of the human mind are
people who
A) ignore reality.
B) see more than others do.
C) understand better.
D) are unintelligent.

Lesson 1 continued:

5

Choose the term the author uses to describe the human tendency to do "wrong for the wrong's sake."
A) proposition
B) perverseness
C) revelation
D) phrenology

6

The impulsive tendency, the author reasons, cannot be a function of self-defense because
A) it occurs only in dangerous situations.
B) human reason controls physical response.
C) criminals usually exhibit the tendency.
D) it sometimes undermines personal safety.

7

As it is used in line 67, the word *circumlocution* most nearly means
A) speaking in a reluctant tone.
B) skill in efficient conversation in discussions about art, science, or history.
C) intentionally dragging out a story by being vague.
D) accidentally giving away secrets or divulging personal information.

8

The main purpose of paragraph 4 (lines 80-110) is to
A) provide an example situation in which perverseness manifests.
B) refute the scientific theories about the cause of human impulsiveness.
C) relate perverseness to a personal anecdote of the narrator.
D) explain the fragile psychology of the human mind.

9

The narrator claims that he is
A) without a conscience.
B) a master of self-discipline.
C) guided by his faith.
D) no match against impulsive behavior.

10

Choose the lines from the passage that provide the best evidence for your answer to the previous question.
A) lines 174-175 ("No sooner…heart")
B) lines 177-178 ("I remembered…attacks")
C) lines 183-184 ("At first…soul")
D) lines 186-188 ("Every succeeding…lost")

11

Of the following choices, the overall passage is best described as
A) the confession of a murderer.
B) an argument against the legal system.
C) a scientific report.
D) a personal narrative.

Lesson 1 continued:

Vocabulary: Context Answers

The following sentences contain vocabulary words used in the reading passage. Choose the answer that best completes the sentence. There may be more than one technically correct answer, but one will better exemplify the italicized vocabulary word than the others will.

1) One of the *faculties* that some people lose in old age is their _____.
   A. savings
   B. relationships
   C. memory
   D. license
   E. coworkers

2) Sophia considered her *innate* desire to help others to be a[n] _____ of her identity.
   A. indicator
   B. essential part
   C. false representation
   D. unnecessary piece
   E. criticism

3) Winifred had no tolerance for David's *sophistry*, so she pointed out his _____ to everyone in attendance at the debate.
   A. miscalculation
   B. ignorance
   C. excellent argument
   D. deceptive reasoning
   E. poor manners

4) Rachel was not offended by Ethan's _____ answer; he was often unintentionally *curt*.
   A. short and impolite
   B. soft and sweet
   C. loud and angry
   D. offensive and thoughtless
   E. quick and excited

5) Microblogging platforms like Twitter require *laconic* writing because each tweet must be _____.
   A. interesting
   B. brief
   C. multifaceted
   D. beautiful
   E. accessible

6) Every time her older brother *deprecates* her, Sally feels _____.
   A. better
   B. upset
   C. belittled
   D. pleased
   E. excited

7) *Gradations* of dress colors at the school dance _____.
   A. changed throughout the night
   B. meant that most wore the same color palette
   C. meant that everyone wore either red or purple
   D. required everyone to wear white
   E. progressed from deep red to lavender

8) Making *impetuous* decisions will not be good for the business; instead, _____.
   A. consider each option carefully
   B. act on impulse
   C. consult with no one
   D. be willing to change
   E. arrive at a solution quickly

Lesson 1 continued:

9) Attempts to compromise brought out Sandy's *petulance*; she was _____.
   A. pleased when everyone agreed
   B. nervous when the compromise took too long
   C. accepting of change
   D. upset when she did not get what she wanted
   E. glad to facilitate the discussion

10) A[n] _____ proved to be the *consummation* of Albert's string of crimes.
   A. arrest
   B. trial
   C. guilty verdict
   D. interrogation
   E. arraignment

11) To Allison's *mortification*, her family shouted her name as she walked out onto the basketball court, _____ her.
   A. pleasing
   B. embarrassing
   C. upsetting
   D. cheering for
   E. relieving

12) What seemed most ridiculous to Aaliyah was the _____ her friends had *concocted*.
   A. idea
   B. window
   C. photograph
   D. outfit
   E. plan

Lesson 1 continued:

Writing Practice

The underlined portion of each sentence possibly contains a flaw related to pronoun use. Select the answer that best corrects the flaw. Select NO CHANGE if the underlined portion is correct.

1) The host asked each of the party guests <u>to bring their</u> dish to the potluck dinner.
   A. NO CHANGE
   B. to bring his or her
   C. to bring one's
   D. to brings their

2) I'm not sure; is it both your brothers or just your brother Ken who <u>has skipped</u> a grade?
   A. NO CHANGE
   B. have skipped
   C. had skipped
   D. are skipping

3) That evening, some of the chickens <u>was eaten</u> by a fox.
   A. NO CHANGE
   B. was ate
   C. have been eaten
   D. were eaten

4) Every cat will meow until <u>their</u> owner remembers to feed it.
   A. NO CHANGE
   B. his
   C. her
   D. its

5) The movie's cast members <u>were rehearsing their lines.</u>
   A. NO CHANGE
   B. was rehearsing their lines
   C. were rehearsing our lines
   D. was rehearsing its lines

6) The laundry detergent restored the grass-stained pants to <u>its</u> original condition.
   A. NO CHANGE
   B. their
   C. it's
   D. the

7) <u>If there are any discrepancies in the paycheck, please make sure to report it to the payroll manager.</u>
   A. NO CHANGE
   B. If there are any discrepancy in the paycheck, please make sure to report it to the payroll manager.
   C. If there are any discrepancies in the paycheck, please make sure to report them to the payroll manager.
   D. If there is any discrepancies in the paycheck, please make sure to report it to the payroll manager.

Lesson 1 continued:

8) The star swimmer always wins because <u>they have</u> no hesitation when the gun signals the start of the race.
   A. NO CHANGE
   B. he or she have
   C. they has
   D. she has

9) I read a book about the Mafia called *The Valachi Papers* <u>that reveal a series of amazing secrets</u> about the mob.
   A. NO CHANGE
   B. *Papers* that reveals a series of amazing secrets
   C. *Papers* that reveal amazing secrets
   D. *Papers*, that reveals a series of amazing secrets

10) Neither Mrs. Herman, the manager, nor the employees want to give up <u>his or her</u> break to attend the company seminar.
    A. NO CHANGE
    B. her
    C. their
    D. one's

Lesson 1 continued:

Vocabulary: Choosing the Right Use

The following sentences contain vocabulary words used in the reading passage. Identify the sentence or sentences that use the italicized vocabulary word properly. We have changed the form of some vocabulary words to provide new contexts; for example, some adjectives and verbs have been used as nouns.

1) A. "Explain to me the *faculty* of having a carpeted ceiling; the idea just sounds useless," said Dan.
    B. My mother has the unexplainable *faculty* of being able to find anything that is missing in my bedroom.
    C. Contestants on the game show had to defend their inventions, discussing the many *faculties* of using each one.
    D. The sociopath exhibits none of the emotional *faculties* that well-adjusted people employ daily, such as caring, closeness, empathy, or compassion.

2) A. As the roller coaster picked up speed, Danica felt the *impulse* of the car as it bumped over the tracks.
    B. The most agonizing aspect of maintaining a diet is resisting the *impulse* to have a piece of chocolate here and there.
    C. Seeing her favorite brand of shoe in the store window, Ms. Shuster was overcome with the *impulse* to immediately purchase a pair.
    D. Alec failed to notice the teacher's negative comments on his essay; needless to say, the *impulse* took him by surprise.

3) A. It is polite not to talk with your friends during a movie, as the chatter might *obtrude* upon the enjoyment of others.
    B. The knights drew their swords and readied their bows and arrows to do battle against the army that was *obtruding* the castle.
    C. The tall new apartment building on Main Street *obtruded* on the citizens' view of the annual fireworks display.
    D. Jerome enlisted security guards to stand outside of his dressing room to make sure that no wild fans could *obtrude* his private space.

4) A. Frankenstein *concocted* a plan to create a new being and bring it to life using the power of lightning.
    B. I could barely believe the itinerary that Mom had *concocted* for Thanksgiving; she expected us to attend four different dinners.
    C. Mr. Gendler quickly *concocted* Amar's suggestion to have class outside, claiming that students would become too easily distracted.
    D. Despite the fact that the congressman had already *concocted* Diana's proposal, she continued to petition for it all over the state.

Lesson 1 continued:

5) A. Doris and Dean *fathomed* their three children into the living room and announced, "We're having another baby!"
   B. A lover of bread, Bethany could not *fathom* what it would be like to have to maintain a gluten-free diet.
   C. Every year, Marvel and DC Comics enthusiasts *fathom* for an event called Comic-Con.
   D. "Kids in high school do not *fathom* just how much fun college is," boasted Maria.

6) A. The "bystander effect" occurs when a person is not *impelled* to intervene in a conflict between two strangers because he or she assumes that someone else will help.
   B. The grumpy old man installed tall electric fences to *impel* the neighborhood kids from trespassing on his property.
   C. "Is it the causes that *impel* you to attend all these charitable fundraisers, or are you just coming for the food?" asked Lorinda.
   D. Soup kitchens do not *impel* homelessness, but they do at least provide an important resource for people in need.

7) A. Fans eagerly awaited the third installment of the book series, as the second novel had had quite an *antagonistic* ending.
   B. Loki the Bearded Dragon, whose favorite activity was eating, seemed to think that being fed crickets was the most *antagonistic* event of the week.
   C. Rory's *antagonistic* roommate purposely left dirty dishes in the sink just to infuriate her.
   D. Whenever Hanna's brother acted *antagonistically* toward her, she usually ended up running to her parents, sobbing.

8) A. The explorer raced through the underground tunnel, hoping to find the luxurious *sentiment* before the falling boulders blocked his path, or worse—crushed him.
   B. As Mindy professed her undying love for Reggie, he realized that he did not hold the same *sentiment* for her.
   C. Legend tells of a hidden *sentiment* buried deep underneath the Roman ruins—a statue made entirely of gold and silver.
   D. Everyone in the courtroom seemed to experience a similar *sentiment*: They felt sympathetic toward the defendant, who seemed to have been framed.

9) A. The *curt* distance between my house and Brenda's allowed us to spend time together almost every day.
   B. "I can't tell if Aimee is sending *curt* messages on purpose, or if she is just really busy," complained Adam.
   C. Billy's *curt* responses to my questions about the scandal indicated just how angry he felt about what had happened.
   D. Even relatively tall people appeared *curt* when standing next to Leonardo, who was almost seven feet.

Lesson 1 continued:

10) A. Perched on a *precipice*, Dylan could see the entirety of another mountain far in the distance.
   B. "Be careful on this particular hike; halfway through, there is a *precipice* without any rails," warned Alberto.
   C. Instead of waiting to be caught, Sabrina took responsibility for her *precipice* and confessed to pulling the fire alarm.
   D. Principal Grudzina soon announced the *precipice* of the student council election: Jason had won by a mere three votes.

11) A. Christopher's mother was furious that her son had so *impetuously* decided to go skydiving that day.
   B. The antique collector could hardly believe how *impetuous* the Egyptian artifact remained in spite of its years buried underground.
   C. Despite the disastrous tornado, most of the Fergusons' farmhouse remained *impetuous*.
   D. Jennie regretted her *impetuous* agreement to repaint the house; she should have considered the summer heat and humidity.

12) A. George often *deprecates* people who are not vegetarian, forgetting that he used to eat meat, too.
   B. As fewer people demanded electric toothbrushes, product prices began to *deprecate*.
   C. After he failed the third chemistry test in a row, Hunter could not help but *deprecate* himself.
   D. Malia feared that increasing the number of required hours of volunteering would *deprecate* the turnout.

Lesson 1 continued:

Synonyms and Antonyms

Match the word with its *antonym*.

1) impel   **A.** dissuade

2) antagonistic   **B.** civil

3) curt   **C.** cautious

4) deprecate   **D.** friendly

5) impetuous   **E.** commend

Match the word with its *synonym*.

6) sentiment   **F.** interrupt

7) impulse   **G.** understand

8) faculty   **H.** compulsion

9) fathom   **I.** cliff

10) concoct   **J.** feeling

11) obtrude   **K.** ability

12) precipice   **L.** devise

END of LESSON 1

Lesson 2

Questions 12–21 are based on the following passage.

This passage discusses the history and potential application of tiny carbon structures called nanotubes.

Carbon, atomic number 6, has plenty of reason to bond with other elements, owing to its high **valence** of four available **electrons**. Covalent bonds between atoms occur when atoms share one or more valence electrons.
5 A carbon atom, having four valence electrons, can bond with four other atoms as long as each has at least one electron to share. In addition, carbon's small **nuclear** radius makes it all the more attractive compared to tetravalent elements that have larger radii, such as silicon,
10 atomic number 14. Put in **practical** terms, the structure formed by two carbons bonded together will be stronger than that of two silicon atoms bonded together.

As a tetravalent element with so many available electrons, carbon has the most potential for bonding to
15 itself, inherently increasing its likelihood of forming long chains and other complex, well-connected structures. This catenation of carbon atoms, depending on the environment in which it occurs, can result in substances as physically diverse as graphite, coal,
20 or diamonds, all of which are pure carbon, but have different atomic arrangements. The practical values of graphite, coal, and diamonds are well known for their physical properties, but there is a more recently discovered allotrope of carbon that might have the
25 potential to revolutionize certain fundamentals of civilization even more than coal power or diamond-tipped saws have. The new arrangement is called the carbon **nanotube**, and it is a frontrunner to overtake concrete and steel as the building material of the future.
30 Few people think of cinder blocks or steel beams when they consider space stations, after all.

In 1985, scientists at Rice University vaporized graphite with a laser and discovered an allotrope of carbon that had been observed in the past but never
35 fully explored: groups of carbon atoms arranged into sphere-like structures. Named buckminsterfullerenes, after American architect Buckminster Fuller, a famous **advocate** of the **geodesic** dome, each fullerene, or "buckyball," **comprised** sixty carbon atoms bonded
40 together in a shape resembling a soccer ball with 12 pentagonal faces, 20 hexagonal **lattices**, and a carbon atom at each corner, where the seams meet on a soccer ball. The buckyball is the most common fullerene found in nature, but it is not the only one; notably,
45 some fullerenes form a cylindrical arrangement called a nanotube.

Carbon nanotubes (CNTs) are structurally perfect, single-wall, hollow carbon molecules connected in a hexagonal formation to form a cylinder. They are
50 typically between 0.7 to 2.0 nanometers in diameter—approximately 100,000 times thinner than a strand of human hair—and hundreds of times their diameters in length. In spite of their size, CNTs have colossal properties. An individual tube possesses a thermal
55 conductivity higher than that of a diamond, demonstrates mechanical strength superior to that of steel, and, in certain forms, has the potential to be more than 1,000 times more conductive than copper. In terms of **tensile** strength, which measures how much linear force must
60 be applied to stretch an object before it fails, nanotubes are the strongest material in history. Depending on how the nanotubes are manufactured and arranged, they have been tested as having upwards of 30 times the tensile strength of steel (see Figure 1).
65 There are countless real-world applications for carbon nanotubes. Because CNTs are both extremely strong and lightweight, they were immediately used to enhance existing materials. Nanotubes within carbon fiber **composite** establish networks within the material
70 that increase its ability to bear the load of the weight and strain placed upon it. Manufacturers have begun to incorporate CNTs in mountain bike handlebars, tennis racquets, and lightweight bicycle frames. "Buckytubes" improve the stiffness, stability, **resiliency**, repulsion
75 power, and vibration control of tennis and badminton racquets and golf club shafts. They lower the weight, as well as the spin, of golf clubs, and they minimize the chance of **abrasion** and make paddling easier in kayaking. **Infusing** nanotubes into ultra lightweight boat
80 hulls have effectively doubled and tripled the fuel range of experimental watercraft, yet without decreasing strength.

The atomic structure and subsequent chemical properties of nanotubes render them excellent filtering
85 agents that could be used to desalinate seawater or remove pollutants from water or air through the use of CNT sponges. In addition to their **conductivity**, CNTs exhibit, in their many forms, many peculiar and useful

electrical properties that will result in their inclusion in
90 **transistors**, circuitry, solar panels, super**capacitors**, and
super-efficient, fast-charging, long-life batteries, some of
which may be created on a printer and measure less than
1 millimeter thick.

CNTs have plenty of microscopic applications, but
95 they are most impressive in their large-scale, world-
changing possibilities. The most ambitious proposal to
date is to use carbon nanotubes to create space elevators.
A space elevator would theoretically comprise a tether
made of carbon nanotube bundles that extends from
100 Earth's surface to a station—perhaps a massive solar-
energy array capable of producing enough energy to
power a whole country—in **geostationary** orbit, as well
as miles of additional tether to hold a counterweight to
offset the hundreds of tons of cable between Earth and
105 the station. Climbers, powered by lasers or otherwise
wireless energy, would ascend and descend the cable
with supplies or deliveries such as satellites to be
launched. Once established, such an elevator would
eliminate the need to burn millions of pounds of fuel for
110 each trip into space. A CNT bridge would have further
value as an energy **conduit** for the **hypothetical** solar
array, if the conductive potential of CNTs is exploited.
The future is bright, but don't shop for space-ride tickets
quite yet: there are a few obstacles to overcome.

115 Presently, the manufacture of single-walled, untangled
nanotubes is extremely specialized, labor intensive, and,
therefore, rare and expensive. Forming a tube that is
one-atom wide is as exacting and difficult as it sounds,
though it is less a matter of making the tube as it is the
120 matter of untangling the tube and stringing the pieces
together. Manufactured nanotubes typically emerge in a
tangled heap of CNTs, some long, some short, but miles
in cumulative length—and all contained in the volume
of a single tablespoon. The longest nanotube on record,
125 created in 2013 by Chinese researchers, measured a
half-meter in length. It is progress, of course, but just to
be used for a bridge cable, for example, a CNT would
need to be a kilometer long. In terms of space bridges,
CNTs will need to be thousands of kilometers long. With
130 time, demand, and **copious** investments, the production
process of nanotubes will improve. Glass, concrete, steel,
and aluminum were once rare and expensive materials,
too, and they went on to become **ubiquitous** and change
civilization. Think of a world without bottles, windows,
135 buildings, or highways. Invest in nanotubes; they're
going to be around for a while.

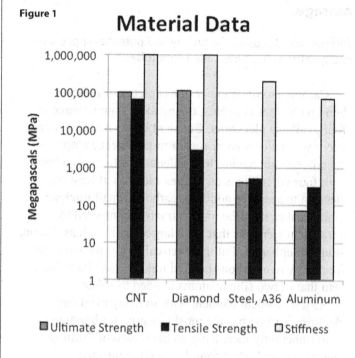

Figure 1

Material Data

Megapascals (MPa)

Ultimate Strength   Tensile Strength   Stiffness

12

According to paragraph 1, an element that has at least
one valence electron available has the potential to

A) lose its electron to another atom, gaining a positive
charge in the process.

B) split into four separate atoms and then combine
with itself.

C) self-combust, if it combines with the right element.

D) bond covalently with another atom that has an
available electron.

13

As it is used in line 17, *catenation* most nearly means

A) self-combining.

B) elimination.

C) resistance.

D) linear shape.

Lesson 2 continued:

14

Choose the lines that provide the best evidence for your answer to the previous question.
A) lines 5-7 ("A carbon...share")
B) lines 10-12 ("Put in...together")
C) lines 14-15 ("carbon has...itself")
D) lines 21-23 ("The practical...properties")

15

The author's tone, when discussing the subject matter of the passage, is best described as
A) indifferent and clinical.
B) guarded optimism.
C) hyperbolic expectations.
D) confident of progress.

16

Which two major properties of CNTs make them a theoretical possibility for use as part of an orbiting solar power array?
A) covalence and strength
B) length and geodesic design
C) tensile strength and conductivity
D) diameter and catenation

17

The passage does *not* include details about which category of CNT application?
A) medical technology
B) electrical systems
C) structural use
D) chemical agents

18

The author of the passage would probably agree with which one of the following statements?
A) CNTs will likely take the place of glass for the manufacture of containers.
B) Presently, CNTs are not worth the labor and money for research.
C) Though CNTs are impressive, they are not likely to replace cement.
D) CNTs will become a common resource in future societies.

19

Choose the lines that provide the best evidence for your answer to the previous question.
A) lines 121-123 ("Manufactured nanotubes...length")
B) lines 124-125 ("The longest...researchers")
C) lines 131-134 ("Glass, concrete...civilization")
D) lines 134-135 ("Think of...highways")

20

The chart provides data about two unrelated materials, but also includes data about
A) the tensile strength of copper.
B) conductivity differences between metals.
C) two allotropes of carbon.
D) buckminsterfullerenes under pressure.

21

According to the chart, the stiffness of carbon nanotubes is rated at
A) about 100,000 MPa more than that of aluminum.
B) more than double that of steel, but no higher than that of diamond.
C) slightly less than that of diamond.
D) 90,000 MPa more than that of steel.

Lesson 2 continued:

Vocabulary: Context Answers

The following sentences contain vocabulary words used in the reading passage. Choose the answer that best completes the sentence. There may be more than one technically correct answer, but one will better exemplify the italicized vocabulary word than the others will.

1) The *practical* white sneakers were not George's favorite, but he knew they would be the _____ running shoes.
   A. most popular
   B. most impressive
   C. least expensive
   D. most useful
   E. longest-lasting

2) Theresa did not expect the material to break when she _____ it; she thought it would have had greater *tensile* strength.
   A. stretched
   B. threw
   C. dropped
   D. wore
   E. washed

3) The mineral *composite* contained _____ substances.
   A. identical
   B. similar
   C. multiple
   D. small
   E. conductive

4) *Infusing* the cake with green food dye caused the dessert to _____.
   A. be speckled with green
   B. turn green throughout
   C. become completely colorless
   D. become half green-colored
   E. be green on the outside

5) Camping for long periods of time requires *resiliency* in order to _____.
   A. cook food quickly
   B. continue sleeping outside
   C. start a fire with wet wood
   D. put up a tent and take it down
   E. withstand harsh conditions

6) I realized that I had to be my own *advocate* when _____.
   A. I felt I deserved a raise at work
   B. no one was available to help me move
   C. my friends and I joined an exercise class
   D. I was trying to get on a crowded subway train
   E. it was time to study for final exams

7) Richard's *hypothetical* solution required _____.
   A. supplies that were unavailable
   B. multiple vaccinations
   C. testing to prove it would work
   D. large amounts of water
   E. a thousand solar panels

Lesson 2 continued:

8) The *copious* amount of paperwork required for the grant application was so _____.
   A. detailed that the organization had to search their archives
   B. general that the newest employee could complete it
   C. minimal that it was quickly done
   D. unnecessary that the group refused to complete it
   E. large that the work had to be divided

9) Police officers have been *ubiquitous* on the scenic highway since the speed limit was decreased; the police are _____, ready to write speeding tickets.
   A. waiting
   B. everywhere
   C. uniformed
   D. quick
   E. hidden

10) If the *abrasion* is not too severe, _____.
   A. your research paper will cover the subject completely
   B. I will make sure the presents arrive on time
   C. the two substances will not stick together
   D. there probably won't be any permanent damage
   E. the electric company can run on back-up power

Lesson 2 continued:

LANGUAGE
MODIFIER PLACEMENT 1

Writing Practice

Each of the following sentences contains a modifying phrase that may or may not be clear or correct. Choose the answer that best corrects the sentence while retaining the intended meaning of the original sentence. Select NO CHANGE if the provided sentence is correct.

1) Undaunted, the rough seas did not prevent the crew from sailing as planned.
   A. NO CHANGE
   B. The rough seas did not prevent the crew from sailing as planned, undaunted.
   C. The undaunted rough seas did not prevent the crew from sailing as planned.
   D. The rough seas did not prevent the undaunted crew from sailing as planned.

2) By pressing a button on the side, water is slowly squirted onto the coffee, producing the proper mix at the proper temperature.
   A. NO CHANGE
   B. By pressing a button on the side, you slowly squirt water onto the coffee, which produces the proper mix at the proper temperature.
   C. By pressing a button on the side, the coffee gets water slowly squirted onto it, producing the proper mix at the proper temperature.
   D. Producing the proper mix at the proper temperature, water is slowly squirted onto the coffee by pressing a button on the side.

3) Winning the election, donors needed millions of dollars.
   A. NO CHANGE
   B. To win the election, millions of donor dollars were needed.
   C. Winning the election required millions of dollars in donations.
   D. Millions of dollars were needed from donors who won the election.

4) After moving to the desert, Mark's breathing became much easier.
   A. NO CHANGE
   B. After moving to the desert, Mark found that his breathing became much easier.
   C. Mark's breathing became much easier after moving to the desert.
   D. After Mark's breathing became much easier, he moved to the desert.

5) Walking through the kitchen, the ice cream in the freezer tempted Jamie, who was on a diet.
   A. NO CHANGE
   B. The ice cream in the freezer tempted Jamie, who was on a diet while walking through the kitchen.
   C. While walking through the kitchen on a diet, Jamie was tempted by the ice cream in the freezer.
   D. While walking through the kitchen, Jamie, who was on a diet, was tempted by the ice cream in the freezer.

6) Doubling the time necessary to complete the project allowed for fewer errors.
   A. NO CHANGE
   B. Doubling the time necessary to complete the project, it allowed for fewer errors.
   C. Doubling the necessary time to complete the project created fewer errors.
   D. Doubling the time to complete the project allowed for fewer necessary errors.

Lesson 2 continued:

7) Completing the interviews, the crew members turned the lights and cameras off, and the participants shook hands.
   A. NO CHANGE
   B. The interviews were complete, the participants shook hands, and the crew turned the lights and cameras off.
   C. Once they had completed the interviews, the crew members turned lights and cameras off, and the participants shook hands.
   D. The lights and cameras went off after completing the interviews, and the participants shook hands.

8) To define some English words, a knowledge of Latin roots is necessary.
   A. NO CHANGE
   B. Defining some English words requires a knowledge of Latin roots that is necessary.
   C. A knowledge of Latin roots is necessary in order to define some English words.
   D. For people to define some English words, there is a need to know that Latin roots are necessary.

9) While studying my biology notes, the ecosystem of the jungle began to make sense.
   A. NO CHANGE
   B. While studying my biology notes, the jungle ecosystem began to make sense.
   C. While I studied my biology notes, the ecosystem of the jungle began to make sense.
   D. The ecosystem of the jungle began to make sense while studying my biology notes.

10) Being in a good mood, the movie turned out to be amazing when I saw it.
   A. NO CHANGE
   B. I was in a good mood, and the movie I saw turned out to be amazing.
   C. The movie turned out to be amazing when I saw it in a good mood.
   D. When I saw the amazing movie, it was because I was in a good mood.

Lesson 2 continued:

Vocabulary: Choosing the Right Use

The following sentences contain vocabulary words used in the reading passage. Identify the sentence or sentences that use the italicized vocabulary word properly. We have changed the form of some vocabulary words to provide new contexts; for example, some adjectives and verbs have been used as nouns.

1) A. Reviewing his notes every day leading up to the final exam would be a *practical* way for Laurence to prepare.
   B. Though purchasing the sturdier table would have been more *practical*, I chose the one that had an interesting pattern and color scheme.
   C. As the *practical* leader of the research team, Monica had to answer only to Mr. Lin, the actual head of the project.
   D. The primary goal of the conference was to assemble scientific minds from all over the nation, but the *practical* goal involved collecting important contact information.

2) A. Because she was a *geodesic* researcher, Ashley stopped to examine almost every boulder on our hike.
   B. Upon closer examination, Fred noticed that the exterior of the spherical *geodesic* dome was actually made up of triangles.
   C. The *geodesic* toy, shaped like a ball, could both expand and contract, depending on how it was handled.
   D. The cavern, rumored to be a *geodesic* treasure, was filled to capacity with geologists hoping to discover something fantastic.

3) A. The UN ambassadors opened up a *conduit* through which they could exchange information.
   B. One *conduit* after the other came into the room and spoke to the class about the difficulty of daily life.
   C. Eventually, the old *conduits* began to develop microscopic holes through which oil was able to leak onto the ground.
   D. Irrigation of the California desert depended on many *conduits* that brought water to the parched land.

4) A. The strings on tennis racquets, especially those that professionals use, should have great *tensile* strength in order to handle the speed at which tennis balls are hit.
   B. The dining room table could hold up to thirty times its weight because of its *tensile* legs.
   C. The elastic tied in Marissa's hair had weak *tensile* strength and broke after being stretched only a bit.
   D. Beach visitors watched in awe as the *tensile* bodybuilder lifted a two-hundred pound barbell over his head.

5) A. The *composite* of Gina's SAT scores made her a competitive college applicant, even though her first trial had yielded poor results.
   B. The garbage truck delivers the neighborhood's trash to a large *composite* once a week.
   C. As a *composite*, the three chemicals reacted poorly and created a dangerous, nearly explosive mixture.
   D. The old house looked beautiful, but John and Lily refused to buy it because of its location next to a foul-smelling *composite*.

Lesson 2 continued:

6) A. Liquids *infuse* depending on what container they are in because they are made up of loosely packed particles.
   B. Abby practiced her dance routine for a year, every month *infusing* it with more new, complex, and difficult moves.
   C. "This mattress *infuses* to the exact shape of your body," said the convincing salesperson.
   D. The victim lost a great deal of blood in the accident; luckily, a donor volunteered to have some of his blood *infused* into her.

7) A. The *hypothetical* idea of cliff-diving did not frighten Wes; once he actually stood before the cliff, though, he felt terrified.
   B. Since the job opportunity was merely *hypothetical*, I did not tell my family about it yet.
   C. The song lyrics contained a *hypothetical* message that you could decipher by combining the second letter of every word in the chorus.
   D. New members had to learn a *hypothetical* handshake that they were then not allowed to divulge to anyone outside of the club.

8) A. *Copious* of Gretel's actions, Jackson secretly followed her in his car to determine how she planned to spend her time that day.
   B. It was strange for Miranda to see her grandfather's barren garden in the winter because she was accustomed to its being *copiously* filled with flowers and vegetation.
   C. Nobody knew for sure who had murdered Susanne, but the police seemed *copious* of her next-door neighbor, who had held a grudge against her for years.
   D. *Copious* with cheer and merriment, the Sterling family danced around their home while singing Christmas carols.

9) A. No one in the house could properly identify the source of the *ubiquitous* noise coming from the back of the closet.
   B. The ending to the famed book series *Tales of Misteronia* was so *ubiquitous* that not even the author's publicist knew what it would be.
   C. "Do you find it interesting how some news stories become *ubiquitous*, while some remain practically unnoticed?" asked Larry.
   D. Jessica believes that the ghosts of her deceased loved ones are *ubiquitous*, traveling with her in spirit with every step she takes.

10) A. We had to *comprise* on our beliefs slightly to reach any type of agreement.
    B. Reading the lengthy book *comprised* an entire weekend, but it was worth it.
    C. After we *comprised* everyone about the rules, the kids picked team names.
    D. The air we breathe *comprises* primarily nitrogen and oxygen.

Lesson 2 continued:

Synonyms and Antonyms

Match the word with its *antonym*.

1) ubiquitous   **A.** drain

2) infuse   **B** real

3) hypothetical   **C.** inefficient

4) practical   **D.** scarce

Match the word with its *synonym*.

5) copious   **E.** compound

6) composite   **F.** abundant

END
of
LESSON 2

Lesson 3

Questions 22–32 are based on the following passage.

This passage describes a little-known element of American history from the Mexican-American War of 1846.

Bullets ricocheted and cannonballs exploded against the walls of San Mateo **Convent**, pelting the crouched defenders with fragments of stone and blanketing them with a haze of sulfurous gunpowder
5 smoke. A company of San Patricios attempted to repel US attackers from the South and West. In spite of heavy casualties, the American soldiers surrounded the fortress. General Antonio López de Santa Anna ordered the San Patricios and a Mexican company to take cover inside
10 the fort. Supplies were running low, and the defenders soon discovered that the cartridges Santa Anna sent with them fit only the San Patricios' weapons; the second regiment was left defenseless. Advancing US soldiers forced the defenders into the convent, where some
15 soldiers attempted to raise a white flag in surrender. Understanding their fate if captured by the US forces, the San Patricios tore down the white flag and continued to fight.

The San Patricios, or Saint Patrick's, Battalion,
20 was not the typical Mexican Army unit of 1847. The 200 soldiers and artillerymen, led by John Riley, marched under a green flag that portrayed St. Patrick on one side and a harp with Mexico's emblem on the other. A caption beneath the logo read "Erin go Bragh," the
25 Anglicized version of *Éirinn go Brách*, or "Ireland Forever." These soldiers, having fought for Santa Anna in the Mexican army against the US in Monterrey, Saltillo, and Buena Vista, were in fact **expatriates**— immigrant **defectors**.

30 John Riley endured a childhood among the Irish west coast's rough terrain and **capricious** weather, exacerbated by the peak of the potato **blight**. Systemic British oppression of Irish Catholics and **exorbitant** taxes had rendered the Irish reliant on the potato crops
35 for both food and commerce; between 1845 and 1852, amid a million deaths from disease and starvation, thousands emigrated to escape the misery. Riley immigrated to Canada and then Michigan, where he enlisted in the US Army, enticed by the prospect of
40 regular wages and steady meals.

Army conditions of the time provided little reprieve from the misery the Irish had fled in their homeland. Bad food, ineffective shelter, and **rampant** disease, especially as the US engaged in the Mexican-American
45 War in 1846, led to the desertion of thousands of soldiers, in addition to the 13,000 whose lives it took throughout the course of the war. For comparison, actual American combat deaths numbered fewer than 200.

Among the deserters was John Riley and the group
50 of immigrants and expatriates he chose to designate the Saint Patrick's Battalion. Citing widespread US Army intolerance against Irish soldiers in denying promotions or even the ability to conduct Catholic Mass, Riley and the men of the St. Patrick's Battalion defected to
55 Mexico, which, at the onset of the war, had actively engaged in recruiting **disaffected** American immigrants to fight for Mexico, claiming that the US "Protestant tyrants," just like their British imperialist counterparts in Ireland, desired to eliminate all Catholics, specifically in
60 Mexico.

Shortly before the US officially declared war, Riley deserted Company K of the 5th US Infantry to join the Mexican army's Legion of Foreigners. Joined by his forty-eight defectors, including mostly immigrants from
65 Ireland but also Germany, France, Italy, and Poland, Riley formed el Batallón de San Patricio. Escaped slaves joined Riley's ranks, as well, motivated to prevent the expansion of the southern slaveholding states of the US, as the abolitionist movement gained momentum in the
70 North.

The **regiment** of foreigners quickly earned a reputation as fierce fighters as they engaged the US in key battles of the Mexican-American War, no doubt motivated by the knowledge that their defection would
75 result in extreme punishment if they were captured. Their luck ran out at Churubusco in 1847.

Out of ammunition, the Mexican soldiers in the convent knew that the battle was over and that to continue fighting would invite needless death. Three
80 attempts to surrender were each blocked by the San Patricios. Finally, US Army Captain James Milton Smith, the leader of the invaders, raised his own handkerchief on a pole and entered the convent, bringing the Battle of Churubusco to an end and sealing the fate
85 of the San Patricios.

Having captured Riley and his deserters, the US Army convened two **courts martial**, one at San Angel and one at Tacubaya, in which all but two of the

Lesson 3 continued:

seventy-two men were sentenced to death. Immediate
90 Mexican fury ensued over the sentence, forcing General
Winfield Scott to consider **appeals** for retrials. At San
Angel, twenty of the twenty-nine men were sentenced
to death, while Tacubaya yielded thirty death sentences.
Because John Riley and a handful of other soldiers
95 had technically defected before the US declared war
on Mexico, their death sentences were reduced to
punishment. Riley received fifty lashes and was twice
branded with the letter "D," for deserter, on his cheek.
  On the morning of September 13, 1847, the
100 remaining thirty living San Patricios were fitted with
nooses and made to stand on the **gallows** as the Battle
of Chapultepec erupted in the distance. As the US
flag ascended in victory over Chapultepec Castle, the
platform dropped and the thirty were hanged.
105 Following the treaty of Guadalupe Hidalgo, which
ended the war, the surviving San Patricios regrouped
with new defectors and formed two new companies.
John Riley grew a beard to cover his branded face and
continued to fight for Mexico until the San Patricios
110 dissolved in August of 1848, and Riley vanished into
obscurity.
  In spite of the war's outcome, and having been
regarded as deserters by the US, Riley and the San
Patricios are lauded as heroes in both Mexico and
115 Ireland, where their actions created an **amicability** and
mutual respect between the two countries, and are said to
have inspired, in part, the Irish War of Independence of
the 20th century.

22

Choose the most appropriate title for the passage.
A) The Story of John Riley
B) Santa Anna's Revenge
C) A Shamrock in Mexico
D) An Unlikely Situation

23

According to the author, the number of combat deaths
during the Mexican-American War
A) exceeded that of all but the American Civil War.
B) were negligible compared to the deaths from
   disease and austere conditions.
C) can be attributed to large numbers of soldiers
   deserting their posts.
D) have no real historical basis because such records
   were not regularly maintained.

24

Choose the lines that provide the best evidence for your
answer to the previous question.
A) lines 32-35 ("Systemic British…commerce")
B) lines 49-51 ("Among the…Battalion")
C) lines 86-89 ("Having captured…death")
D) lines 43-48 ("Bad food…200")

25

The passage begins with details specific to the Battle
of Churubusco. At which point in the passage does the
author continue the story where it leaves off?
A) paragraph 6 (line 61)
B) paragraph 7 (line 71)
C) paragraph 8 (line 77)
D) paragraph 9 (line 86)

Lesson 3 continued:

26

The author starts the passage by using a technique called *in medias res*, which means "in the middle of things." What is the author's probable intent in using such a device?

A) The author begins with an exciting part of the narrative because it will best capture the attention of the reader.

B) The author is providing evidence that he or she directly witnessed the events that occurred during the battle, establishing credibility.

C) The author invents a fictional scene in order to help readers understand what went on at the battle.

D) The details of the battle provide character background for John Riley, who is the focus of the overall passage.

27

Riley's battalion under the Mexican army is best described as having consisted of

A) regular US soldiers who worked as mercenaries in between tours of duty.

B) various immigrants of European descent, as well as escaped slaves.

C) entirely Irish immigrants to the US.

D) a mixture of both Catholic and Protestant immigrants.

28

Choose the lines that provide the best evidence for your answer to the previous question.

A) lines 45-47 ("led to...war")

B) lines 49-51 ("Among the...Battalion")

C) lines 51-55 ("Citing widespread...Mexico")

D) lines 63-67 ("Joined by...well")

29

The author of the passage would agree with which one of the following statements?

A) The Mexican-American War was an act of American imperialism.

B) The immigrants were deserters and deserved to suffer their fate.

C) Only those who endured what the immigrants endured can pass judgment on their decisions.

D) The Irish battalion compromised US standing among other countries.

30

The best meaning for the word *disaffected* as it is used in line 56 is

A) worried.

B) loyal.

C) troublesome.

D) rebellious.

31

According to the passage, the Irish soldiers refused to surrender at Churubusco because

A) the soldiers knew there would be harsh consequences if captured.

B) the soldiers had enough supplies within the fort to withstand a lengthy siege.

C) they were exceptionally loyal to General Santa Anna.

D) they were dedicated to freeing the escaped slaves who had joined their ranks.

32

Choose the answer that is *not* one of the grievances listed in the passage as a motive for the immigrants' desertion of the US army.

A) religious persecution

B) forced labor

C) disease

D) inadequate shelter

Lesson 3 continued:

Vocabulary: Context Answers

The following sentences contain vocabulary words used in the reading passage. Choose the answer that best completes the sentence. There may be more than one technically correct answer, but one will better exemplify the italicized vocabulary word than the others will.

1) *Rampant* hunger plagued the remote village after the drought; neighboring towns hoped it would not _____.
   A. continue
   B. return
   C. be lethal
   D. increase prices
   E. spread

2) Though Annabelle enjoyed traveling to Europe, she could never imagine becoming an *expatriate*; instead, she wanted to _____.
   A. become a dual citizen
   B. visit foreign countries, not live in them
   C. attend school in Europe
   D. leave Europe, but not permanently
   E. live abroad and never visit home

3) Riley's friends accused her of being a *defector*, but she had no control over the decision to _____.
   A. use outdated study guides
   B. move away
   C. bring the dogs to the shelter
   D. transfer to a rival high school
   E. leave the football game early

4) Aiden's family was frustrated by their mother's *capricious* nature; every time they started to plan their vacation, she _____.
   A. took charge of the decision
   B. complained about money
   C. asked them to wait
   D. left the house
   E. changed her mind

5) The Paulsens refused to pay the _____ charge because they felt it was *exorbitant* for the amount of work done.
   A. old management's
   B. previously agreed upon
   C. ridiculously high
   D. total, undiscounted
   E. hourly, not daily,

6) The author fell into *obscurity* after publishing his first short story, which explains why _____.
   A. everyone reads his stories
   B. he became rich
   C. he did not make a lot of money
   D. students read about him in history class
   E. his work is unknown

Lesson 3 continued:

7) As a member of the first *regiment*, Cassidy moved to a new location _____.
   A. that had new houses
   B. with her family
   C. for a new job
   D. with her Army battalion
   E. in a better school district

8) The *prospect* of a new car _____.
   A. made Ralph think about getting one
   B. caused great happiness in Ralph
   C. enabled Ralph to drive
   D. helped all of Ralph's friends
   E. was a decision Ralph needed to make

9) When Renee _____ her exam grade from her teacher, he said that no *appeal* would motivate him to grade more quickly.
   A. questioned
   B. requested
   C. took
   D. saw
   E. received

10) Laura wanted *amicability* in her break-up with Jack so that they would _____.
    A. be civil to each other in the future
    B. never see each other again
    C. speak openly about their feelings
    D. raise their voices at each other
    E. get rid of their mutual friends

11) After the class president went back on her campaign promises, *disaffected* students stopped _____.
    A. being friendly to her
    B. attending student council meetings
    C. disagreeing with her
    D. supporting her
    E. running for student government

12) A _____ was caused by an unexplainable *blight* that struck local farms.
    A. fertilizer surplus
    B. food shortage
    C. bad disease
    D. lengthy drought
    E. vermin infestation

Lesson 3 continued:

Writing Practice

Some of the following sentences are fragments, comma splices, or run-ons. Choose the answer that best corrects the sentence while retaining the intended meaning of the original sentence. Select NO CHANGE if the provided sentence is correct.

1) Proving more disorienting, it was either the poor weather conditions or the headlights obscuring the visitor's vision.
   A. NO CHANGE
   B. Obscuring the vision of the visitor, the poor weather conditions or the headlights proved more disorienting.
   C. Whether the poor weather conditions or the headlights proved more disorienting. They obscured the visitor.
   D. Whether it was the poor weather conditions or the headlights that proved more disorienting, something obscured the vision of the driver.

2) As an amateur astronomer, Clara likes to travel away from the city and stargaze through a telescope because it makes her feel connected to the universe.
   A. NO CHANGE
   B. As an amateur astronomer, Clara likes to travel away from the city and stargaze through a telescope, it makes her feel connected to the universe.
   C. Clara, an amateur astronomer, likes to travel away from the city and stargaze though a telescope it makes her feel connected to the universe.
   D. Although she is only an amateur astronomer, Clara likes to stargaze through a telescope away from the city, it makes her feel connected to the universe.

3) Idioms seem similar in meaning differ in wording: I prefer "Flies don't enter a closed mouth" to "Silence is golden."
   A. NO CHANGE
   B. Idioms seeming similar in meaning differing in wording: I prefer "Flies don't enter a closed mouth" to "Silence is golden."
   C. Idioms that seem similar in meaning differ in wording. I prefer "Flies don't enter a closed mouth" to "Silence is golden."
   D. Idioms seeming similar in meaning differ in wording; and I prefer "Flies don't enter a closed mouth" to "Silence is golden."

4) When Steven stepped on the basketball court for the championship game, he felt confident the team would win.
   A. NO CHANGE
   B. When Steven stepped on the basketball court. He felt confident the team would win the game.
   C. Steven felt confident the team would win the game; and stepped on the basketball court.
   D. At the championship game and Steven was feeling confident his team would win.

Lesson 3 continued:

5) Harry met his wife at the bookstore as soon as they locked eyes that first time, they knew it was meant to be.
   A. NO CHANGE
   B. Harry met his wife at the bookstore: as soon as they locked eyes that first time; they knew it was meant to be.
   C. Harry met his wife at the bookstore, and as soon as they locked eyes that first time, they knew it was meant to be.
   D. Harry met his wife at the bookstore, as soon as they locked eyes that first time, they knew it was meant to be.

6) Ron moved into his new apartment, hauling furniture upstairs, unpacking boxes, and exhausted.
   A. NO CHANGE
   B. Ron, while moving into his new apartment, hauling furniture upstairs, unpacking boxes, and he was exhausted.
   C. As Ron moved into his apartment, hauled furniture upstairs, and unpacked boxes; he became exhausted.
   D. After moving into his new apartment, hauling furniture upstairs, and unpacking boxes, Ron felt exhausted.

7) I believe you realize that labeling people because of their country of origin often leads directly down the path to racial epithets.
   A. NO CHANGE
   B. I believe you realize labeling of people because of their country of origin. This often leads directly down the path to racial epithets.
   C. Labeling people because of their country of origin often leads directly down the path to racial epithets. Which is something I believe you realize.
   D. I believe you realize that to label people because of their country of origin leading directly down the path to racial epithets.

8) We left for our vacation to the Bahamas on Tuesday, the flight was long and tiring.
   A. NO CHANGE
   B. When the flight was long and tiring, we left for our vacation on Tuesday.
   C. The long and tiring flight to the Bahamas when we left for our vacation.
   D. We left for our vacation to the Bahamas on Tuesday. The flight was long and tiring.

9) Right after Duane and his hockey team had lost the game Duane and his parents.
   A. NO CHANGE
   B. In the ice rink with his parents; right after Duane and his hockey team had lost the game.
   C. In the ice rink right after Duane and his hockey team had lost the game, his parents were waiting with an ice cream cone to cheer him up.
   D. In the ice rink right after Duane and his hockey team had lost the game. His parents cheered him up with an ice cream cone.

10) My mother was proud of me at the academic awards ceremony it was last week.
   A. NO CHANGE
   B. My mother was proud of the academic awards I received at the ceremony last week.
   C. At the awards ceremony last week, my mother was proud; because of my achievements.
   D. The many awards I received at the ceremony last week. My mother was proud of me.

Lesson 3 continued:

11) Because Mendelian genetics used to teach principles of heredity do not work for human characteristics, which are usually determined by multiple genes.
   A. NO CHANGE
   B. Not working for human characteristics, Mendelian genetics used to teach principles of heredity, which are usually determined by multiple genes.
   C. Mendelian genetics, used to teach principles of heredity, do not work for human characteristics, which are usually determined by multiple genes.
   D. Usually determined by multiple genes, Mendelian genetics used to teach principles of heredity, do not work for human characteristics.

12) Even though both of the models were impressive during their respective casting calls.
   A. NO CHANGE
   B. Even though both of the models were impressive during their respective casting calls, neither received a call back about the photo shoot.
   C. Both of the models were impressive during their respective casting calls, neither one got called back for further work by that photographer.
   D. Even though, both of the models were impressive during their respective casting calls. Neither one was contacted about a job.

13) The winter, with its gusty wind, thick snowfall, and ability to keep us all tucked away inside our homes.
   A. NO CHANGE
   B. The winter: with its gusty wind, thick snowfall, and ability to keep us all tucked away inside our homes.
   C. With its gusty wind, thick snowfall, and ability to keep us all tucked away inside our homes this winter.
   D. The winter, with its blustering wind, thick snowfall, and ability to keep us all tucked away inside our homes, seemed like it would never end.

14) Wanda was so nervous before the date at the restaurant that she couldn't stop moving her leg up and down under the table as she waited for Troy to arrive.
   A. NO CHANGE
   B. Wanda was so nervous. Before the date at the restaurant, that she couldn't stop moving her leg up and down under the table; she waited for Troy to arrive.
   C. Wanda was so nervous before the date at the restaurant; that she couldn't stop moving her leg up and down under the table as she waited for Troy to arrive.
   D. Wanda was so nervous: Before the date at the restaurant, as she waited for Troy to arrive, that she couldn't stop moving her leg up and down under the table.

15) Whenever it's raining and I arrive at my destination only to realize I forgot my umbrella.
   A. NO CHANGE
   B. Unfortunately, when it's raining and I arrive at my destination only to realize that I forgot my umbrella.
   C. Because it's raining and I arrive at my destination only to realize I forgot my umbrella.
   D. Whenever it's raining and I arrive at my destination only to realize I forgot my umbrella, I get both annoyed and, worse, soaked.

Lesson 3 continued:

Vocabulary: Choosing the Right Use

The following sentences contain vocabulary words used in the reading passage. Identify the sentence or sentences that use the italicized vocabulary word properly. We have changed the form of some vocabulary words to provide new contexts; for example, some adjectives and verbs have been used as nouns.

1) A. While my father enjoyed the taste of Brussels sprouts, my mother felt sheer *appeal* toward them.
   B. *Appeal* toward spiders likely has to do with the fact that their having eight legs seems creepy.
   C. Georgio's mother sent an *appeal* to the court, insisting that they had made a mistake—her son would never have robbed a bank.
   D. Bronte's *appeal* suggested that the court issue a retrial of the case of *Bronte Flores vs. the State of New Jersey.*

2) A. Whatever your interest, there likely exists a *convent* for it: For example, last year, Sheila attended one about dental hygiene.
   B. Shirley opted out of college and, instead, decided to pursue her religious devotion by studying at a *convent* in Europe.
   C. The *convent* took place at a museum in Florida and hosted thousands of eager anthropologists.
   D. The *convent* set a strict curfew for the young nuns: They were to be in bed by 11:00 pm.

3) A. Cinna, an *expatriate* from Chile, came to the United States in 1989 and built a business from the ground up.
   B. Often, towns will exchange *expatriates*; for example, Colorado City trades its tomatoes for grapefruit from Florida.
   C. Macadamia nuts and papaya are two of the most important and valuable *expatriates* from the state of Hawaii.
   D. "*Expatriates* make this country so much more diverse and interesting," commented Jasper.

4) A. One *regiment* waited in the bunker until the other one signaled that it was safe to emerge.
   B. Brent must abide by his daily morning *regiment* of going for a run and then having breakfast; otherwise, he will be irritable.
   C. The leader of the *regiment*, General Seeding, gave his troops a passionate speech before they began the raid.
   D. The basketball game had the usual *regiment* at practice—running laps around the gym, doing drills, and working on plays.

5) A. Taxes paid throughout his life amounted to well over a million dollars—quite an *exorbitant* sum.
   B. The *exorbitant* cost of living in San Diego often deters people from settling down there.
   C. The young boy received suspension from school for engaging in alarmingly *exorbitant* behavior.
   D. *Exorbitant* adolescents cannot, under the law, go to jail, but juvenile detention centers can be just as traumatizing.

Lesson 3 continued:

6) A. Cara failed to notice the *rampant* part of the sidewalk and, consequently, tripped over it.
   B. Once *rampant* with poverty, the town now had improved schools and more job opportunities.
   C. The doctor recommended that Ricky keep his injured leg *rampant* with a pillow while he rests.
   D. In the summer, *rampant* bees and mosquitos worry Piper, who is allergic to both of those species.

7) A. Dr. Jenkins gave his class quite a *capricious* lecture on the importance of proper preparation for the final exam.
   B. Dad provided *capricious* details as to where we were going on our excursion, so when we ended up at an amusement park, I was quite surprised.
   C. "Though the island is magnificent, the weather patterns there are *capricious*, so make sure you pack for all occasions," advised Kim.
   D. The sign on the door seemed oddly *capricious*: It said, "Something Dangerous in Here."

8) A. Merely the *prospect* of meeting her idol in person was enough motivation for Leona to travel 40 miles to the coffee shop he frequented.
   B. The horrors of Hurricane Katrina led to thousands of volunteers offering *prospect* to those affected.
   C. With *prospect* from my artistic parents, I created a mosaic mural in our backyard.
   D. Deterred by the *prospect* of a snowstorm, we chose to stay inside and drink hot chocolate.

9) A. "These sunglasses will protect your eyes from the sun's *blight*," said Mom, handing me her pair.
   B. Having sat in the dark for a couple hours, Mike had trouble adjusting to the *blight* of the chandelier.
   C. Tanya, descended from farmers, applied for a master's program in botany because she wanted to be able to develop potential cures for various types of *blight*.
   D. The mold in the school cafeteria, if not professionally removed, would certainly become a serious *blight*.

10) A. It is imperative that salespeople maintain *amicability* with customers whom they are trying to persuade to buy a product.
    B. Tom had woken up early with the *amicability* of going for a run, but he ended up watching morning cartoons instead.
    C. I had had noble *amicability* when I decided to trim my neighbor's bushes for him, but he still got angry that I had not done it properly.
    D. Dianne chose a puppy based on *amicability*; the one that seemed the friendliest was the one that she selected.

Lesson 3 continued:

11) A. It took almost two weeks and countless cups of tea for Tasha's horrible cold to become completely *disaffected*.
   B. After my preferred candidate won election to the city council, she quickly became extremely *disaffected* and took great interest in her duties.
   C. Until he became *disaffected* from the flu, Jack had no choice but to stay home from school and miss soccer practice.
   D. The *disaffected* cult member continued preaching at the passersby, without care that no one was listening.

12) A. The author's *obscurity* began because of his refusal to meet with fans or the press.
   B. Marla, a lawyer, demonstrated her great *obscurity* by standing up straight and speaking in a loud, confident voice.
   C. The once-popular band The Dizzy Boats seemed to disappear into *obscurity* after their lead singer left the group to pursue a solo career.
   D. Barney definitely had incredible artistic talent; unfortunately, he lacked the *obscurity* to defend his work to critics.

Lesson 3 continued:

VOCABULARY
SYNONYMS & ANTONYMS

Synonyms and Antonyms

Match the word with its *antonym*.

1) rampant   **A.** native

2) capricious   **B.** reasonable

3) expatriate   **C.** fame

4) obscurity   **D.** unfriendliness

5) exorbitant   **E.** devoid

6) amicability   **F.** predictable

Match the word with its *synonym*.

7) disaffected   **G.** rebellious

8) appeal   **H.** disease

9) prospect   **I.** plea

10) blight   **J.** possibility

END
of
LESSON 3

Lesson 4

Questions 33–42 are based on the following passage.

This article explains the pharmaceutical value of marine sponges.

Sponges, which belong to the **phylum** *Porifera*, are some of the simplest animals. Even since the Proterozoic Eon, about 635 million years ago, they haven't changed much. The cells of sponges do not form organs or tissues
5   like those of other animals; *Porifera* also contain unique **biochemical compounds**, which make sponges particularly significant to medical science. Scientists are especially interested in sponges' secondary **metabolites**, which are chemicals that are not involved in normal
10 growth, development, or reproduction. Some secondary metabolites defend sponges against **pathogens** such as viruses, bacteria, fungi, and algae—a function of high interest to humanity.

A chemist named Werner Bergmann can be credited
15 for launching **pharmaceutical** interest in sponges. In 1945, Bergmann identified a new species of sponge, *Cryptotethya crypta* (later renamed *Tectitethya crypta*). In his laboratory, Bergmann dissolved compounds from the sponge by placing it in an instrument called a soxhlet
20 extractor in which acetone, a **solvent**, is boiled in the bottom of a flask. The vapors from the boiling acetone rise to the top of the device, where they condense on a water-cooled condenser and drip onto the sponge, dissolving it. As dissolved compounds from the sponge
25 collect below, they can be isolated for further study. Over the course of a few years, Bergmann discovered two crystalline compounds that he named spongothymidine and spongouridine. Spongothymidine demonstrates optic activity: its asymmetrical carbon atoms rotate polarized
30 light as it passes through them (imagine it as a vertical mail slot that rotates a few degrees as flat envelopes pass through it), and it has an ultraviolet absorption spectrum similar to that of thymidine. Thymidine is a nucleoside composed of a thymine base, a building block of DNA,
35 attached to a sugar called deoxyribose. Thymine is also the base of spongothymidine, although its connected sugar is arabinose. Spongouridine has characteristics like those of uridine, a component of RNA, which is a photocopy of DNA that makes proteins. Both of these
40 compounds have important implications in medicine.

The two compounds Bergmann discovered are secondary metabolites that appear to interfere with DNA and RNA replication as a defense mechanism. Seymour Cohen, another scientist involved in *Porifera* research,
45 proposed that this defense mechanism could be used to inhibit the growth of cancer cells. He and other researchers **synthesized** a **derivative** of spongothymidine known as arabinosyl cytosine (ara-C). Ara-C has become one of the primary agents in chemotherapy and is used to
50 treat **systemic** cancers such as leukemia. The base and sugar of ara-C are similar enough to the human cytosine, deoxyribose, a nucleoside, that ara-C is accepted and incorporated into DNA; but ara-C is different enough that it kills the cancer cells by stopping the synthesis of DNA.
55 As the development of anticancer drugs continued through the 1960s, Bernard Randall Baker synthesized vidarabine (ara-A) from spongothymidine and spongouridine. Ara-A works much like its counterpart ara-C, but it most effectively interferes with the synthesis
60 of viral DNA. Ara-A is used against herpes simplex and varicella zoster viruses, which include chicken pox and **shingles**. In 1964, scientists derived an antiviral called azidothymidine (AZT) from *Cryptotethya crypta*. AZT was found to be effective against **retroviruses**, which use
65 an enzyme called reverse transcriptase to create single-stranded DNA from an RNA template. At the time, AZT had limited application because there were no known human retroviruses. This changed with the onset of the AIDS epidemic in the early 1980s. Scientists began using
70 AZT to prevent the replication of the human immunodeficiency virus that causes AIDS. AZT even prevents HIV transmission in certain instances, including from mother to child during birth or after a needle-stick injury. It remains one of the leading treatments of HIV;
75 however, because the virus may become AZT-resistant over time, it is often used in conjunction with other medications.

The discovery of a medical application for AZT nearly twenty years after it was first synthesized has
80 sparked a resurgence in research into the pharmaceutical potential of sponges. Marine biologists explore oceans in submersible vehicles, searching caverns, crevices, and rocky areas for unique sponge species. They collect small pieces from multiple sponges in order to obtain
85 representative samples and then break the sponges down with acetone just as Bergmann did over half a century ago. So far, scientists have found thousands of chemical compounds, and, given the **myriad** types of sponges, there could be thousands more to discover.
90 Pollution and rising ocean temperatures threaten the fragile ecology of sponges' habitats, which, in turn, damages the habitats of microorganisms residing in the sponges. At 33° C (91° F), the beneficial **symbiosis** between sponges and microbes breaks down, and coral
95 begins to bleach, which further damages the relationship. Symbiotic bacteria make up a significant percentage of the body weight of sponges and contribute to chemical defenses and the processing of nutrition and waste; these contributions are part of what makes sponges so medically
100 valuable. Preserving *Porifera* and their potential life-saving compounds will require global protection of the oceans and coral reefs in which they thrive.

Lesson 4 continued:

33

Choose the most appropriate title for this passage.
A) The Overrated *Porifera*
B) The Cure for Cancer
C) In Search of the Miracle Drug
D) The Lifesaving Potential of Sponges

34

Choose the answer that best describes how ara-C functions when used as a tool in the treatment of cancer.
A) The compound mimics thymidine and then spontaneously converts to a nucleoside.
B) It tricks cancer cells into incorporating it, which causes the cells to die.
C) Ara-C is toxic to the healthy cells adjacent to cancer cells; killing the healthy cells denies resources to the cancer cells.
D) The ara-C replaces the DNA of the host cell with healthy DNA.

35

Choose the lines that provide the best evidence for your answer to the previous question.
A) lines 46-48 ("He and...(ara-C)")
B) lines 48-50 ("Ara-C has...leukemia")
C) lines 50-54 ("The base...DNA")
D) lines 55-58 ("As the...spongouridine")

36

The author of the passage can be said to be writing under which one of the following assumptions?
A) The audience knows what chemotherapy is.
B) Antiviral drugs such as AZT exist only in theory.
C) No one is researching *Porifera*.
D) Few people will agree to dedicate more resources to sponge research.

37

In explaining optic activity, the author uses an analogy in which light is represented by
A) rotating wind.
B) carbon atoms.
C) flat envelopes.
D) boiling water.

38

Choose the answer that best describes the main difference between thymidine and spongothymidine, according to the author.
A) the temperature at which each breaks down
B) the species of sponge in which each originates
C) the type of cells each affects
D) the type of sugar molecule each is connected to

39

As it is used in line 93, the word *symbiosis* describes a relationship in which
A) two living things depend on each other.
B) a single organism benefits from another.
C) more than two living things live within ten meters of each other.
D) microorganisms live on the surface of higher-order animals.

Lesson 4 continued:

40

Choose the lines that provide the best evidence for your answer to the previous question.
A) lines 90-91 ("Pollution and...habitats")
B) lines 93-95 ("At 33° C...bleach")
C) lines 96-98 ("Symbiotic bacteria...waste")
D) lines 100-102 ("Preserving *Porifera*...thrive")

41

The details of AZT's having existed so long without a purpose is included in the passage as a way to
A) demonstrate that pharmaceutical companies invest only in drugs that will make money.
B) emphasize how many years researchers have known about the potential of sponges, yet still remain reluctant about funding research.
C) connect the discovery of thymine to the value of sponge research.
D) advocate for the importance of research and protection of sponges, even if their products do not have a readily apparent use.

42

Choose the best description of the overall tone of the passage.
A) defensive and self-conscious
B) objective and clinical
C) erratic and confident
D) biased and smug

Lesson 4 continued:

Vocabulary: Context Answers

The following sentences contain vocabulary words used in the reading passage. Choose the answer that best completes the sentence. There may be more than one technically correct answer, but one will better exemplify the italicized vocabulary word than the others will.

1) One morning, Norm glanced out the window and *myriads* _____.
   A. of cars were in his driveway
   B. of songs were playing on his stereo
   C. of his family sat in the car
   D. of snowflakes had covered the ground
   E. of dreams faded instantly away

2) *Derivative* of _____, the modern overuse of antibiotics is now creating a great deal of worry.
   A. horrible bacteriological diseases
   B. the need for sterile conditions
   C. the first one, which is penicillin
   D. a need to become healthy again
   E. new advances in science

3) _____ are caused by foreign *pathogens*.
   A. Diseases
   B. Coughs
   C. Acts of violence
   D. Injuries
   E. Crimes

4) Water can _____ many substances, which is why it is sometimes called "the universal *solvent*."
   A. saturate
   B. dissolve
   C. be absorbed by
   D. be substituted for
   E. greatly alter

5) Using _____, Fredrick was finally able to *synthesize* the chemical.
   A. multiple sources
   B. emails from his teacher
   C. an equation
   D. a diagram
   E. a reliable source

6) Doctors told Emily that her disease was quickly becoming *systemic* after they saw that _____.
   A. she was no longer contagious
   B. her condition was not improving
   C. multiple body parts were affected
   D. it remained in her lungs
   E. she continued to get sicker

7) To understand _____, doctors must take classes in *biochemistry*.
   A. reactions between chemicals
   B. biology's effects on chemicals
   C. classifications of species
   D. how chemicals affect living beings
   E. the periodic table of elements

Lesson 4 continued:

8) Relationships between dogs and pet owners are examples of *symbiosis* because _____.
A. dogs and humans should not live together, but continue to anyway
B. both dogs and humans benefit from being together
C. they remain independent of each other
D. both dogs and humans represent something to each other
E. dogs and humans can instantly love one another

9) In order to try to _____, Reina wants to enter the *pharmaceutical* industry.
A. discover a new species of bird
B. locate more galaxies
C. develop a cure for cancer
D. plan therapies for sports injuries
E. harness renewable energy sources

Lesson 4 continued:

Writing Practice

The underlined portion of each sentence provides two pronouns that are often used incorrectly. Choose the pronoun that completes the sentence correctly.

1) Never ask for <u>who</u> / <u>whom</u> the bell tolls; it tolls for thee.

2) The senatorial candidate, <u>who</u> / <u>whom</u> had been in a scandal, gave an evasive answer to the reporter.

3) Athena is the goddess <u>who</u> / <u>whom</u> the Romans replaced with Minerva.

4) According to Sun Tzu, <u>who</u> / <u>whom</u> wrote *The Art of War*, war is rooted in deception.

5) Good advice: To those <u>who</u> / <u>whom</u> the rumors target, keep your head high.

6) The newscasters, in <u>who</u> / <u>whom</u> trust is placed, shorten, lengthen, or frame events so as to distort things without actually lying.

7) Lily, <u>who</u> / <u>whom</u> had been described as being "a mediocre actress," was praised after her emotional performance in *Accident*.

8) Rose decided to go to the park with <u>who</u> / <u>whom</u>?

9) Gail, <u>who</u> / <u>whom</u> plays the viola, practices five nights a week.

10) Emma, <u>who</u> / <u>whom</u> the teacher had humiliated before, despised the class on principle.

11) Bill, <u>who</u> / <u>whom</u> was attempting to scare his girlfriend on Halloween, hid in the shadows.

12) Allison is the girl <u>who</u> / <u>whom</u> people call when they need a sympathetic ear.

13) <u>Who</u> / <u>Whom</u> shall we say is responsible for the corruption in City Hall?

14) The lawyer asked pointedly, since she knew the answer, "These follow-up evaluations show that <u>who</u> / <u>whom</u> was committing fraud?"

15) For the men <u>who</u> / <u>whom</u> the United Nations charged with being war criminals, the trial had little chance of ending well.

Lesson 4 continued:

Vocabulary: Choosing the Right Use

The following sentences contain vocabulary words used in the reading passage. Identify the sentence or sentences that use the italicized vocabulary word properly. We have changed the form of some vocabulary words to provide new contexts; for example, some adjectives and verbs have been used as nouns.

1) A. The fly's *compound* eye is made up of an array of smaller, individual eyes, which gives the fly a wide field of view.
   B. Deb *compounded* the dough by beating it with her fist and rolling it out flat.
   C. Only those who have lived through the *compound* years of the war can know what it is like to truly want peace.
   D. Darryl's *compound* decision to run the stop sign led to a $75 ticket.

2) A. "Cutting down so many trees in the forest will surely hurt the *phylum* of birds that dwells there," asserted Pamela.
   B. Sea anemones and jellyfish are different species, but they are classified in the same *phylum*.
   C. The *phylum Nematoda* consists of 20,000 species, but *Placazoa* includes only one.
   D. During the recession, the *phylum* of the wealthy town drastically declined, as many people needed to live somewhere more affordable.

3) A. The *pathogen* of the storm swept through all of Connecticut and just missed New York.
   B. "You probably feel ill because the *pathogen* that causes the flu infected your system," said the doctor.
   C. The bluegrass band traveled on tour this year; the tour's *pathogen* spanned all across the country.
   D. Fungal *pathogens* are the leading cause of diseases in crops and other types of plants.

4) A. The *solvent* quickly absorbed the unknown substances to form a highly reactive compound.
   B. The water into which Marco poured the salt acted as a *solvent*. He used the solution to rinse out his mouth.
   C. After searching for days, the team of investigators finally discovered fingerprints in the office, a *solvent* that would certainly provide a suspect.
   D. With so many *solvents* against him, it was difficult to believe that Marty did not steal the highly prized dog.

5) A. Betsy was so elated about winning the science fair that joy practically *synthesized* from her.
   B. The chemical engineer *synthesized* a compound found in flowers by combining several proteins in a lengthy process.
   C. Elephants not only use instinct to understand their world, they are also able to *synthesize* past experiences to solve problems, validating the axiom "An elephant never forgets."
   D. Educators were able to *synthesize* the best parts of history curricula from around the state into a program that suited the school perfectly.

Lesson 4 continued:

6)   A.   The school PTA's warring factions eventually developed a *symbiotic* relationship, which improved the students' chances of visiting Washington, D.C.

       B.   Scientists found a strange *symbiosis* between the flowers and the soil they grew in, which allowed the flowers to flourish without depleting the dirt of nutrition.

       C.   Donna's mother rushed her to the hospital when her illness reached a level of *symbiosis*.

       D.   "General Hospital needs to expand its emergency room if it is going to be able to accommodate all the patients whose fevers have reached *symbiosis*," Jared told his wife.

7)   A.   Apathy and laziness seemed *systemic* among the seniors who had already been admitted to college and had no real work left to complete.

       B.   The little girl preferred playgrounds to organized sports, as running around a playground was much less *systemic*.

       C.   The new *systemic* schedule at Elena's summer camp bothered her; she had appreciated the older system, which allowed campers more freedom.

       D.   At first, only the town's elementary school students had to wear uniforms, but then, the rule became *systemic* throughout the school district.

8)   A.   As a *pharmaceutical* sales representative, Jeremy possessed a wealth of knowledge about different medicines.

       B.   "Did you see the article about the doctor who illegally charged his patients extra for medicine?" asked Luke about the *pharmaceutical* malpractice lawsuit.

       C.   The motivational speaker provided the audience with several *pharmaceutical* dilemmas to consider as though they might truly happen.

       D.   The phrase "Are you crazy?" is usually a *pharmaceutical* question, not a serious one.

9)   A.   Gerald's reflection bounced between the mirrors at the carnival allowing him to see *myriad* versions of himself.

       B.   *Myriad* atoms make up a single molecule of water.

       C.   The only reason lions can exist in the wild is because of their *myriad* prey that lives on the plains.

       D.   In only an hour, the neighborhood experienced a *myriad* of thunderstorms.

10)   A.   All the prequels and sequels of *Star Wars* are only *derivatives* of the original—and not nearly as good.

       B.   After we located the *derivative*, making another pair of pliers was easy.

       C.   A *derivative* of modern English is Latin.

       D.   "Come and See Me" is just a mindless *derivative* of the great song called "Shine on Brightly."

Lesson 4 continued:

Synonyms and Antonyms

Match the word with its *antonym*.

1) synthesize   **A.** independence

2) symbiosis   **B.** limited

3) pathogen   **C.** deconstruct

4) myriad   **D.** cure

Match the word with its *synonym*.

5) systemic   **E.** thinner

6) solvent   **F.** localized

7) derivative   **G.** offshoot

END
of
LESSON 4

Lesson 5

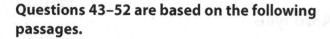

Questions 43–52 are based on the following passages.

The first passage is adapted from a 1921 essay by Scott Nearing in which he comments on the US entry into World War I in 1917. The second passage is adapted from a 1960 speech by President Dwight D. Eisenhower in which he discusses the changes to US society wrought by World War II.

Passage 1

Anyone who is familiar with its history will realize at once that the United States is passing through some of the more advanced stages in the development of empire. The name "**Republic**" still remains; the traditions of the
5 Republic are cherished by millions; the republican forms are almost intact, but the relations of the United States to its conquered territory and its subject peoples; the rapid maturation of the **plutocracy** as a governing class or **caste**; the shamelessness of the exploitation in which the
10 rulers have **indulged**; and the character of the forces that are now shaping public policy, proclaim to all the world the fact of empire.

The chief characteristics of empire exist in the United States. Here are conquered territory; subject
15 peoples; an **imperial**, ruling class; and the exploitation by that class of the people at home and abroad. During generations, the processes of empire have been working, unobserved, in the United States. Through more than two centuries, the American people have been busily laying
20 the foundations and erecting the imperial structure. For the most part, they have been unconscious of the work that they were doing, as the dock laborer is ordinarily unconscious of his part in the mechanism of industry. Consciously or unconsciously, the American people
25 have reared the imperial structure, until it stands, today, imposing in its grandeur, upon the spot where many of the founders of the American government hoped to see a republic.

The entrance of the United States into the war did
30 not greatly alter the character of the forces at work, nor did it in any large degree change the direction in which the country was moving. Rather, it brought to the surface of public attention factors of American life that had been evolving, unnoticed, for generations.
35 The world situation created by the war compelled the American imperial class to come out in the open and to occupy a position that, while wholly inconsistent with the traditions of American life, is nevertheless in keeping with the demands of imperial necessity. The ruling class in the
40 United States has taken a logical step and has made a logical stand. The masters of American life have done the only thing that they could do in the interests of the imperial forces that they represent. They are the victims, as much as were the Kaiser and the Czar on the one hand, and the Belgians and
45 the Serbs on the other, of that imperial necessity that knows no law save the preservation of its own most sacred interests.

Certain liberal American thinkers have taken the stand that the incidents of 1917-1918 were the result of the failure of the President, and of certain of his advisers, to follow the
50 theories which he had **enunciated**, and to stand by the cause that he had espoused. These critics overlook the incidental character of the war as a factor in American domestic policy. The war never assumed anything like the importance in the United States that it did among the European **belligerents**.
55 On the surface, it created a **furor**, but underneath, the big fact staring the administration in the face was the united front of the business interests and their organized demands for action. The far-seeing among the business men realized that the plutocratic structure the world over was in peril and
60 that the fate of the whole imperial **régime** was involved in the European struggle. The Russian Revolution of March 1917 was the last straw. From that time on, the entrance of the United States into the war became a certainty as the only means of "saving (capitalist) civilization."
65 The thoughtful student of the situation in the United States is not deceived by personalities and names. He realizes that the events of 1917-1918 have behind them generations of causes which lead logically to just such results; that he is witnessing one phase of a great process
70 in the life of the American nation—a process that is old in its principles yet ever new in its **manifestations**.

Traditional liberties have always given way before imperial necessity. An examination of the situation in which the ruling class of the United States found itself in 1917, and
75 of the forces that were operating to determine public policy, must convince even the enthusiast that the occurrences of 1917 and the succeeding years were the logical outcome of imperial necessity. To what extent that explanation will account for the discrepancy between the promise of 1776
80 and the twentieth-century fulfillment of that promise must appear from a further examination of the evidence.

Lesson 5 continued:

Passage 2

We now stand ten years past the midpoint of a century that has witnessed four major wars among great nations. Three of these involved our own country. Despite these **holocausts**, America is today the

5 strongest, the most influential, and most productive nation in the world. Understandably proud of this preeminence, we yet realize that America's leadership and prestige depend, not merely upon our unmatched material progress, riches, and military strength, but on

10 how we use our power in the interests of world peace and human betterment.

Throughout America's adventure in free government, our basic purposes have been to keep the peace; to foster progress in human achievement; and to

15 enhance liberty, dignity and integrity among people and among nations. To strive for less would be unworthy of a free and religious people. Any failure traceable to arrogance or our lack of comprehension or readiness to sacrifice would inflict upon us grievous hurt both at

20 home and abroad.

Progress toward these noble goals is persistently threatened by the conflict now engulfing the world. It commands our whole attention, absorbs our very beings. We face a hostile **ideology**—global in scope,

25 atheistic in character, ruthless in purpose, and **insidious** in method. Unhappily, the danger it poses promises to be of indefinite duration. To meet it successfully, there is called for, not so much the emotional and transitory sacrifices of crisis, but rather those which enable us to

30 carry forward steadily, surely, and without complaint the burdens of a prolonged and complex struggle—with liberty the stake. Only thus shall we remain, despite every **provocation**, on our charted course toward permanent peace and human betterment.

35 Crises there will continue to be. In meeting them, whether foreign or domestic, great or small, there is a recurring temptation to feel that some spectacular and costly action could become the miraculous solution to all current difficulties. A huge increase in newer elements

40 of our defense; development of unrealistic programs to cure every ill in agriculture; a dramatic expansion in basic and applied research—these and many other possibilities, each possibly promising in itself, may be suggested as the only way to the road we wish to travel.

45 But each proposal must be weighed in the light of a broader consideration: the need to maintain balance in and among national programs—balance between the private and the public economy, balance between cost and hoped for advantage—balance between the

50 clearly necessary and the comfortably desirable; balance between our essential requirements as a nation and the duties imposed by the nation upon the individual; balance between actions of the moment and the national welfare of the future. Good judgment seeks balance

55 and progress; lack of it eventually finds imbalance and frustration.

The record of many decades stands as proof that our people and their government have, in the main, understood these truths and have responded to them

60 well, in the face of stress and threat. But threats, new in kind or degree, constantly arise. I mention two only.

A vital element in keeping the peace is our military establishment. Our arms must be mighty, ready for instant action, so that no potential **aggressor** may be

65 tempted to risk his own destruction.

Our military organization today bears little relation to that known by any of my **predecessors** in peacetime, or indeed by the fighting men of World War II or Korea.

Until the latest of our world conflicts, the United

70 States had no armaments industry. American makers of **plowshares** could, with time and as required, make swords as well. But now we can no longer risk emergency improvisation of national defense; we have been compelled to create a permanent armaments

75 industry of vast proportions. Added to this, three and a half million men and women are directly engaged in the defense establishment. We annually spend on military security more than the net income of all United States corporations.

80 This conjunction of an immense military establishment and a large arms industry is new in the American experience. The total influence—economic, political, even spiritual—is felt in every city, every State house, every office of the Federal government. We

85 recognize the imperative need for this development. Yet we must not fail to comprehend its grave **implications**. Our toil, resources, and livelihood are all involved; so is the very structure of our society.

In the councils of government, we must guard

90 against the acquisition of unwarranted influence, whether

sought or unsought, by the military industrial complex. The potential for the disastrous rise of misplaced power exists and will persist.

95 We must never let the weight of this combination endanger our liberties or democratic processes. We should take nothing for granted. Only an alert and knowledgeable citizenry can compel the proper meshing of the huge industrial and military machinery of defense with our peaceful methods and goals, so that security

100 and liberty may prosper together.

Akin to, and largely responsible for the sweeping changes in our industrial-military **posture**, has been the technological revolution during recent decades.

In this revolution, research has become central; it

105 also becomes more formalized, complex, and costly. A steadily increasing share is conducted for, by, or at the direction of, the Federal government.

Today, the solitary inventor, tinkering in his shop, has been overshadowed by task forces of scientists in

110 laboratories and testing fields. In the same fashion, the free university, historically the fountainhead of free ideas and scientific discovery, has experienced a revolution in the conduct of research. Partly because of the huge costs involved, a government contract becomes virtually

115 a substitute for intellectual curiosity. For every old blackboard there are now hundreds of new electronic computers.

The prospect of domination of the nation's scholars by Federal employment, project allocations, and the

120 power of money is ever present—and is gravely to be regarded.

Yet, in holding scientific research and discovery in respect, as we should, we must also be alert to the equal and opposite danger that public policy could itself

125 become the captive of a scientific technological **elite**.

It is the task of **statesmanship** to mold, to balance, and to integrate these and other forces, new and old, within the principles of our democratic system—ever aiming toward the supreme goals of our free society.

43

According to passage 1, which element is *not* a characteristic of an empire?
A) a ruling class
B) conquered lands
C) dependence on machines
D) exploitation of the working class

44

In passage 1, the author's tone toward the ruling class is best described as
A) empathetic.
B) pitiful.
C) judgmental.
D) furious.

45

Choose the lines that provide the best evidence for your answer to the previous question.
A) lines 9-10 ("the shamelessness…indulged")
B) lines 13-14 ("The chief…States")
C) lines 18-20 ("Through more…structure")
D) lines 24-25 ("Consciously or…structure")

46

According to passage 1, the US entered World War I because
A) it was personal to most citizens.
B) of cruel treatment of the French.
C) the US was at more risk than any other nation.
D) US businesses insisted on it.

47

As it is used in passage 1, line 59, *plutocratic* most nearly means
A) military.
B) wealthy.
C) elderly.
D) lower-class.

Lesson 5 continued:

48

In passage 2, Eisenhower describes two major threats to the US. The threats are best described as
A) a weakened military and a stall in technological progress.
B) communism and a technology gap between the world powers.
C) the military industrial complex and the rule of the technological elite.
D) an overabundance of inventions and a growing arms industry.

49

Choose the answer that best summarizes the implication of the following lines from passage 2 (lines 108-115):

> Today, the solitary inventor, tinkering in his shop, has been overshadowed by task forces of scientists in laboratories and testing fields. In the same fashion, the free university, historically the fountainhead of free ideas and scientific discovery, has experienced a revolution in the conduct of research. Partly because of the huge costs involved, a government contract becomes virtually a substitute for intellectual curiosity.

A) In order for the country to retain its inventors, the government will need to provide more funds through university research departments.
B) What used to be real creativity is now funded and dictated by the government.
C) The only successful inventors are those who have chosen to receive funding from the universities, who, in turn, influence the inventors' ideas.
D) Intellectual curiosity is far superior to the bureaucratic, war-driven practical needs of a government in league with business.

50

As it is used in passage 2, line 125, *elite* most nearly means
A) open-minded researchers.
B) best at their jobs.
C) devious plotters.
D) exclusive group.

51

The authors of both passages describe groups who have the power to influence the government. In passage 2, the group is designated the "military industrial complex." In passage 1, Nearing calls the group
A) the united front of business interests.
B) the Kaiser and the Czar.
C) Russian immigrants in America.
D) the European belligerents.

52

The author of passage 1 writes as though the government is already subject to the influence and control of certain groups. Choose the answer that best describes how passage 2 is different with regard to the immediacy of the problem.
A) Passage 2 is a call-to-arms about outside influences upon the government but much less specific about the sources of influence.
B) Eisenhower disregards the role of business as it pertains to the problem.
C) Passage 2 is an entreaty to trust those elected to deal with the influences.
D) Eisenhower writes passage 2 as a warning to avoid preventable imbalances of power.

Lesson 5 continued:

Vocabulary: Context Answers

The following sentences contain vocabulary words used in the reading passages. Choose the answer that best completes the sentence. There may be more than one technically correct answer, but one will better exemplify the italicized vocabulary word than the others will.

1) Steve, a presidential candidate, *enunciated* his beliefs to the crowd so that they could not be _____.

   A. quoted directly
   B. denied later
   C. misinterpreted
   D. heard clearly
   E. adopted by others

2) *Belligerents* forced officers to put an end to the otherwise peaceful protest due to _____.
   A. noise
   B. supplies
   C. size
   D. obstruction
   E. violence

3) Because he was _____, Donald believed that a *plutocracy* would be best for all.
   A. generous
   B. diplomatic
   C. very poor
   D. conservative
   E. very wealthy

4) Wei proposed that student government be established as a *republic* in which _____.
   A. students vote for representatives to govern
   B. teachers act as representatives of the students
   C. students attend every student council meeting
   D. student council positions are determined by GPA
   E. one student makes all of the decisions

5) The Indian *caste* system, which _____, has been in place for hundreds of years.
   A. creates jobs for those unable to find their own
   B. separates people based on social class
   C. punishes criminals in court
   D. uses taxes for public works
   E. ensures fair treatment

6) Some believe that natural disasters are *manifestations* of a higher power's wrath, which can _____.
   A. happen anywhere
   B. be brutal
   C. take many forms
   D. heal the damage
   E. be dangerous

Lesson 5 continued:

7) As a result of _____, Britain was an *imperial* superpower in the nineteenth century.
   A. economic prosperity
   B. conquering many nations
   C. colonial rebellions
   D. poor transportation
   E. urbanization

8) The new administration created a *furor* with their new policies, _____.
   A. improving the condition of the school
   B. pleasing students and teachers alike
   C. reducing homework indefinitely
   D. upsetting students greatly
   E. including new parking restrictions

9) Rather than seeking a resolution of the conflict through _____, the international council determined that *statesmanship* would be the most beneficial means of negotiation.
   A. diplomacy
   B. new legislation
   C. violence
   D. trade agreements
   E. taxation

10) Marissa's *insidious* disease made her ill _____.
   A. quickly
   B. gradually
   C. mildly
   D. completely
   E. easily

11) Rosie was excited to meet the political *elite* who were visiting her university because she aspired to be _____ like them.
   A. sweet and accommodating
   B. unforgiving and strict
   C. thin and attractive
   D. powerful and successful
   E. interesting and smart

12) Marinah knew instantly that Coco had been the *aggressor* in the cat fight because Coco was known for her _____.
   A. sweet disposition
   B. irritability
   C. sharp claws
   D. indifferent attitude
   E. fluffy coat

13) Oliver was unsure if he wanted to be aligned with a group whose *ideology* was so different from his; he didn't know if he could reconcile their _____.
   A. different methods
   B. previous dispute
   C. physical differences
   D. differing beliefs
   E. unequal power

14) Blake knew that there would be _____ what he had done, but he could not anticipate all possible *implications*.
   A. questions about
   B. consequences for
   C. disbelief about
   D. solutions for
   E. concern over

Lesson 5 continued:

15) Preston's elaborate _____ was unnecessary; the protestors needed very little *provocation* to begin marching.
   A. apology
   B. questioning
   C. discussion
   D. call to action
   E. plan

16) The student body's *posture* toward their new administration was not positive; similarly, the _____ of the administration toward the students was distrust.
   A. attitude
   B. carriage
   C. conduct
   D. behavior
   E. concern

17) Emma was asked to leave a note for _____, just as her *predecessors* had done for her.
   A. her supervisor
   B. her replacement
   C. the district manager
   D. her coworkers
   E. the night staff

Lesson 5 continued:

Writing Practice

The underlined portion of each sentence possibly contains a flaw related to the construction of the sentence.
Select the answer that best corrects the flaw. Select NO CHANGE if the underlined portion is correct.

1) Though at first, she had agreed to the task begrudgingly and <u>there was hesitance</u>, Hannah soon found that going on a run every morning improved her health.
   A. NO CHANGE
   B. hesitant
   C. with hesitance
   D. hesitantly

2) This morning, Kendall double-checked his suitcases, <u>his passport was found</u>, and ate breakfast in preparation for his flight to Indonesia.
   A. NO CHANGE
   B. found his passport
   C. he found his passport
   D. finding his passport

3) George's wife often served as his muse; he wrote many short stories, poems, and <u>plays</u> based on their relationship.
   A. NO CHANGE
   B. plays were written
   C. his plays
   D. writing plays

4) In preparation for opening night, cast members advertised the play, practiced stage direction, <u>and their lines</u>."
   A. NO CHANGE
   B. and their lines were rehearsed
   C. and rehearsed their lines
   D. and also their lines

5) The police squad discovered bundles of cash and a fake passport hidden in her closet, which helped them conclude that the money had been stolen <u>and leaving</u> the country was the final step of her master plan.
   A. NO CHANGE
   B. to eventually leave
   C. leaving
   D. and that leaving

Lesson 5 continued:

6) Nina planned to choose a fun movie and <u>watch</u> it with her children after dinner.
   A. NO CHANGE
   B. watching
   C. could watch
   D. had watched

7) Wendy, last year's cross-country star athlete, made a brief appearance at the homecoming game, <u>running and cheering for</u> the home team on her way to the library.
   A. NO CHANGE
   B. running for and cheering
   C. running by and cheering for
   D. she ran and cheered for

8) The doctor assured the little girl that the booster shot would be quick, easy, and <u>no pain</u>.
   A. NO CHANGE
   B. painless
   C. painlessly
   D. happen painlessly

9) My dog was not allowed to sit on the couch, on the table, <u>or not the</u> counter.
   A. NO CHANGE
   B. or the
   C. or on the
   D. and not on the

10) I decided to write my college essay about a few of my favorite topics: animals that hibernate, plants' adaptation to winter, and <u>to preserve the environment</u>.
    A. NO CHANGE
    B. about preserving the environment
    C. preserve the environment
    D. preservation of the environment

Lesson 5 continued:

Vocabulary: Choosing the Right Use

The following sentences contain vocabulary words used in the reading passages. Identify the sentence or sentences that use the italicized vocabulary word properly. We have changed the form of some vocabulary words to provide new contexts; for example, some adjectives and verbs have been used as nouns.

1)   A. Construction workers dug an *indulge* for the new cables that need to be placed underground.
   B. During World War I, troops huddled in their *indulges* as gun fire peppered the air around them.
   C. The bride and groom *indulged* in a week-long celebration of their nuptials at a family estate in the Hamptons.
   D. Bruce could not help but *indulge* in a piece of chocolate cake at Cindy's birthday party.

2)   A. William used a *posture* to brace the young maple tree he planted several weeks ago.
   B. Eleanor required a *posture* to straighten her spine before the problem worsened.
   C. Frederick's *posture* toward the delegates betrayed distaste for the bickering exchanged between each member.
   D. Charles refused to make his *posture* known until the two factions settled their disputes civilly.

3)   A. The president's *imperial* nature made him unpopular among voters who favored a more egalitarian leader.
   B. "It is *imperial* we use our influence as a force for good," Jane told the other protesters.
   C. The *imperial* army invaded each of the kingdom's surrounding territories and devastated everything in its wake.
   D. Ursula knew it was *imperial* she finish her English essay before the busy weekend.

4)   A. "It took the doctor forty-five minutes to remove the *caste* from my leg," James informed his dubious friends.
   B. Harold and Susanne live within a rigid *caste* system, making it forbidden for them to be seen in public together.
   C. Fiona belongs to a *caste* that has a low position in her country's hierarchy.
   D. The deceased man's family ordered a plaster *caste* of his face—a common tradition among grieving relatives.

5)   A. Prince Andrew's *régime* became more popular after his army defeated the French.
   B. The artist's *régime* has been displayed outside the bank for fifty years.
   C. Museums in Paris embarked on a bidding war for the opportunity to show Michelangelo's famous *régime*.
   D. The art museum's new *régime* made innovative changes to its exhibits and drew hundreds of guests to the annual New Year's Eve gala.

Lesson 5 continued:

6) A. Our local *furor* is required to poll residents for their opinion about the next referendum.
    B. Xavier's controversial campaign for class president sparked a *furor* among the student body.
    C. Advertisement executives did not anticipate the *furor* their campaign caused among viewers.
    D. "Grover County has not had a *furor* for two decades, and they have done just as well as any other county," Representative Williams told his constituents.

7) A. Despite the *holocausts* caused by both wars in Europe, the continent rebuilt itself in the wake of each tragedy.
    B. Bystanders near the science museum saw *holocausts* projected into the center of the town square depicting Comet Hale-Bopp.
    C. "*Holocausts* are heinous acts against humanity that must be avoided through nonviolent diplomacy," Derek explained.
    D. Dr. Cather earned a spot on the team of experts commissioned to develop new technology for *holocausts* used by NASA.

8) A. Last week, the president *enunciated* his plan to lower taxes.
    B. The president had a person standing next to her who *enunciated* the speech in sign language so the deaf could understand it.
    C. The principal's *enunciation* made it against the dress code for students to wear open-toed shoes.
    D. Laborers across the country rebelled against the king's new taxation *enunciation*, which raised the price of bread and milk.

9) A. Smartphones allow people to download *implications* at lightning speeds, giving them access to unprecedented amounts of information.
    B. Annemarie did not understand the *implications* of Denny's comments until it was too late to fix the situation.
    C. Members of the school board could not hide the negative *implications* of their annual report.
    D. Technology students of this generation must have a sound knowledge of how to create and enhance *implications* for public use.

10) A. Pierre could not understand how his brother became enamored with a hostile *ideology* that ignored common sense.
    B. Political *ideologies* have the power to shape an individual's relationship with society, but they should not prevent a person from treating others with respect.
    C. "Our *ideology* depicts the geographical makeup of each part of the country," Keith explained.
    D. Lawrence has created hundreds of valuable *ideologies* that are often used in history textbooks to provide students with a visual of the landscape.

Lesson 5 continued:

11) A. Senator Dunston and his colleagues employed their *plutocracy* to get a piece of complicated legislation through Congress.
   B. Powerful bankers and businessmen formed the nation's ruling *plutocracy* for thirty years.
   C. Tyler used his *plutocracy* to lead the team to victory during the final round of the tournament.
   D. "I will not allow our nation to fall into the hands of a greedy *plutocracy*," the president exclaimed in his speech.

12) A. *Aggressors* examined Jasmine's farm and determined that her tractor was up to standards, but her production of ethanol was not.
   B. Principal Simmons listened to several students and teachers explain who they believe was the *aggressor* in that morning's fistfight.
   C. Several international officials denied allegations that they were *aggressors* in the escalating tensions between Spain and France.
   D. "If any of you are interested in becoming *aggressors*, please speak to Dr. Ryman—head of the Department of Agriculture—before you leave today," Dean Richards said.

13) A. Corey and his colleagues had respect for their *predecessors* at the company, who brought sales to an unprecedented level of success.
   B. "If you *predecessor* your husband, you can arrange for the funeral and burial to be taken care of beforehand," Bernice's sister said.
   C. Orson's *predecessor*, Colonel Nielson, lacked the skills and integrity the position required during a time of war.
   D. Most parents assume they will *predecessor* their children, but sometimes they are forced to face the tragedy of a child's premature death.

14) A. Allison crafted her final *provocation* carefully and was rewarded with an A from her English professor.
   B. Hilda's *provocation* contained too many errors for her club to use as its manifesto.
   C. "I will not rise to even address Mr. Feinstein's ridiculous *provocation*," the young lawyer declared.
   D. Ursula ridiculed Ben for his poor wardrobe choice, but he refused to respond to her *provocation*.

15) A. Exercise in the morning gives people healthy, *insidious* energy to get them through the day.
   B. Eating vegetables provides *insidious* vitamins and minerals to build up the body's immune system.
   C. Air pollution has an *insidious* effect on people's health, and most won't know anything is wrong with them until it's too late.
   D. The movie critic's *insidious* comments about Kimberly's acting bothered her greatly and would definitely affect the film's potential audience.

Lesson 5 continued:

16) A. George Washington exhibited excellent *statesmanship* during his time as president, stressing the need for unity between people of different views.
   B. Each person seated in the convention room decided good *statesmanship* was the only reasonable way to reach a solution to the problem.
   C. Mr. Eacker was called to fill the open *statesmanship* position left vacant by Gregory's death.
   D. The *statesmanship* is a prestigious position for anyone seeking a career in political campaigning.

17) A. The *elite* of Detroit are forced to frequent local shelters in order to have a place to sleep at night.
   B. The New Haven Military School, established in 1878, helps prepare some of the most *elite* students in the country for careers as officers.
   C. Karen and her friends volunteered to feed the destitute and the poor *elite* in her city.
   D. The Academy Awards ceremony celebrates the work of *elite* members of the film community.

18) A. Karl Marx's political *manifestations*, published in 1848, incited revolutions around the world.
   B. One *manifestation* of a warmer climate in the Arctic is that polar bears have great difficulty finding food.
   C. Newly appointed board members amended the company's marketing policies to limit the effect of damaging *manifestations* in the old regulations.
   D. Vivian crafted the environmental group's first two *manifestations* and published them on their local senator's office door.

19) A. Vernon fastened his new shed with steel *belligerents*, hoping their strength would hold it together for years to come.
   B. General McNamara ordered his *belligerents* on the front line to cease fire after the opposing army surrendered.
   C. The construction crew ran out of *belligerents* one week into the project, which stalled the bridge's progression for several days.
   D. *Belligerents* fighting during those years faced a decade of drudgery and economic depression.

20) A. Our country's founders laid the foundation for a *republic* that would be maintained by elected officials at the state and national levels.
   B. In the late 18th century, French revolutionaries overthrew King Louis XVI to establish a *republic*.
   C. Three powerful businessmen from each district formed their own *republic* to replace the nation's democratically elected officials.
   D. Corruption ran rampant through the self-appointed leadership of their *republic* for twenty years until it was overthrown to form a democracy.

Lesson 5 continued:

Synonyms and Antonyms

Match the word with its *antonym*.

1) elite   **A.** pacifist

2) insidious   **B.** abstain

3) belligerent   **C.** inferior

4) enunciate   **D.** innocent

5) manifest   **E.** mumble

6) indulge   **F.** disappear

Match the word with its *synonym*.

7) furor   **G.** attacker

8) provocation   **H.** rule

9) caste   **I.** suggestion

10) régime   **J.** philosophy

11) ideology   **K.** stance

12) aggressor   **L.** status

13) implication   **M.** aggravation

14) posture   **N.** rage

15) predecessor   **O.** ancestor

END
of
LESSON 5

Lesson 6

Writing and Language Test

A set of questions accompanies each passage. The questions will ask you to make editorial decisions that improve or correct language, grammar, and construction errors in the paragraphs, including any accompanying graphics. Read the passage and then choose the best answer to each of the questions. In some instances, no change will be necessary.

Questions 1–11 are based on the following passage.

— 1 —

In the United States, it seems that as soon as a president is elected, news media and political **pundits** start **speculating** on who will run for the next presidency. Politicians themselves announce their plans to run for president more than a year before the actual election. Campaign season in the US is much longer than campaign seasons { **1** } in other countries. In Australia and the United Kingdom, campaigning lasts about six weeks; in France, presidential { **2** } candidates only campaign two weeks before the first ballot. US elections were not always this way; the trend of people **heralding** presidential runs so far in advance began in 1975 with Jimmy Carter's presidential bid.

— 2 —

American politicians like Thomas Jefferson and Andrew Jackson spent years **inconspicuously** gaining support for planned presidential { **3** } runs. The candidates used to wait at least until the calendar year of the election to make their announcement public. That historic trend changed when Mr. Carter kicked off his Iowa campaign early, in part because Iowa moved its **caucuses** to January during the 1972 election cycle. Carter's efforts to gain attention early paid off, and, despite starting as a little-known former Georgia governor, he won the election. Other politicians took notice; since 1976, most presidential hopefuls have been announcing their campaigns well over a year in advance. This extended campaigning is tied not only to gaining more media coverage, but also { **4** } to success in earlier primaries and getting more funding.

1

A) NO CHANGE
B) from other
C) to some
D) in the other

2

A) NO CHANGE
B) campaign only, candidates
C) only candidates campaign
D) candidates campaign only

3

Choose the best revision to connect the sentences at the underlined portion.
A) runs; therefore,
B) runs; the
C) runs, while the
D) runs because

4

A) NO CHANGE
B) the success
C) to succeeding
D) having success

Lesson 6 continued:

— 3 —

{ 5 } [1] <u>As previously mentioned in the essay, in 1972, Iowa moved its caucus to January, and other states followed.</u> [2] Other states also took similar measures. [3] Historically, New Hampshire holds the first **primary** after the Iowa caucus on the second Tuesday of March, but in 1972, Florida tried to compete by having its primary election the same day. [4] New Hampshire changed its primary to March seventh. [5] This **jockeying** to hold the first primaries has continued, and by 2012, the Iowa caucus was on January third, and five other states held their primaries in January. [6] In order to be competitive in the polls, candidates have to declare their campaigns before the Iowa caucus, so the earlier scheduling for nomination events forces them to campaign before the election year. { 6 }

— 4 —

Protracted campaigning gives candidates more time to raise money and gain recognition; it also means that it costs more to run. Jimmy Carter raised $13.6 million for his 1976 presidential campaign; Barack Obama raised $414 million for his 2008 presidential campaign, eight times more than Carter, even when adjusted for **inflation**. Candidates need increasingly more money to conduct long-term campaigns that require them to focus their efforts on their presidential bids instead of { 7 } <u>their other job,</u> such as governing states. Some candidates leave their jobs or political office in order to run for president. The full-time job of campaigning and { 8 } <u>to fund the campaign</u> makes it almost impossible for less wealthy people to run for president. The fact that most presidential hopefuls are rich is nothing new to politics, but the difference in wealth between candidates and the average American has become more pronounced, on average, in recent decades. This wealth factor, in addition to seemingly endless campaign seasons, causes many Americans to feel detached from politics. Polls conducted by the Pew Research Center during the 2004, 2008, and 2012 elections found that at least half of Americans considered the presidential campaigns too long.

5

Choose the best revision to replace the underlined sentence.
A) When, in 1972, as stated before, Iowa moved its caucus to January.
B) When Iowa moved its caucus to January, other states followed.
C) Iowa, in 1972, moved its caucus to January, with other states following, as mentioned.
D) Iowa followed the other states when, in 1972, it moved its caucus to January.

6

One sentence in paragraph 3 is unnecessary and redundant. Choose the sentence that should be deleted.
A) sentence [5]
B) sentence [4]
C) sentence [3]
D) sentence [2]

7

A) NO CHANGE
B) they're other jobs
C) their job
D) their other jobs

8

A) NO CHANGE
B) work to fund the campaign
C) funding the campaign
D) to get funds for the campaign

Lesson 6 continued:

— 5 —

[1] Even political parties are re-evaluating the current campaign season. [2] In 2011, the GOP tried to delay the nominating system until February sixth and provided incentives for states to have later primaries; while a number of states bucked and held primaries in January, there were many primaries in March or later. { 9 } [3] Canada's longest campaign season in the nation's modern history was eleven weeks long. [4] Perhaps if the Democrat and GOP leadership can encourage states to delay their primaries or, better yet, establish a system of primaries closer to Election Day, the US campaign season can become more reasonable. { 10 } { 11 }

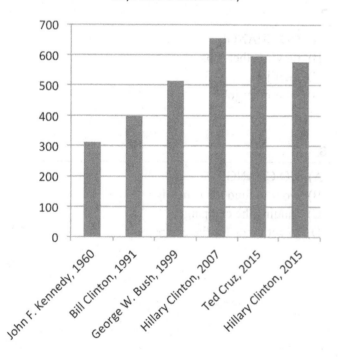

Presidential Candidacy Announcements

■ Days before Election Day

9

Sentence 3 seems to stray from the main topic of paragraph 5. The sentence should be moved to
A) paragraph 1 because it provides an example of another country's campaign length.
B) paragraph 2 because it supports the historical details of US political campaigns.
C) paragraph 3 because it is specific to an individual state's process.
D) paragraph 4 because it implies the massive funding required to run a successful campaign.

10

Which data, if inserted on the chart, would better tie the chart to the author's historical example in the passage?
A) average candidacy announcement length for countries other than the US
B) an analysis of the gap between Bill and Hillary Clinton's campaigns
C) an explanation for the increase in announcement lead times between John F. Kennedy and George W. Bush
D) Jimmy Carter's announcement because he is used as an example of the first candidate to campaign early

11

What information cannot be taken from the graph?
A) The length of the campaign season will continue to decrease.
B) Hillary Clinton spent approximately twice as much time campaigning than John F. Kennedy.
C) The longest time spent campaigning was in the 21st century.
D) The total amount of time in all Clinton campaigns is greater than the other three candidates.

Lesson 6 continued:

Vocabulary: Context Answers

The following sentences contain vocabulary words used in the reading passage. Choose the answer that best completes the sentence. There may be more than one technically correct answer, but one will better exemplify the italicized vocabulary word than the others will.

1) There was a *caucus* held at the high school in order to _____.
   A. plan a student orientation for the incoming freshman
   B. raise money for a local charity
   C. decide on dates for the home football games
   D. choose candidates for the mayor
   E. discuss whether to build a library in an open lot

2) *Speculating* about her grade led to _____ failure for Fiona, though, in fact, she passed.
   A. complete
   B. virtual
   C. partial
   D. imagined
   E. clear

3) The _____ were examples of the two towns *jockeying* for control of the lake.
   A. joint boating tournaments
   B. protests outside of town halls
   C. equal divisions
   D. collaborative clean-up crews
   E. colorful fish

4) Quan went into the movie theater as *inconspicuously* as possible because the film had already begun and he did not want to _____.
   A. cause a disturbance
   B. miss any of it
   C. see the movie
   D. know who was in it
   E. watch the opening credits

5) Due to *inflation* and other factors, a two-bedroom home _____.
   A. is far larger than other homes
   B. is less expensive than it would have been in the past
   C. has grown in size recently
   D. has only one floor, rather than two
   E. costs more than it did twenty years ago

6) Adelman needed more votes than _____ in order to win the *primary* election.
   A. all candidates combined
   B. the other political party
   C. the majority
   D. others in her political party
   E. she had last week

Lesson 6 continued:

7) Employees gathered to protest their newly *protracted* work day because they did not want _____.

A. their benefits revoked
B. shortened holiday hours
C. to work extended hours
D. fewer hours
E. continued monitoring

8) For the hundredth anniversary of the war's final battle, well-known history *pundits* Shaw and Cooper released a new book containing _____.

A. photographs of the battlefield
B. their opinions about the effects of the war
C. assorted essays about the war
D. firsthand accounts from the front lines
E. multiple sources

9) Dominic burst through the door, *heralding* good news from the hospital: He _____ that his newly born nephew was healthy.

A. exclaimed
B. knew
C. thought
D. hoped
E. was happy

Lesson 6 continued:

Writing Practice

Each of the following sentences contains a modifying phrase that may or may not be clear or correct. Choose the answer that best corrects the sentence while retaining the intended meaning of the original sentence. Select NO CHANGE if the provided sentence is correct.

1) Wally received a birthday card from his grandma in the mail.
   A. NO CHANGE
   B. In the mail, Wally received a birthday card from his grandma.
   C. Wally received a birthday card in the mail from his grandma.
   D. From his grandma, Wally received a birthday card in the mail.

2) I needed some extra money because Mom only gave me five dollars for my allowance last week.
   A. NO CHANGE
   B. I needed some extra money because Mom gave me only five dollars for my allowance last week.
   C. I needed some extra money because Mom gave me five dollars allowance only last week.
   D. Mom only gave me five dollars allowance last week, so I needed some extra money.

3) The realtor sold the house to the buyer with the brick patio.
   A. NO CHANGE
   B. The realtor sold, to the buyer, the house with the brick patio.
   C. The realtor sold the house with the brick patio to the buyer.
   D. The house with the brick patio, the realtor sold to the buyer.

4) The doctor said that quickly running improves a person's health.
   A. NO CHANGE
   B. The doctor quickly said that running improves a person's health.
   C. The doctor said that running quickly improves a person's health.
   D. The doctor said that running improves a person's health quickly.

5) He bought a cat for his daughter called Fluffy.
   A. NO CHANGE
   B. He bought a cat called Fluffy for his daughter.
   C. A cat called Fluffy is the cat he bought his daughter.
   D. Fluffy bought a cat for his daughter.

6) During his trip across the country, Carl nearly drove twelve hours a day.
   A. NO CHANGE
   B. Carl nearly drove twelve hours a day during his trip across the country.
   C. During his trip across the country, Carl drove nearly twelve hours a day.
   D. During his trip, Carl drove twelve hours a day nearly across the country.

Lesson 6 continued:

LANGUAGE
MODIFIER PLACEMENT 2

7) The blue coat was too big in the store.
   A. NO CHANGE
   B. The blue coat in the store was too big.
   C. In the store, the blue coat was too big.
   D. The big blue coat was in the store.

8) Mr. Clark said after spring break he would return our exams.
   A. NO CHANGE
   B. Mr. Clark said he would after spring break return our exams.
   C. After spring break, Mr. Clark said he "would return our exams."
   D. Mr. Clark said he would return our exams after spring break.

9) When three years old, my dad bought a new car.
   A. NO CHANGE
   B. When I was three years old, my dad bought a new car.
   C. My dad bought a new, three-year-old car.
   D. A three-year-old car is what my dad bought.

10) Marchers in the parade were handing out candy in bright wrappers to children.
   A. NO CHANGE
   B. Marchers were handing out candy in bright wrappers to children in the parade.
   C. Marchers in the parade were handing out candy to children in bright wrappers.
   D. Marchers were handing out candy in bright wrappers in the parade to children.

Lesson 6 continued:

Vocabulary: Choosing the Right Use

The following sentences contain vocabulary words used in the reading passage. Identify the sentence or sentences that use the italicized vocabulary word properly. We have changed the form of some vocabulary words to provide new contexts; for example, some adjectives and verbs have been used as nouns.

1) A. Members of the past two *caucuses* began vehement infighting when attempting to choose their candidate.
    B. Certain types of *caucuses* appear only every seventeen years, and their emergence brings a steady buzzing sound to the summer season.
    C. *Caucuses* got into Gregory's house through a hole in his screen door, forcing him to spend the rest of the day removing them.
    D. Many people have lost their faith in the effectiveness of state *caucuses* throughout the country and have moved to create a new system of selecting a candidate.

2) A. On our local radio station, political *pundits* from Washington, D.C. expressed their well-formed ideas.
    B. "I don't have time to train the new *pundits* with my current course load," Hector told the academy's commandant.
    C. Corrupt city officials tried to ban *pundits* from airing opinions, fearing they would persuade constituents to vote against those people already in office.
    D. As a *pundit*, Jane was not able to navigate the training obstacle course quickly enough, but she eventually improved her time.

3) A. Janice's *protracted* speech lasted two class periods and still failed to make any significant points.
    B. Kurt *protracted* a new office building for his law firm in the bustling city center.
    C. Mr. Judd's lecture was so *protracted* and pedantic that some students stopped paying attention after the first hour of class.
    D. Cara's construction company built the *protracted* school in record time, which curtailed the traveling time of local students.

4) A. Our local *primary* lacked basic rations such as fruits and vegetables, leaving residents to make meals with high-calorie, processed foods.
    B. New Jersey's *primary* attracted record-breaking crowds to voting stations across the state.
    C. Vera's parents made her quit her job at the *primary* until her mathematics grade improved by at least ten percentage points.
    D. "Our state's *primary* does not accurately represent the will of the people because so few eligible voters actually voted," Brian claimed.

Lesson 6 continued:

5) A. The school boasted *inconspicuously* about its rise in student enrollment and high standardized test scores.
   B. The *inconspicuous* tree stood in the middle of the barren desert, looking like some form of alien growth.
   C. Brenda's friends moved *inconspicuously* into their hiding places as she opened the door to her surprise birthday party.
   D. A large American flag floated *inconspicuously* above the governor's mansion.

6) A. Aaron could not *jockey* his company into a competitive position with other, more valuable institutions.
   B. "Stop *jockeying* around. I know a lie when I hear it," Dean said quietly to his friend.
   C. Karen and Sue began *jockeying* for the lead role in their school's production of West Side Story.
   D. "It is wildly inappropriate that two of our town's most respected leaders are *jockeying* for monetary contributions," the mayor said.

7) A. Prices were *speculating* rapidly as the supply of cotton became increasingly unstable.
   B. Students cannot do well on exams by *speculating* about the correct answers.
   C. Journalists wasted their time *speculating* about the outcome of the World Series instead of covering the earthquake in California.
   D. *Speculating* weather makes it difficult for us to enjoy spring break.

8) A. Bobby could not stop himself from *heralding* his candidacy a year in advance.
   B. Kim prevented candidates from *heralding* for votes in front of her shop.
   C. *Heralding* is such a complicated art form that most students opt to study more traditional forms, such as painting and sculpture.
   D. The Museum of Modern Art began exhibiting *heralding* pieces in the mid-1940s.

9) A. *Inflation* has led to a drastic spike in common goods and services.
   B. "Jamie doesn't understand the financial intricacies of *inflation*," Ian told his mother.
   C. Hilda used an *inflation* to travel across the Hudson River on the first day of spring.
   D. The new camp counselors were unable to locate *inflations* for the children to use during the rowing tournament.

Lesson 6 continued:

Synonyms and Antonyms

Match the word with its *antonym*.

1) speculate

2) inconspicuous

3) protracted

4) inflation

A. shortened

B. deflation

C. know

D. obvious

Match the word with its *synonym*.

5) pundit

6) jockey

7) herald

E. compete

F. commentator

G. signify

END
of
LESSON 6

Lesson 7

Questions 12–22 are based on the following passage.

— 1 —

Have you ever looked at a cloud and thought, "Hey, that looks like a { **12** } dragon?"! That might surprise you. If { **13** } it were a child, it could inspire flights of imagination. Or maybe you looked at an electrical outlet and realized it resembled a face with a **gaping** mouth. That might make you smile or cause you to look for more examples of the same thing. Seeing images or faces in other objects is a **phenomenon** called pareidolia. Pareidolia happens when the mind { **14** } implies images or sounds as familiar patterns when no pattern actually exists. The term is derived from the Greek words *para*, meaning "alongside" or "beyond," and *eidolon*, meaning "form" or "image."

— 2 —

[1] So, what causes pareidolia? [2] Psychologists once thought it was a symptom of **psychosis**, but have since determined that it is a natural human tendency. [3] In his { **15** } book: *The Demon Haunted World*, scientist Carl Sagan **posits** that the tendency is linked to the evolutionary need to quickly identify faces. [4] Infants recognize faces as soon as they can see, and babies who can better read facial moods and respond appropriately are more likely to survive. [5] Our brains are so efficient at identifying facial patterns that they sometimes construct false positives. [6] This evolutionary model also works with **auditory** pareidolia. [7] When our ancestors heard a rustle in the leaves, it could have been the wind or a predator. [8] Assuming that it was a { **16** } predator, and running away cost less—even if the noise was actually the wind—than assuming the noise was the wind and possibly being killed by a saber-toothed tiger. [9] Sometimes, there really is a pattern that looks like a face. [10] Basically, pareidolia exists because falsely identifying patterns that aren't there is less potentially dangerous than not perceiving actual patterns. { **17** }

12

A) NO CHANGE
B) dragon"!
C) dragon!"?
D) dragon?"?

13

A) NO CHANGE
B) you were
C) it was
D) you was

14

A) NO CHANGE
B) infers
C) discerns
D) portrays

15

A) NO CHANGE
B) book;
C) book—
D) book

16

A) NO CHANGE
B) predator, running
C) predator, and running does
D) predator, because running

17

Choose the sentence that should be deleted from paragraph 2 because it does not contribute to the main idea.
A) sentence [3]
B) sentence [5]
C) sentence [7]
D) sentence [9]

Lesson 7 continued:

— 3 —

These false positives occur more frequently than you might think. Finding human faces in things is the most common form of pareidolia. For example, people have seen the "Man in the Moon" for **millennia**, and { 18 } the figure is so old that it has been mythologized in Chinese and Norse myths and Medieval Christian lore. More recently, in 1976, the spacecraft Viking 1 photographed a rocky plateau on Mars that many people interpreted as a face. The so-called "Face on Mars" can be seen as such only from certain angles and in specific lighting, much like a shadow puppet. Perhaps these images indicate an **inclination** to see ourselves or similar beings on other worlds; however, there are plenty of pareidolia incidents on Earth, and they don't all relate to geography. { 19 } Take the smiley face, for example. In actuality, the image is simply two dots and an arc drawn within a circle, yet it is composed in such a way that people associate it with a human face and emotion. These "faces" can then be used to convey emotion in a variety of applications, from emoticons in text messages to pain charts in doctors' offices.

— 4 —

Pareidolia is sometimes triggered intentionally for learning or psychological purposes. Hermann Rorschach's inkblot test is the most famous example of using pareidolia to understand personality and emotional functions. The Rorschach test consists of ten cards, all with symmetrical inkblots of **ambiguous** design. { 20 } The general idea is that the viewer's interpretations of the blots should indicate subconscious personality and cognition, variables such as motivations, response tendencies, and confusion, personal and interpersonal relationships, and emotions. For years, the Rorschach test was used to hint at mental disturbances in patients undergoing psychiatric therapy. Though modern psychologists question the value of the inkblot test, it demonstrates how pareidolia can be used to induce or reveal human emotion.

18

A) NO CHANGE
B) the figure has been
C) the figure, so old, that it has been
D) the figure, having been seen for so long, has been

19

A) NO CHANGE
B) There is
C) Also
D) Consider

20

Choose the best revision for the underlined portion of the sentence.
A) The viewer's interpretations
B) In general, the idea is that the viewer's interpretations
C) The interpretations of the view
D) The idea, in general, is that the viewer's interpretations

Lesson 7 continued:

LANGUAGE PASSAGE

— 5 —

Whether created intentionally or not, pareidolia causes us to respond to stimuli in ways we would not otherwise. By seeing faces in objects, we can strangely relate to them just as they appear to relate to us. It induces a greater, **albeit** inexact, connection to the world.

— 6 —

Pareidolia is also used in advertising. In some cases, the pareidolia transmits a **subliminal** message intended to appeal to the audience's subconscious; however, with the popularization of pareidolia, sparked by images of "things with faces" being shared on the Internet, advertisers now tend to make pareidolia an object of humor. One credit card company produced a commercial that depicted objects that appeared to have sad faces, explained how the credit card works, and then showed objects with happy faces. A footwear company advertises its shoes with a picture of a hand holding a shoe so that the fingernails look like eyes and the opening of the shoe looks like a mouth. The company's motto is, "You are what you wear." Pareidolia is used to make certain objects seem like { 21 } <u>an extension</u> of the self. Cars are especially pareidolic. People readily see faces in the grills and headlights of cars, and a scientific study shows that most customers prefer cars that look **dominant**, angry, or powerful. With this knowledge, car manufacturers can design vehicles with "faces" that are likely to appeal to the largest number of customers—all by turning the brain's false positives into real positives. { 22 }

21

A) NO CHANGE
B) an extra part
C) extensions
D) extension

22

Paragraph 5 does not seem to fit the logical flow of ideas in the passage. The paragraph should be relocated to

A) precede paragraph 1 as an introduction.
B) follow paragraph 3 because it introduces the use of pareidolia as a psychological tool.
C) follow paragraph 2 because it explains the biology of pareidolia.
D) the end of the passage, as a conclusion.

Lesson 7 continued:

Vocabulary: Context Answers

The following sentences contain vocabulary words used in the reading passage. Choose the answer that best completes the sentence. There may be more than one technically correct answer, but one will better exemplify the italicized vocabulary word than the others will.

1) Hugh's persistent _____ led to a diagnosis of *psychosis.*
   A. nausea
   B. fatigue
   C. snoring
   D. delusions
   E. friendliness

2) The *ambiguous* painting was confusing to Raquel because it _____.
   A. was very large
   B. was created in a foreign country
   C. was very complicated
   D. could be interpreted in multiple ways
   E. could be easily described

3) Jean was glad to have an opportunity, *albeit* short, to meet the prominent scientist; a brief meeting was _____.
   A. frustrating
   B. distracting from the problem
   C. very inconvenient
   D. much appreciated
   E. better than no meeting

4) It is _____ the *phenomenon* of a UFO.
   A. nothing special to experience
   B. common to see
   C. easy to explain
   D. possible to request
   E. extremely rare to witness

5) In shock, Maritza's *gaping* _____ at the sight of the tornado on the horizon.
   A. lips formed a frown
   B. mouth hung open
   C. eyes filled with tears
   D. shriek echoed
   E. worries increased

6) Gina's _____ has been heightened since losing her vision; she relies on *auditory* stimuli to get around.
   A. sense of smell
   B. sensitivity to light
   C. emotional response
   D. sense of hearing
   E. balance

7) For _____, humans have lived as family units; countless *millennia* have passed, and this fact remains a common thread in the human experience.
   A. thousands of years
   B. the purpose of sleep
   C. hundreds of years
   D. the duration of their lives
   E. protection from predators

8) Scout was the more *dominant* dog, which was evident when he _____ Spot.
   A. overpowered
   B. cuddled with
   C. licked
   D. fought with
   E. was frightened by

Lesson 7 continued:

9) Ever since he started volunteering, Tommy had an *inclination* to help others, _____ that would stay with him for the rest of his life.
   A. a distaste
   B. a tendency
   C. a hobby
   D. an obligation
   E. an experience

10) Esther read that advertisements could affect _____ with their *subliminal* messages.
   A. her eyesight
   B. people who didn't see the ads
   C. her mind
   D. the environment
   E. aquatic life

11) Latisha, a cancer researcher, *posited* that cancer is caused by a contagious microbe, so the Centers for Disease Control investigated her _____.
   A. guess
   B. suggestion
   C. lie
   D. discovery
   E. cure

Lesson 7 continued:

Writing Practice

The underlined portion of each sentence possibly contains an error related to the use of restrictive and nonrestrictive clauses. Select the answer that best corrects the flaw. Select NO CHANGE if the underlined portion is correct.

1) <u>George Washington, the first president of the United States, refused</u> to serve a third term.
   A. NO CHANGE
   B. George Washington, the first president, of the United States, refused
   C. George Washington the first president of the United States, refused
   D. George Washington the first president of the United States refused

2) Norm studies ancient languages for <u>enjoyment which is a hobby that's not easy for me to understand.</u>
   A. NO CHANGE
   B. enjoyment a hobby that's not easy for me to understand.
   C. enjoyment, which is a hobby, that's not easy for me to understand.
   D. enjoyment, which is a hobby that's not easy for me to understand.

3) <u>Jerry, who lives down the street, is jealous of my new Ferrari which cost over $100,000.</u>
   A. NO CHANGE
   B. Jerry who lives down the street, is jealous of my new Ferrari, which cost over $100,000.
   C. Jerry, who lives down the street, is jealous of my new Ferrari, which cost over $100,000.
   D. Jerry, who lives down the street is jealous of my new Ferrari which cost over $100,000.

4) We looked for <u>anyone who was interested in helping decorate the cafeteria for the dance that would be held next Wednesday night.</u>
   A. NO CHANGE
   B. anyone, who was interested in helping decorate the cafeteria for the dance, that would be held next Wednesday night.
   C. anyone, who was interested in helping decorate the cafeteria for the dance that would be held next Wednesday night.
   D. anyone who was interested in helping decorate the cafeteria for the dance which would be held next Wednesday night.

5) <u>Mark and his friend Carlos who didn't show up for practice were</u> cut from the team.
   A. NO CHANGE
   B. Mark and his friend Carlos, who didn't show up for practice were
   C. Mark and his friend Carlos, who didn't show up for practice, were
   D. Mark and his friend Carlos who didn't show up for practice, were

Lesson 7 continued:

6) No classes that are required courses will be available in the evening because those are all classes which offer college credit.
   A. NO CHANGE
   B. No classes that are required courses, will be available in the evening because those are all classes, which offer college credit.
   C. No classes that are required courses will be available in the evening because those are all classes that offer college credit.
   D. No classes, which are required courses, will be available in the evening because those are all classes which offer college credit.

7) Old Professor Marks, who tries to impress her students with her knowledge of modern slang usually just ends up embarrassing herself.
   A. NO CHANGE
   B. Old Professor Marks, who tries to impress her students, with her knowledge of modern slang, usually just ends up embarrassing herself.
   C. Old Professor Marks who tries to impress her students with her knowledge of modern slang usually just ends up embarrassing herself.
   D. Old Professor Marks, who tries to impress her students with her knowledge of modern slang, usually just ends up embarrassing herself.

8) My mother who had been cheated when she purchased her first home years ago refuses to buy any house that Silvers Builders is involved with.
   A. NO CHANGE
   B. My mother, who had been cheated when she purchased her first home years ago, refuses to buy any house that Silvers Builders is involved with.
   C. My mother who had been cheated when she purchased her first home refuses to buy any house, that Silvers Builders is involved with.
   D. My mother, who had been cheated when she purchased her first home years ago, refuses to buy any house, that Silvers Builders is involved with.

9) "Any physician who overeats, smokes, and doesn't exercise has no right to advise any of his or her patients about their health," David angrily exclaimed.
   A. NO CHANGE
   B. Any physician who overeats, smokes, and doesn't exercise, has no right to advise
   C. Any physician, who overeats, smokes, and doesn't exercise has no right to advise,
   D. Any physician, who overeats, smokes, and doesn't exercise, has no right to advise

10) For more than six weeks, Vic traveled around Europe with the student, who lives next door to him.
   A. NO CHANGE
   B. Vic traveled around Europe, with the student who lives next door to him.
   C. Vic traveled around Europe with the student who lives next door to him.
   D. Vic traveled around Europe with the student, who lives next door, to him.

Lesson 7 continued:

Vocabulary: Choosing the Right Use

The following sentences contain vocabulary words used in the reading passage. Identify the sentence or sentences that use the italicized vocabulary word properly. We have changed the form of some vocabulary words to provide new contexts; for example, some adjectives and verbs have been used as nouns.

1) A. Jolene and Sydney *posited* for their group's website until they had raised enough money to pay the server fees.
   B. Mr. Quinn *posits* that the connection between the monarchy and the people became frayed over years of tension.
   C. "I am not willing to *posit* that Bertha will be able to run the club after she graduates," Anna said.
   D. Allison was not able to finish reading all the *posits* her teacher posted online the night before, making her unprepared for class.

2) A. "I've established that Jim is suffering from *auditory* hallucinations, so he must continue with psychological therapy," Dr. Pym explained.
   B. The new student had an *auditory* problem that made it nearly impossible for him to remain seated for long.
   C. Polly failed the *auditory* presentation course because she was unable to get over her fear of public speaking.
   D. One amazing *auditory* dancer after the other took the stage, until there were over fifty people performing.

3) A. Naval commanders acquired a *subliminal* watercraft to use during training operations.
   B. "I won't let my children watch television because advertisements use *subliminal* messages to influence viewers," Tina explained.
   C. Carl spent ten years researching the use of *subliminal* messages to inspire fear in the enemy during times of war.
   D. Otto designed the code for a digital scale model of the destroyed *subliminal* ship.

4) A. Even though Christianity has millions of followers in the world, the Roman Catholic Church has existed for only about two *millennia*.
   B. During summer vacation, June took part in a Roman feast that had been a tradition for *millennia*.
   C. "My mother has been working for that company for two *millennia*, and she still loves going in every day," Kirsten said.
   D. Wall paintings on the cave proved it had been continually inhabited for at least two *millennia* before France became a country.

Lesson 7 continued:

5) A. Lisa had the opportunity to see the *phenomenon* of the aurora borealis in Alaska during her family's vacation.
   B. "Peter has been training for this *phenomenon* for a year. He has a good chance of finishing in less than three hours," Gene said.
   C. Any *phenomenon* JoAnn can participate in this year will definitely help her self-esteem.
   D. The development of several new fast food establishments in the town center was an unappealing *phenomenon* to many residents.

6) A. Lana has been using *psychosis* to study for her exam since last week, so it's safe to assume she will do extremely well.
   B. *Psychosis* is a difficult disease to cure because patients have trouble with their balance.
   C. Marianne's grandfather suffered from a severe form of *psychosis*, which left him institutionalized for twenty years.
   D. "I've spent my entire academic career studying the genetic and environmental factors that lead to different forms of *psychosis*," Dr. Lynn told her students.

7) A. Nadia had a strong *inclination* not to support her husband in his campaign for town mayor.
   B. Students became outraged that there were no *inclinations* on campus for people in wheelchairs to use.
   C. "I have no *inclination* to see that movie; I already read the book and know how it turns out," Ivan told his friends.
   D. The cyclists' *inclination* cracked after months of intense use leading up to the semifinals.

8) A. "Our students love *gaping* for microscopic invertebrates along the edge of the pond," Ms. Kreacher told the principal.
   B. Corporal Dern wrapped a cloth around the *gaping* wound on his leg until he reached the mobile army hospital.
   C. Joey lost his fishing net while *gaping* from the side of his canoe.
   D. Fern foolishly fell into the *gaping* hole her brothers dug on the beach because she was too distracted by dolphins near the shore.

9) A. The principal's *ambiguous* speech made it clear that violations of other students' rights were unacceptable.
   B. "The ending of the film was completely *ambiguous*; I couldn't tell what happened to the main character," Abdul lamented.
   C. Alisha crafted a piece of legislation so *ambiguous* that it was immediately approved by astute members of the Senate.
   D. Mr. Kessler's instructions were *ambiguous*, making it difficult for students to complete their laboratory assignment.

Lesson 7 continued:

10) A. Candace campaigned for healthier school lunches and secured a position as a *dominant* member of the school's PTA.

  B. Lions are *dominant* animals in the food chain of the African plains.

  C. Deirdre felt so *dominant* on her sister that she decided to carry out this task on her own for the first time in several months.

  D. Pete became *dominant* on an intake of sugar every day at 3:00 pm, which helped him get through the rest of the day.

11) A. Polly was not able to attend the play, *albeit* her dog required emergency care after it fell ill.

  B. *Albeit* Leo was late to school on Wednesday, his teachers would not allow him to go on the class field trip.

  C. Yolanda presented an interesting, *albeit* overly broad, introduction to the Revolutionary War.

  D. Tracy found an inexpensive, *albeit* out of the way, alternative to the hotel she booked for her family's vacation.

Lesson 7 continued:

Synonyms and Antonyms

Match the word with its *antonym*.

1) ambiguous   **A.** sanity

2) inclination   **B.** aversion

3) dominant   **C.** specific

4) psychosis   **D.** inferior

Match the word with its *synonym*.

5) phenomenon   **E.** speculate

6) posit   **F.** oddity

7) auditory   **G.** hearing

END
of
LESSON 7

Lesson 8

Questions 23–33 are based on the following passage.

Two percent of the US population—roughly 7.5 million people—suffer from some type of speech **impediment**, and we have become fairly **adept** at identifying and empowering them. It is rare today to see speech impediments as the center of jokes, as with historic cartoon characters such as the lisping Sylvester the Cat or the stuttering Porky Pig. The field continues to improve, and careers in research, counseling, and therapy are dedicated to helping people overcome impediments.

Besides a stricter, more **comprehensive** definition of speech problems, other recent developments in **neurology** and genetics are also contributing to the dialogue surrounding speech disorders. In a study focused on stuttering, { 23 } <u>84 percent %</u> of patients interviewed reported a relative who currently stutters or had experienced stuttering in the past. Scientists have identified three **genes** linked to stuttering, and connectivity issues between the auditory and motor **cortexes** of the brain likely contribute to errors in proper articulation. Because of the genetic discovery, **natal** diagnosis and early treatment are becoming more viable options in the treatment of childhood stuttering.

Considering the current challenges in traditional methods of { 24 } <u>treatment, that includes</u> praise and repetition, these biological developments could signal a breakthrough. After all, more than half of those who undergo traditional behavioral treatment suffer **relapse**. Early **diagnoses** are usually not determined until grade school, at which point both the brain and behavior have { 25 } <u>become habituated; less receptive</u> to treatment. Furthermore, the subjective speech tests used rely on categorizing symptoms that overlap between disorders and can result in wrong diagnoses and even incorrect treatments, exacerbating the problem. { 26 } <u>On the other hand, the</u> three genes linked to stuttering are not exclusive to speech problems, meaning that multiple genes and combinations of those genes could cause similar issues. Consequently, these biological and genetic determinations, assuming they are adopted in mainstream medicine, will still likely be used in conjunction with more traditional methods of treatment.

{ 27 } <u>Consequently,</u> stuttering frequently disappears spontaneously, with about 35% of youthful stutterers exhibiting symptoms for longer than two { 28 } <u>years however once</u> stuttering has been part of a person's life for five years, only 18% recover. Girls, for whatever reason, seem to lose symptoms faster than boys do.

23
A) NO CHANGE
B) 84 per cent
C) 84%
D) 84% percent

24
A) NO CHANGE
B) treatment, which include
C) treatment, that includes,
D) treatment; which includes

25
A) NO CHANGE
B) become habituated and less receptive
C) habituated and receptive
D) become habituated; therefore, less receptive

26
A) NO CHANGE
B) Understandably—the
C) Otherwise: the
D) The

27
A) NO CHANGE
B) Sadly
C) Interestingly
D) Expectedly

28
A) NO CHANGE
B) years; however, once
C) years however, once
D) years: however, once

Lesson 8 continued:

LANGUAGE PASSAGE

From genetics to neurology, the field of Speech Language **Pathology** (SLP) is often interdisciplinary. { 29 } With Speech Language Pathologists (SLPs) work with a variety of individuals, including health care professionals, educators, behavior consultants, and parents. They also work in a variety of workplaces, including hospitals, Skilled Nursing Facilities (SNFs), Long-Term Acute Care (LTAC) facilities, hospice, home healthcare, community health organizations, and within educational districts. Recent technology and official clearance has even opened the field to more remote areas via Skype and similar programs.

Nevertheless, the focus of SLPs is very much on communication and aero-mechanical or digestive disorders involving swallowing or respiration, for example. They also treat both physical and emotional causes for these disorders and are involved in every step of the process, from initial screening, assessment, and diagnosis, to later consultation, treatment, and counseling.

According to the field's leading organization, the American Speech-Language-Hearing Association (ASHA), the salary range for an SLP is anywhere between $40,000 and { 30 } $90,000 dollars, with the median at $61,000, based on their 2014 School Survey. To be eligible for a career in the field, however, candidates require rigorous **prerequisite** schooling, as well as advanced classes and the training of later candidates in order to maintain their licenses.

29

Choose the answer that corrects an error in the underlined sentence.
A) Delete the acronym.
B) Insert a semicolon after "individuals."
C) Delete "With" to repair the fragment.
D) Insert an apostrophe after "parents."

30

A) NO CHANGE
B) 90,000 thousand dollars
C) $90,000 thousand
D) $90,000

Lesson 8 continued:

To begin with, { **31** } <u>a degree must be received by candidates from an accredited school, a master's degree</u> that has a program in communicative sciences and disorders. A **doctorate** is optional, but to contribute to a career in SLP, it should be either **clinical** science or in a field related to a specific career goal. In either case, candidates must complete 400 clinical hours of observation and complete Knowledge and Skills Acquisition (KASA) exams. After the graduate degree, candidates must pass the national Praxis exam for SLP and work as a Clinical **Fellow** (CF) for between { **32** } <u>five to thirty-five hours a</u> week, for at least 36 weeks, for no less than 1,260 hours. At that point, and assuming satisfactory performance, ASHA awards the CCC (Certificate of Clinical **Competence**) and a full state license. { **33** }

31

Choose the best revision of the underlined portion of the sentence.

A) candidates must receive a master's degree from an accredited school

B) candidates must have received from an accredited school, a master's degree,

C) a master's degree must be received by the candidate from an accredited school

D) receipt of a master's degree from an accredited school must be obtained by the candidate

32

A) NO CHANGE

B) forty hours

C) a period of 5 to 35 hours per

D) 5 to 35 hours a

33

The author would like to insert the following sentence at this point in the passage:

> Becoming qualified in the field of SLP is not easy, but the effort ensures a rewarding, interesting career helping those who need it most.

Should the writer make the addition here?

A) No, because it provides no details regarding the career process.

B) Yes, because it links the end of the passage to the introduction and provides a conclusion.

C) No, because the main subject of the passage is about patients, not therapists.

D) Yes, because it connects the psychological aspect of SLP to the biological research.

Lesson 8 continued:

Vocabulary: Context Answers

The following sentences contain vocabulary words used in the reading passage. Choose the answer that best completes the sentence. There may be more than one technically correct answer, but one will better exemplify the italicized vocabulary word than the others will.

1) Frank visited _____ before he received an accurate *diagnosis*.
   A. a skilled carpenter for treatment
   B. his mother in the hospital
   C. someone with a similar illness
   D. an emergency clinic
   E. four doctors about his symptoms

2) If a person is unusually *adept* at a job, he or she will probably _____.
   A. do it very well
   B. completely fail at it
   C. succeed in other things
   D. ignore it for a while
   E. dislike whatever it is

3) _____ Pat had to complete all of the *prerequisite* materials.
   A. After finishing his history class,
   B. During the difficult class,
   C. After earning his degree,
   D. Before taking the advanced course,
   E. He had already taken all of the classes, so

4) Rosa's new gym membership was *comprehensive*, unlike her old membership, which _____.
   A. included everything: gym access, tanning, and fitness classes
   B. was more expensive than she could afford
   C. included access only to equipment
   D. was extremely complicated
   E. she renewed yearly

5) Scientists noticed _____, so they took samples to determine what caused the *pathology*.
   A. similar nuclei in the cells
   B. particularly strong structures in the cell
   C. irregularities in the cell's structure
   D. that the cells were moving
   E. cellular growth

6) Varsha was nervous to begin her *clinical* courses in medical school because she would be _____.
   A. working with real patients
   B. doing new research
   C. completing vast amounts of homework
   D. working with different professors
   E. working in dangerous areas

7) Madison's *doctoral* program awarded _____.
   A. medical licenses
   B. admission to all applicants
   C. high-paying jobs
   D. scholarships to needy students
   E. the highest academic degree

8) *Natal* cardio surgery was a new field when Nina was _____, so she did not receive treatment for her heart condition immediately.
   A. born
   B. a child
   C. sick
   D. young
   E. injured

Lesson 8 continued:

9) Doctors thought that the antibacterial medicine had _____ until Sonny had a *relapse*.
   A. worsened the illness
   B. cured the infection
   C. not been working
   D. caused an allergic reaction
   E. treated the sickness's symptoms

11) The Writing Committee had concerns about Violet's _____, so she showed them samples of her previously published material to prove her *competence*.
   A. over-qualification for the job
   B. unprofessional resume
   C. compensation demands
   D. busy schedule
   E. ability to complete quality work

10) Shawn's nervousness was an *impediment* that made public speaking _____, but with practice, he improved.
   A. impossible
   B. simple
   C. an important skill
   D. difficult
   E. hilarious

12) Cindy depended on other *fellows* from the university to _____.
   A. pay her college tuition bills
   B. update her with the latest surgical trends
   C. work with other students
   D. be equal to her employers
   E. tell her the truth about the dress she had chosen

Lesson 8 continued:

Writing Practice

The following sentences contain words that are often misused. Choose the correct word in each sentence.

1) <u>Inferring</u> / <u>Implying</u> that the teacher wanted a positive response, Jordan said, "Yes, it is."

2) Because of the drought and subsequent famine, thousands of people have wanted to <u>emigrate</u> / <u>immigrate</u> from their home country for years.

3) On the witness stand, the defendant calmly said, "Had I known that my friends were planning something <u>elicit</u> / <u>illicit</u>, I never would have participated."

4) Everyone tried, but no one could <u>assure</u> / <u>insure</u>, let alone convince me, that skydiving was safe enough for me to do it.

5) My roommates talked about the differences <u>among</u> / <u>between</u> getting a job and staying in college.

6) Nothing could be further from the truth. I never <u>implied</u> / <u>inferred</u> that I would go there!

7) I've known her <u>fewer</u> / <u>less</u> than a month, but I know we'll get married soon.

8) The process of <u>emigrating</u> / <u>immigrating</u> to the United States can take as long as two years.

9) It was difficult to <u>elicit</u> / <u>illicit</u> a response from the bored students, but the next day, everything seemed to change.

10) <u>Fewer</u> / <u>Less</u> horses raced in the Kentucky Derby this year than last year, and <u>fewer</u> / <u>less</u> money was wagered.

11) Do you have enough <u>assurance</u> / <u>insurance</u> to pay for the cost of replacing your home if there's a fire?

12) <u>Among</u> / <u>Between</u> the last four presidents, which two were millionaires before they entered office?

13) Must I be completely <u>explicit</u> / <u>implicit</u> with you? Can't you understand the gist of the conversation without my coming out directly and saying that you hurt my feelings?

Lesson 8 continued:

Vocabulary: Choosing the Right Use

The following sentences contain vocabulary words used in the reading passage. Identify the sentence or sentences that use the italicized vocabulary word properly. We have changed the form of some vocabulary words to provide new contexts; for example, some adjectives and verbs have been used as nouns.

1) A. The novel's *prerequisite* was an eloquent appraisal of the author's achievements.
   B. Introduction to Chemistry is a mandatory *prerequisite* for upper-level science courses at the university.
   C. "Her *prerequisite* to Bill's book was illogical and too personal," Viola exclaimed.
   D. Carrie did not fulfill enough of the research *prerequisites* for her thesis to be given scholarly approval.

2) A. Greta overcame her anger, a serious *impediment* to job advancement, after several years of intense therapy and practice.
   B. Workers in the mid-1800s used *impediments* in the construction of the Washington Monument.
   C. Even though *impediments* have become an obsolete building tool, many still exist in museums around the country.
   D. The major *impediment* to peace after the long war was the fact that many soldiers brought their weapons back from the battlefields.

3) A. Every student athlete is required to get a *clinical* at the start of each academic year.
   B. "*Clinical* trials for the new medication begin on Monday," Dr. Judith told the board.
   C. Each doctor completed forty hours of *clinical* observation by the end of the semester.
   D. Mindy's *clinical* proved that she was healthy enough to participate in the field hockey season.

4) A. Gilda *relapsed* into a painful illness from which she felt she would not recover again.
   B. Danny's *relapse* into alcohol dependency caused his parents to begin an intervention with his closest friends and relatives.
   C. Laura *relapsed* on the sidewalk and fractured her arm in two places upon impact.
   D. Despite his parents' warning, Johnny tried to balance on a thin wall and *relapsed* before anyone could catch him.

5) A. Dr. Niemen spent his career studying the *pathology* of lung disease, leading to groundbreaking research.
   B. Bert's *pathology* raised his spirits because the doctor assured him he would need only two weeks of rehabilitation.
   C. A team of doctors could not determine a uniform *pathology* for Bernard's illness.
   D. New York City's new research hospital specializes in the *pathology* of 20/20 vision.

Lesson 8 continued:

6)   A.   Coach Lee's offensive line became *adept* at dodging blocks from the opposing team's defense.
      B.   Maria was an *adept* athlete who frequently missed the soccer ball when she attempted to kick it.
      C.   Adulthood requires the *adept* management of work schedules, domestic chores, and personal engagements.
      D.   Ricky is extremely *adept* and accidentally broke his grandmother's antique vase.

7)   A.   Fyodor pinned a *fellow* to his date's shirt before they left for the school dance.
      B.   "The store ran out of *fellows* moments before I got there. It ruined my date's outfit," Alana said.
      C.   Nelson became a distinguished *fellow* in the medical residency program at Chicago General Hospital.
      D.   Tyrell and Cleo were the only *fellows* from their program to attend the hospital's anniversary gala.

8)   A.   The linguist exhibited *competence* in several Romance languages, including Spanish, French, Portuguese, and Italian.
      B.   The *competence* at this year's tournament became heated when the Wizards and the Cyclones came head to head in the final round.
      C.   St. Anne's offered stiff *competence* at the playoff game, defeating the long-reigning champions, St. Helen's.
      D.   Harriet had little to no *competence* in solving quadratic equations, so Ms. Lowell offered to tutor her after school.

9)   A.   Alan possessed a *comprehensive* computer that could analyze complex equations in a matter of minutes.
      B.   Professor Reid created a *comprehensive* lesson plan for his substitute to use during the week of his absence.
      C.   Kyra's trip to Europe was advertised as "*comprehensive*" because it involved a week in Ireland.
      D.   The registrar's office contains a *comprehensive* list of each student and faculty member at the university.

10)   A.   The soccer team made a fantastic *natal* play in the last ten seconds of the game to win the championship.
      B.   If there is a natural, untouched area left to discover in Africa, Dr. Prince, the *natal* explorer and scientist, will locate it.
      C.   Obstetricians often prescribe pre-*natal* vitamins to pregnant women, which contribute to a healthy development of the fetus.
      D.   *Natal* diagnoses are vital to the treatment and eradication of childhood illnesses and diseases.

Lesson 8 continued:

VOCABULARY
SYNONYMS **&** ANTONYMS

Synonyms and Antonyms

Match the word with its *antonym*.

1) clinical   **A.** aid

2) impediment   **B.** narrow

3) adept   **C.** emotional

4) comprehensive   **D.** unskilled

Match the word with its *synonym*.

5) diagnosis   **E.** return

6) fellow   **F.** expertise

7) relapse   **G.** determination

8) competence   **H.** requirement

9) prerequisite   **I.** associate

END
of
LESSON 8

Lesson 9

Questions 34-44 are based on the following passage.

— 1 —

Technology has shown { **34** } <u>for a very many years now</u> that the human race is capable of conquering even the most deadly and threatening diseases out there. It is often the simple passage of time, in addition to research and discovery, that leads us to make significant strides in medicine and science. However, we do tend to think of these advances as somewhat beyond our **cognizance**, particularly if we are not personally involved in or knowledgeable about the field. But what about an advancement that is as simple as downloading an app to { **35** } <u>your phone.</u>

— 2 —

A new application called Folding@Home manages to achieve { **36** } <u>alot</u> by asking people to do very little. The application remotely accesses the massive computing power of smartphones to contribute to research about cures and treatments for Alzheimer's, a disease that progressively **deteriorates** the brain in middle or old age, and currently affects over five million Americans.

— 3 —

Even though this **affliction** harms so many people, it is poorly understood, so researchers and scientists work hard to learn more about it { **37** } <u>each and every day, right now, most</u> of our knowledge about Alzheimer's lies in the results of the disease rather than its causes. Generally speaking, Alzheimer's is a memory disorder that kills and damages brain cells. People who suffer from it will initially experience increased forgetfulness and some mild confusion. Symptoms typically get worse with age, though the rate of progression varies from case to case. Especially in the early stages of the disease, people with Alzheimer's are often unaware of { **38** } <u>one's</u> forgetfulness, even though it seems obvious to everyone around them.

34

The underlined portion of the sentence should be
A) revised to "so many years now."
B) preceded by a semicolon.
C) preceded by a comma.
D) revised to say "for years."

35

A) NO CHANGE
B) your phone?
C) your phone"?
D) one's phone.

36

A) NO CHANGE
B) allot
C) much
D) a lot

37

A) NO CHANGE
B) every day. Right now, most
C) each and everyday. Right now, most
D) everyday; right now, most

38

A) NO CHANGE
B) the
C) their
D) they're

Lesson 9 continued:

— 4 —

{ 39 } <u>So, its safe</u> to say that Alzheimer's is a horrible disease, not just in its **prevalence**, but also in the way it manifests. It's devastating to watch a loved one unwillingly surrender all of his or her memories and experience the fear that accompanies confusion and disorientation.

— 5 —

An app that has the potential to help find a cure for such a disease is nothing short of a miracle. But how can a simple mobile app achieve so much? The answer is in how the disease itself works.

— 6 —

In order to even begin to understand it, we first need to delve into how Alzheimer's develops in the brain. Again, doctors and researchers currently know very little about the origins of the disease, but there are { 40 } <u>a couple of</u> key, observable **abnormalities** that shed some light on this issue. Those **anomalies** are all related to proteins in the brain, which are essentially machines inside the cells that keep us alive and healthy. { 41 }

— 7 —

Alzheimer's begins with anomalies of proteins in the brain. Abnormal clusters of chemically "sticky" proteins, called **plaque**, build up between **neurons** in the brain and interfere with cell-to-cell communication. Some plaque develops naturally with age, but is not typically a health threat when limited. In a normal, healthy brain, plaques have a role in activating cells in the immune system that trigger inflammation and devour disabled cells. When the brain produces too many of these proteins, however, it becomes **prone** to diseases like Alzheimer's. Tangles, which are twisted fibers of protein that form inside of dying cells, further threaten the brain. These proteins are vital for an internal support-and-transport system that carries nutrients and other essential materials, so, when a protein becomes tangled, the system fails and causes the death of the affected brain cells. These types of abnormalities occur even in the healthiest brains, but they happen much more frequently in a brain with Alzheimer's.

39

A) NO CHANGE
B) It's safe
C) So; it's safe
D) So—its safe

40

A) NO CHANGE
B) few
C) a whole lot of
D) three

41

Choose the revision that best changes paragraph 6 to improve the overall passage.
A) Move paragraph 6 to follow paragraph 3 because it describes the symptoms of Alzheimer's.
B) Delete paragraph 6 because it does not contribute any important details.
C) Move it to the end because it summarizes the passage.
D) Insert a line about how the app will affect the battery life of smartphones.

Lesson 9 continued:

— 8 —

[1] Generally speaking, proteins normally function through a process called folding, in which they assemble in very specific ways and take on uniquely different shapes. [2] The process occurs within milliseconds, making it extremely difficult to observe and study. [3] When a protein folds { 42 } <u>wrongly</u>, the consequences can be **calamitous** and can lead to the development of a disease like Alzheimer's. [4] Studying the folding process is difficult because it requires vast amounts of computer power. [5] Because protein folding happens too quickly to study it in real time, computer simulations provide the only method for { 43 } <u>it to be observed by researchers which look closely at these complex processes</u>. [6] However, as fast as those milliseconds of folding occur in reality, the process is so complex that it could take a computer an entire day to simulate just 50 nanoseconds! [7] That's fifty millionths of a second! { 44 }

— 9 —

Folding@Home borrows the computing power of your own smartphone, adding it to a giant team of supercomputers, all of which are working towards solving these protein folding problems. For the app to work, you need only to download it (for free) to your phone, open up a browser, and allow the program to run in the background of all your phone's other daily functions. With little effort, you can contribute to finding a cure for one of the most prevalent diseases out there.

— 10 —

Because this application and its related research are still relatively new, the results have yet to be fully documented. So far, many of the developers behind this research have earned awards for their admirable work, and they continue to learn more about the mysterious process of protein folding as they work toward the ultimate goal of wiping out Alzheimer's.

42

A) NO CHANGE
B) accidentally
C) incorrectly
D) not the right way

43

Choose the best revision for the underlined portion of the sentence.
A) the observation of researchers
B) researching by observers who look at the complex processes closely
C) processes to be observed by researchers
D) researchers to observe these complex processes

44

Paragraph 8 should be divided into two paragraphs. Choose the sentence that should begin the new paragraph.
A) sentence [2]
B) sentence [3]
C) sentence [4]
D) sentence [7]

Lesson 9 continued:

Vocabulary: Context Answers

The following sentences contain vocabulary words used in the reading passage. Choose the answer that best completes the sentence. There may be more than one technically correct answer, but one will better exemplify the italicized vocabulary word than the others will.

1) After his eyesight *deteriorated*, Ken _____.
   A. could see much better
   B. had problems in the dark
   C. could not see well, even with glasses
   D. went to the family doctor
   E. told his family about it

2) As a child, swimming had made Laura _____ ear infections; now, though, she is *prone* to ankle injuries from running.
   A. used to having
   B. more likely to get
   C. immune to
   D. worry about
   E. less likely to get

3) When she counted the votes, Jaelyn noticed that _____ and began an investigation into the *abnormalities*.
   A. the results reflected recent political polls
   B. the candidates had similar last names
   C. the ballots were very clearly printed
   D. her favorite candidate had won
   E. some ballots had been altered

4) The researchers dismissed the most recent results as *anomalies* because they were _____ their older data.
   A. unusual compared to
   B. similar to
   C. consistent with
   D. well done compared to
   E. much newer than

5) The tornado was referred to as _____ after its *calamitous* effects.
   A. a disaster
   B. a minor incident
   C. a big storm
   D. little as possible
   E. damaging

6) _____ will help improve your *cognizance* of current events.
   A. Listening to audiobooks
   B. Reading the news
   C. Voicing your opinion
   D. Having no interest
   E. Taking a vacation

7) Due to the *prevalence* of cell phones, _____.
   A. it's difficult for most people to afford them
   B. I keep mine in a protective case
   C. it's best not to give out your phone number
   D. call signals are weak in remote areas
   E. pay phones have nearly all disappeared

8) Few people emerge unscathed after enduring an *affliction* such as _____.
   A. getting ignored by their favorite celebrities
   B. a ten-year civil war
   C. running out of gas on the way to a new job
   D. a three-day power outage
   E. early winter weather

Lesson 9 continued:

Writing Practice

The following sentences contain words that are often misused. Choose the correct word in each sentence.

1) Before Lyndon could complete the paper, she had to do <u>farther</u> / <u>further</u> research into the causes of the war.

2) Slowly but surely, new hospitals were constructed, and the community <u>raised</u> / <u>rose</u> to prominence as the state's central area for medical treatment.

3) No matter where Roger was <u>setting</u> / <u>sitting</u>, it seemed as if the eyes of the man in the painting were staring directly at him.

4) As a joke, we glued a quarter to the concrete, hoping it looked like it was just <u>laying</u> / <u>lying</u> there, and people would try to pick it up.

5) I'm not going <u>irregardless</u> / <u>regardless</u> of how amazing you say the magician is because, to tell you the truth, magic bores me.

6) The CEO angrily exclaimed, "With that type of <u>advice</u> / <u>advise</u>, the company will go broke in a month!"

7) <u>Explicit</u> / <u>Implicit</u> in what I said was the idea that people need to stop complaining and accept responsibility for their actions.

8) The school had a competition to see which athletes could jump the <u>farthest</u> / <u>furthest</u>.

9) Can you please help me? I am trying to <u>raise</u> / <u>rise</u> this pile of boards so they will be easy to use when constructing the roof.

10) After looking it over, but not signing it, Nick <u>set</u> / <u>sat</u> the contract down on the lawyer's desk and walked out of the room.

11) <u>Its</u> / <u>It's</u> imperative that you attend the meeting because that's when we will discuss the new rule and decide <u>it's</u> / <u>its</u> fairness.

12) <u>Sometimes</u> / <u>Sometime</u> / <u>Some time</u>, I wish you'd take my feelings seriously instead of ignoring them like you do.

13) It seems as if there's a problem with the two of you fighting over who controls the remote <u>everyday</u> / <u>every day</u>.

Lesson 9 continued:

Vocabulary: Choosing the Right Use

The following sentences contain vocabulary words used in the reading passage. Identify the sentence or sentences that use the italicized vocabulary word properly. We have changed the form of some vocabulary words to provide new contexts; for example, some adjectives and verbs have been used as nouns.

1) A. Researchers in Austin are studying the *prevalence* of measles in young children across the state.
   B. Principal Peters vowed to reduce the *prevalence* of truancy in his school by enforcing stricter punishments for students who skip class.
   C. Hubert has a *prevalence* for chocolate and other sweets, causing him to have many cavities over the years.
   D. Karen's behavior shows she has a *prevalence* for being in charge of large groups of people.

2) A. Turner needed to put just the right amount of *affliction* on the bowling ball to hit the last two standing pins.
   B. Grandma said that the *afflictions* she suffered in life taught her to appreciate every moment.
   C. Though the disease had rendered his arms and legs useless, Tim succeeded in spite of his *affliction*.
   D. The marathon runner padded her sneakers to prevent *affliction* on her heels during the long, hot race.

3) A. "Many people are *prone* to getting sick during the winter season, so be sure to rest and drink fluids," the public service announcement said.
   B. Jeremy's mother claims her son has always been *prone* to clumsiness and small accidents, even as a child.
   C. The instrument was sturdy and *prone*, making it easy for young Amal to master her introductory book of melodies within two weeks.
   D. Officer Stern's desk was *prone* against damage because it had a protective layer covering its surface.

4) A. When Judith begins her construction projects, she cordons off the necessary *abnormalities* with a tape measure.
   B. Derek noticed several *abnormalities* in the color and shape of an insect he discovered on his daily hike.
   C. "The *abnormalities* for the owl sanctuary were infringed upon by the new mini-mart," Harrison told the media.
   D. "It is imperative that *abnormalities* in newborns are identified immediately to avoid long-term health risks," Dr. Heisman explained.

5) A. Liver *neurons* take significantly longer to repair than intestinal ones, which can lead to liver disease among those who drink heavily.
   B. Terry learned about the developmental process of *neurons* in Ms. Stein's science class last year.
   C. Ian's illness stemmed from the misfiring of *neurons* in his brain, which interfered with normal cell-to-cell communication.
   D. The hospital's most skilled doctors examined the *neurons* in Rafael's brain after his car accident.

Lesson 9 continued:

6)   A.   The list of attendees at Angelica's party has reached such *calamitous* numbers that she must add another table to the dining area.

     B.   Last year's earthquake had *calamitous* effects on the island's lucrative exporting industry.

     C.   The *calamitous* stock market crash of 1929 sent the nation's economy into a major depression.

     D.   The *calamitous* sale of tickets for the band's tour led to a major boost in album sales.

7)   A.   Yolanda's *anomalies* malfunctioned during the plane's first test ride, but she was able to make a safe emergency landing.

     B.   Professor Reeves could not account for the *anomalies* in his research experiment, rendering it unusable by other researchers.

     C.   Several *anomalies* in the case puzzled detectives for three days until a key piece of information put everything in perspective.

     D.   "We questioned whether the newly manufactured *anomalies* would be able to withstand scrutiny by officials," the company's CEO explained.

8)   A.   After a week of fumbling around in confusion, Derek had gained enough *cognizance* to understand how everything worked at his new summer job.

     B.   With great *cognizance*, Cadence watched TV all morning, unaware that his dog was eating his favorite baseball glove.

     C.   For five dollars, the fortuneteller down the street will read your *cognizance* about what will happen in the future.

     D.   When they became *cognizant* of the scandal, thousands of people began calling for the mayor's resignation.

Lesson 9 continued:

Synonyms and Antonyms

Match the word with its _antonym_.

1) calamitous   **A.** immune

2) abnormality   **B.** regularity

3) prone   **C.** fortunate

Match the word with its _synonym_.

4) prevalence   **D.** weaken

5) anomaly   **E.** misery

6) cognizance   **F.** irregularity

7) affliction   **G.** awareness

8) deteriorate   **H.** abundance

END
of
LESSON 9

Lesson 10

Essay

The optional essay portion of the 2016 SAT allocates 50 minutes to read a short passage and respond with a well-organized analytical essay based on observations of the passage (no opinions or personal experiences—all the information needed to write the essay will be contained within the passage).

Three criteria of the essay will be scored: reading, analysis, and writing. After completing an essay, evaluate your writing using the scoring guide provided on pages 196-197.

Prompt

Choose one of the two passages from **Lesson 5** and reread it.

As you read the passage, consider how the author uses the following elements:

- **evidence** – the use of facts, examples, data, research, etc., to support claims

- **reasoning** – the development of ideas and the connection of evidence in support of the argument

- **style** – persuasive language, word choice, emotional appeals, and figurative language that add power to ideas

Write an essay in which you explain how the author builds an argument to persuade his audience of his point about the development of American government and society in the post-war 20th century. In your essay, analyze how the author uses one or more of the elements listed above to strengthen the logic and persuasiveness of his argument. Be sure that your analysis focuses on the most relevant features of the passage.

Your essay should not explain whether you agree with the author's claims, but rather how the author builds an argument to persuade his audience.

SUMMIT

UNIT TWO
Lesson 11

Reading Test

Each passage or pair of passages, some of which are accompanied by graphics such as maps, charts, or graphs, is followed by a set of questions. Read the passage and then choose the best answer to each of the questions.

Questions 1–11 are based on the following passage.

This passage is adapted from Herman Melville's *Moby-Dick*, published in 1851.

Call me Ishmael. Some years ago—never mind how long precisely—having little or no money in my purse, and nothing particular to interest me onshore, I thought I would sail about a little and see the watery
5 part of the world. It is a way I have of driving off the spleen and regulating the circulation. Whenever I find myself growing grim about the mouth; whenever it is a damp, drizzly November in my soul; whenever I find myself involuntarily pausing before coffin warehouses,
10 and bringing up the rear of every funeral I meet; and especially whenever my hypos get such an upper hand of me, that it requires a strong moral principle to prevent me from deliberately stepping into the street, and methodically knocking people's hats off—then, I
15 account it high time to get to sea as soon as I can. This is my substitute for pistol and ball. With a philosophical **flourish** Cato throws himself upon his sword; I quietly take to the ship. There is nothing surprising in this. If they but knew it, almost all men in their degree, some
20 time or other, cherish very nearly the same feelings towards the ocean with me.

There now is your **insular** city of the **Manhattoes**, belted round by wharves as Indian isles by coral reefs— commerce surrounds it with her surf. Right and left, the
25 streets take you waterward. Its extreme downtown is the **battery**, where that noble **mole** is washed by waves, and cooled by breezes, which a few hours previous were out of sight of land. Look at the crowds of water-gazers there.

30 But look! Here come more crowds, pacing straight for the water, and seemingly bound for a dive. Strange! Nothing will content them but the extremest limit of the land; loitering under the shady lee of yonder warehouses

will not suffice. No. They must get just as nigh the water
35 as they possibly can without falling in. And there they stand—miles of them—leagues. Inlanders all, they come from lanes and alleys, streets and avenues—north, east, south, and west. Yet here they all unite. Tell me, does the magnetic virtue of the needles of the compasses of all
40 those ships attract them thither?

Once more, say you are in the country; in some high land of lakes. Take almost any path you please, and ten to one it carries you down in a **dale**, and leaves you there by a pool in the stream. There is magic in it.
45 Let the most absent-minded of men be plunged in his deepest **reveries**—stand that man on his legs, set his feet a-going, and he will infallibly lead you to water, if water there be in all that region. Should you ever be athirst in the great American desert, try this experiment, if your
50 caravan happen to be supplied with a **metaphysical** professor. Yes, as everyone knows, meditation and water are wedded forever.

But here is an artist. He desires to paint you the dreamiest, shadiest, quietest, most enchanting bit of
55 romantic landscape in all the valley of the Saco. What is the chief element he employs? There stand his trees, each with a hollow trunk, as if a hermit and a crucifix were within; and here sleeps his meadow, and there sleep his cattle; and up from yonder cottage goes a sleepy
60 smoke. Deep into distant woodlands winds a mazy way, reaching to overlapping spurs of mountains bathed in their hill-side blue. But though the picture lies thus tranced, and though this pine-tree shakes down its sighs like leaves upon this shepherd's head, yet all were vain,
65 unless the shepherd's eye were fixed upon the magic stream before him. Go visit the Prairies in June, when for scores on scores of miles you wade knee-deep among Tiger-lilies—what is the one charm wanting?—Water— there is not a drop of water there! Were Niagara but a
70 **cataract** of sand, would you travel your thousand miles to see it?

Lesson 11 continued:

Now, when I say that I am in the habit of going to
sea whenever I begin to grow hazy about the eyes, and
begin to be over conscious of my lungs, I do not mean
75 to have it inferred that I ever go to sea as a passenger.
For to go as a passenger you must needs have a purse,
and a purse is but a rag unless you have something in it.
Besides, passengers get seasick—grow quarrelsome—
don't sleep of nights—do not enjoy themselves much,
80 as a general thing;—no, I never go as a passenger; nor,
though I am something of a **salt**, do I ever go to sea
as a Commodore, or a Captain, or a Cook. I abandon
the glory and distinction of such offices to those who
like them. For my part, I abominate all honorable
85 respectable toils, trials, and tribulations of every kind
whatsoever. It is quite as much as I can do to take
care of myself, without taking care of ships, barques,
brigs, schooners, and what not. And as for going as
cook,—though I confess there is considerable glory in
90 that, a cook being a sort of officer on ship-board—yet,
somehow, I never fancied broiling fowls;—though once
broiled, judiciously buttered, and judgmatically salted
and peppered, there is no one who will speak more
respectfully, not to say reverentially, of a broiled fowl
95 than I will. It is out of the **idolatrous** dotings of the old
Egyptians upon broiled ibis and roasted river horse, that
you see the mummies of those creatures in their huge
bake-houses the pyramids.

No, when I go to sea, I go as a simple sailor, right
100 before the mast, **plumb** down into the forecastle, aloft
there to the royal mast-head. True, they rather order me
about some, and make me jump from **spar** to spar, like
a grasshopper in a May meadow. And at first, this sort
of thing is unpleasant enough. It touches one's sense
105 of honor, particularly if you come of an old established
family in the land, the Van Rensselaers, or Randolphs,
or Hardicanutes. And more than all, if just previous to
putting your hand into the tar-pot, you have been lording
it as a country schoolmaster, making the tallest boys
110 stand in awe of you. The transition is a keen one, I assure
you, from a schoolmaster to a sailor, and requires a
strong **decoction** of Seneca and the **Stoics** to enable you
to grin and bear it. But even this wears off in time.

What of it, if some old hunks of a sea-captain
115 orders me to get a broom and sweep down the decks?
What does that **indignity** amount to, weighed, I mean,
in the scales of the New Testament? Do you think

the archangel Gabriel thinks anything the less of me,
because I promptly and respectfully obey that old hunks
120 in that particular instance? Who ain't a slave? Tell me
that. Well, then, however the old sea-captains may
order me about—however they may thump and punch
me about, I have the satisfaction of knowing that it
is all right; that everybody else is one way or other
125 served in much the same way—either in a physical or
metaphysical point of view, that is; and so the universal
thump is passed round, and all hands should rub each
other's shoulder-blades, and be content.

Again, I always go to sea as a sailor, because they
130 make a point of paying me for my trouble, whereas they
never pay passengers a single penny that I ever heard
of. On the contrary, passengers themselves must pay.
And there is all the difference in the world between
paying and being paid. The act of paying is perhaps
135 the most uncomfortable **infliction** that the two orchard
thieves entailed upon us. But BEING PAID,—what will
compare with it? The **urbane** activity with which a man
receives money is really marvelous, considering that we
so earnestly believe money to be the root of all earthly
140 ills, and that on no account can a moneyed man enter
heaven. Ah! how cheerfully we **consign** ourselves to
perdition!

Finally, I always go to sea as a sailor, because of
the wholesome exercise and pure air of the forecastle
145 deck. For as in this world, head winds are far more
prevalent than winds from astern (that is, if you never
violate the Pythagorean maxim), so for the most part the
Commodore on the quarter-deck gets his atmosphere
at second hand from the sailors on the forecastle. He
150 thinks he breathes it first; but not so. In much the same
way do the commonalty lead their leaders in many other
things, at the same time that the leaders little suspect it.
But wherefore it was that after having repeatedly smelt
the sea as a merchant sailor, I should now take it into my
155 head to go on a whaling voyage; this the invisible police
officer of the Fates, who has the constant surveillance
of me, and secretly dogs me, and influences me in some
unaccountable way—he can better answer than anyone
else. And, doubtless, my going on this whaling voyage,
160 formed part of the grand program of Providence that was
drawn up a long time ago.

1

From paragraph 1 (lines 1-21) a reader can infer that the narrator believes
A) in enduring his depression because he knows that it will get better.
B) that death should not have the negative connotation that tradition has placed upon it.
C) the ocean can bring out feelings of unrest in the human mind.
D) that man has a tendency to do violence if he finds no better release.

2

As it is used in line 11, *hypos* most nearly means
A) beliefs.
B) desires.
C) anxieties.
D) morals.

3

On land, the narrator of the passage is employed as a
A) school teacher.
B) merchant.
C) captain of a whaling vessel.
D) portrait painter.

4

Choose the lines from the passage that provide the best evidence for your answer to the previous question.
A) lines 101-103 ("True, they...meadow")
B) lines 110-111 ("The transition...sailor")
C) lines 116-117 ("What does...Testament")
D) lines 129-132 ("Again, I...of")

5

The purpose of paragraphs 2, 3, 4, and 5 (lines 22-71) is to
A) glorify the life of a ship's captain.
B) outline the dangers of humanity's attraction to the sea.
C) suggest an alternative to fits of violence.
D) explain that human beings are drawn to water instinctively.

6

As it is used in line 81, *salt* most nearly means
A) conscientious objector.
B) experienced sailor.
C) restless soul.
D) uneducated laborer.

7

Choose the statement that best paraphrases the author's argument in paragraph 8 (lines 114-128).
A) Those who have power over others will continue to have it, so learn to endure them.
B) Only people who learn to disregard their jobs will be happy.
C) Every person is slave to another to some degree, so be happy and get along.
D) A person must explore different careers in order to find the one that makes him or her happy.

Lesson 11 continued:

8

The author spends half the passage discussing why he goes to sea only as a common sailor instead of as a ship's officer. In the author's explanation as to why he does not care to have a leader's responsibilities on a ship (lines 143-161), he offers which reason for his choice?

A) Commodores may not associate with the crew freely, as friends.

B) Leaders often enjoy the thrills of the sea undeservedly.

C) The value of the experience is worth more than the salary of a captain.

D) Leaders are usually second to see and experience new things.

9

Choose the lines from the passage that provide the best evidence for your answer to the previous question.

A) lines 154-155 ("I should...voyage")

B) lines 159-160 ("my going...Providence")

C) lines 147-149 ("the Commodore...forecastle")

D) lines 145-146 ("For as...prevalent")

10

The general purpose of this passage is to

A) describe the narrator's motives.

B) express the importance of art in one's life.

C) dissuade the meek from ocean voyages.

D) explain the austere conditions of life at sea.

11

According to the author, what is ironic about the eagerness with which people receive wages for work performed?

A) the agreement to settle for the immediate payment of lower wages versus waiting a few days for full payment

B) the knowledge that most of the workers will waste the money immediately

C) the illiteracy of those who cannot even be certain as to whether they were paid enough

D) the popular belief that money is the cause of problems

Lesson 11 continued:

Vocabulary: Context Answers

The following sentences contain vocabulary words used in the reading passage. Choose the answer that best completes the sentence. There may be more than one technically correct answer, but one will better exemplify the italicized vocabulary word than the others will.

1) The *idolatrous* manner in which Theodore _____ bothered Brenda.
   A. tried to force answers from her
   B. pulled the school fire alarm
   C. reprimanded her for littering
   D. defended his love for money
   E. stole money from his many clients

2) The _____ is the most *urbane* part of the city.
   A. rusted bridge that overlooks the state park
   B. factory that constantly pollutes the air
   C. wall that hosts the work of street artists
   D. street with all the museums and galleries
   E. avenue with many abandoned homes

3) Rachel *consigned* one night a week to volunteer at the animal shelter because she _____.
   A. decided it wasn't worth her time
   B. enjoyed working with the dogs
   C. had been grounded for a month
   D. couldn't get a ride there
   E. needed to spend more time studying

4) When we traveled to the *dale*, _____.
   A. the mountains completely obscured the sun
   B. we could see the skyscrapers in the distance
   C. we couldn't hear each other over the waves
   D. the number of people overwhelmed us
   E. the usher told us to silence our cellphones

5) "You may want to _____ so that no one regards you as *insular* about the argument," said Maxine.
   A. withdraw your support
   B. express your opinion
   C. consider both sides
   D. ignore other ideas
   E. participate in person

6) Walker's state of *reverie* began when he _____.
   A. got seasick from the rocking of the boat
   B. was so scared by the horror movie that he couldn't sleep
   C. bought his first car
   D. lost his backpack at the station
   E. remembered the beautiful autumns in New Hampshire

7) Angelique considered the *metaphysical* _____ to be too much to bear.
   A. weight of the used couch
   B. way her father had spoken to her
   C. heat from the blazing sun
   D. number of final exams
   E. concept of nothing after death

8) The *flourishes* on the letters of the signature _____.
   A. looked like normal handwriting
   B. turned the name into a work of art
   C. were a reddish-brown color
   D. can be translated by a linguist
   E. reminded Heather of cinnamon

Lesson 11 continued:

9) Do you think Taylor felt any *indignity* after _____?
   A. winning a Perfect Attendance award
   B. she was caught cheating on the SAT
   C. her childhood home was torn down
   D. her parents surprised her with a puppy
   E. she forgot how to play Texas Hold'em

10) "What an absolute *infliction*!" exclaimed Anne-Marie, referring to the _____.
   A. horrible famine
   B. ugly highway accident
   C. newly planted garden
   D. man's newborn daughter
   E. challenging math problem

Lesson 11 continued:

Writing Practice

The underlined portion of each sentence possibly contains a flaw related to pronoun use. Select the answer that best corrects the flaw. Select NO CHANGE if the underlined portion is correct.

1) Getting a pilot's license is difficult; many fail at their first attempt.
   A. NO CHANGE
   B. his or her
   C. his
   D. one's

2) Nobody realizes that eating kale is a good way to provide their bodies with antioxidants.
   A. NO CHANGE
   B. his or her body
   C. their body
   D. its body

3) Only some of the glass figurines has been damaged in last week's earthquake.
   A. NO CHANGE
   B. was
   C. had been
   D. would have been

4) Before his relatives arrived, Devon made sure everything was in its place.
   A. NO CHANGE
   B. were in their
   C. were in its
   D. was in their

5) After reviewing the evidence, the jury has reached their verdict.
   A. NO CHANGE
   B. have reached their
   C. has reached its
   D. have reached its

6) At the playground, all parents must supervise her children.
   A. NO CHANGE
   B. his or her
   C. their
   D. his

7) Peanut butter and jelly are favorites of mine for a snack.
   A. NO CHANGE
   B. is the favorites of mine
   C. are my favorites
   D. is a favorite of mine

8) Cars running red lights is one reason accidents occur.
   A. NO CHANGE
   B. Cars running red lights are one reason accidents occur.
   C. Cars that run red lights are one reason accidents occur.
   D. Cars running red lights are reasons accidents occur.

9) My brother, like many other teenagers, believes everything they read on the Internet.
   A. NO CHANGE
   B. he or she reads
   C. he reads
   D. they have read

10) The butler happily noticed that none of the silverware had lost their shine.
   A. NO CHANGE
   B. have lost its
   C. have lost their
   D. had lost its

Lesson 11 continued:

Vocabulary: Choosing the Right Use

The following sentences contain vocabulary words used in the reading passage. Identify the sentence or sentences that use the italicized vocabulary word properly. We have changed the form of some vocabulary words to provide new contexts; for example, some adjectives and verbs have been used as nouns.

1) A. Signs along the path warn hikers that if they stand too close to the edge, they risk falling into the *dale*.
   B. We could go the direct way to Grandma's or take the scenic route that will take us past farms and through a *dale*.
   C. The mountain climbers double-checked their gear and supplies before approaching the *dale* and beginning their ascent.
   D. Some *dales* surpass the height of several skyscrapers.

2) A. During the holiday season, many people will *consign* old coats and other winter apparel for those in need.
   B. Since the company sent him two cheap screwdrivers by mistake, Jake *consigned* one of them to his trashcan.
   C. Over dinner, Taylor's father *consigned* him about curfew and keeping up with his studies.
   D. Once a decision was made, the president *consigned* the country about the new laws that would go into effect immediately.

3) A. Todd's invention did not work until he was struck by a *reverie* and redrew his blueprints until he had a functioning product.
   B. Mark was distracted by his *reveries* until his friend tapped him on the shoulder, and he realized the teacher had asked him a question.
   C. The author's *reveries* for his novels are the people he sees on his commute every day, and he imagines what each person's life is like.
   D. A common icebreaker among adults is for them to tell strangers what they wanted to be when they grew up and other *reveries*.

4) A. The magician waved his wand with a *flourish* before dropping the curtain to reveal his missing assistant.
   B. Jim bought *flourishes* at the home store that are supposed to make his front lawn grow better.
   C. To interest her students, Professor Carr stood at the front of the class and, with a *flourish*, rapidly combined the two chemicals to create a reaction.
   D. The *flourish* on Dianne's face revealed to us that she was not looking forward to the surprise party.

5) A. Valerie spent hours each day pondering *metaphysical* ideas, such as the meaning of life.
   B. The body builder made his presence known at the gym so that everyone would get a look at his *metaphysical* torso.
   C. While the writer's essay is interesting, it is filled with *metaphysical* concepts that have no practical use.
   D. With the intent to win the race, the NASCAR driver upgraded his vehicle until it was in *metaphysical* shape.

Lesson 11 continued:

6) A. The numerous *inflictions* on the impoverished villagers led them to rebel against their king.
      B. George's suit gave him the *infliction* that he was wealthy and a successful businessman.
      C. A lion's mane provides him with an *infliction* that he is a regal creature.
      D. The fictitious prince's *infliction* transformed him into a monster every evening.

7) A. Although towns in the Wild West used to thrive on the prospect of striking gold, they are now *insular* and falling apart.
      B. After the party, Jerry's *insular* home was trashed since his guests had not bothered to help clean up after themselves.
      C. Despite the brilliance of the financial genius, she was an *insular* person who had no friends and thought only about making money.
      D. Realizing that he had been deserted, the survivor of the plane crash accepted his *insular* state and took stock of what was available to him.

8) A. The stereotypical *urbane* family has four members, a dog, and a white picket fence.
      B. Evan is always saying he is going to move to the city when he grows up because he cannot stand the *urbane* lifestyle.
      C. The doorman at the front of the hotel was dressed elegantly and greeted all the guests in an *urbane* manner.
      D. Judging by the high-quality paper and the neatness of the script on the wedding invitation, Gary's cousins must be fairly *urbane* and sophisticated.

9) A. Vivian divorced her husband after she found out about his *idolatrous* affair with her dog walker.
      B. Connor makes fun of his sister for her *idolatrous* obsession with her "favorite celebrity of all time."
      C. Archaeologists learned a lot about the decline of Ancient Rome by studying the *idolatrous* commentaries of its corrupt emperors.
      D. The new blockbuster is rated PG-13 for crude language and *idolatrous* behavior.

10) A. To strike an enemy when his back is turned is an act of cowardice and *indignity*.
      B. Lindsey had to endure the *indignity* of her roommate's lack of respect for her belongings.
      C. The *indignity* Josh felt when his mother—in front of his fiancée—criticized his bad choice in women was indescribable.
      D. The comedian would often lose his audience members when telling a story, but he had great *indignity* and timed the punch lines perfectly.

Lesson 11 continued:

Synonyms and Antonyms

Match the word with its *antonym*.

1) insular   **A.** open-minded

2) indignity   **B.** barely

3) urbane   **C.** honor

4) plumb   **D.** unsophisticated

Match the word with its *synonym*.

5) infliction   **E.** daydream

6) consign   **F.** pain

7) reverie   **G.** embellishment

8) flourish   **H.** give

END
of
LESSON 11

Lesson 12

Questions 12–22 are based on the following passage.

This passage discusses the looming challenge of how to dispose of nuclear waste.

Thirty nations worldwide depend on electricity generated by nuclear **reactors**. As of 2015, the United States alone had 60 nuclear power plants and 100 nuclear reactors. One MW (megawatt) of electricity
5 powers roughly 1,000 households, and most power plants have an energy production capacity between 1,000 and 3,000 MW. A coal power plant, for comparison, requires more than 1,000 pounds of coal to generate each MW hour; a nuclear reactor produces the same amount
10 of energy using seven grams of uranium. In one day, a small handful of uranium can produce more energy than twelve tons of coal, and it can produce it without greenhouse emissions. In spite of its obvious efficiency and nonexistent emissions, however, nuclear energy is
15 not without its own unique problems; chiefly, what to do with the waste.

Uranium Oxide (UO_2) is the most common nuclear fuel in use. Rods containing the fuel are inserted into a reactor until the **fission** of the fuel becomes **critical**.
20 This causes a sustained nuclear chain reaction to occur. Each fission reaction triggers another through the release of a **neutron**. The neutrons cause the heavy uranium to split into lighter elements, generating massive amounts of energy. Once fission has exhausted the uranium, the
25 **depleted** rod is extracted from the reactor.

Nuclear waste is, simply, used nuclear fuel (See Figure 1). The substance bears no outward difference from the combination of uranium, oxygen, and steel that initially enters the reactor—both the charge and
30 discharge of a reactor consist of fuel rods, which are hollow, metal rods filled with stacks of pelletized nuclear fuel; however, the discharge's changed composition is not something that can simply be buried or tossed into a recycle bin. Nuclear waste falls into
35 two categories—low-level waste and high-level waste. Low-level waste consists of objects that have been either **compromised** by **radioactive** material or exposed to neutron radiation. Typically, low-level waste is the byproduct of laboratories, hospitals, or power plants—
40 items such as rags, medical tubes, mops, filters, injection needles, etc. Spent reactor fuel, though, is high-level waste, and it is so radioactive that a person standing in its **proximity** would receive a lethal dose of radiation within seconds.

45 The exact composition of spent fuel depends on the type of fuel used, the amount of time that the reactor was in operation, and how long the spent fuel is then left in the reactor. Spent fuel usually comprises plutonium, as well as minor actinides such as neptunium, curium,
50 americium, and the fission products. Minor actinides are largely responsible for the radioactivity of nuclear waste, but they are highly fissionable in fast reactors if reclaimed from the rods. The minor fission products are less useful; they can render the remaining rods unstable.

55 Annually and worldwide, nuclear power plants produce approximately 200,000 cubic meters of low- to intermediate-level waste and 10,000 cubic meters of high-level waste. Though these numbers are tiny compared to the amount of other forms of industrial
60 hazardous waste, the question remains of how to dispose of this material. Low-level waste can be stored on site until it has decayed enough to be treated as regular trash or until the waste accumulates enough to be shipped to low-level waste disposal sites. Because it is relatively
65 low in radiation, low-level waste poses little threat. High-level waste is extremely hazardous when it has not yet decayed to the point at which the radioactivity has **diminished** significantly (See Figure 2), which depends on the waste element's **half-life**.

70 Most spent nuclear fuel is stored on the reactor sites in storage ponds lined with concrete and steel. The waste is submerged and stacked on metal racks lined with neutron absorbers. Circulating water blocks radiation and ensures the pools remain cool. Pond
75 construction varies from one power facility to the next, but typically, the pond is encased in a sealed steel vault or a transportable, multi-purpose canister, the latter of which simplifies the eventual shipping of the material to a reprocessing or disposal facility. Red-hot spent fuel
80 rods sit in the pond, cooling for years before they are transported, though in depressed countries, spent fuel can continue to pile up for decades, untreated, owing to the lack of resources. If cooling systems fail, or pools are allowed to evaporate, spent fuel can catch fire or explode
85 catastrophically, destroying facilities and spewing widespread contamination.

Even when the thermal threat is reduced, and the spent fuel has cooled, it is still highly radioactive.

Lesson 12 continued:

Advancements in the modern nuclear industry now allow
90 for the reprocessing of fuel rods, in which the leftover
uranium and actinides can be refined into new fuel;
however, recycling reduces only a portion of spent fuel
worldwide. The remaining fuel must be kept in secure,
enclosed facilities strong enough to withstand natural
95 disasters while ensuring the long-term containment of
the hazardous substances. "Long term," as it applies to
nuclear waste, does not mean decades, but thousands or
millions of years.

Historically, the best option for nuclear waste
100 disposal has been to bury it deep in the ground, isolated
from any human influence. Presently, in the United
States, 75,000 metric tons of high-level waste are stored
at 120 different facilities near power plants. The waste
is as secure as economically feasible, but it is far from
105 permanently and safely stored. A permanent solution to
dig a deep geological **repository** a half-mile beneath
Yucca Mountain, Nevada, had been in the works since
the 1980s, but funding for the project was terminated
in 2011, after $9 billion had already been spent, due

110 to political pressure, local concerns over the safety of
the population, and the potential hazards in regularly
transporting all the nation's radioactive waste.

Most of the objections to a permanent storage
facility are founded in lingering fears of misunderstood
115 technology (though nuclear power has been in use for
seventy years). Scenes of Chernobyl after the blast,
the Three Mile Island crisis, or the irradiated ghost
town of Fukushima, have led many people to equate all
things nuclear with certain danger; in truth, however,
120 spent-fuel incidents, in spite of the juggling of so many
"hot potatoes," are extremely rare, and those that have
occurred have done so because the fuel had been left
in its temporary holding pool far beyond its intended
duration. The solution for the 75,000 tons of United
125 States nuclear waste is not to continue piling it in
warehouse containers, but to ensure the health and safety
of future generations by depositing it somewhere safe.
Until interstellar barges are perfected, which might be a
while, underground storage is the only solution.

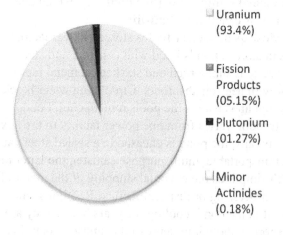

Figure 1: Typical Nuclear Waste Composition

Uranium (93.4%)

Fission Products (05.15%)

Plutonium (01.27%)

Minor Actinides (0.18%)

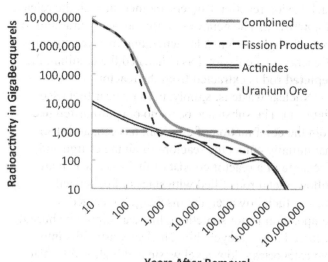

Figure 2: Spent Nuclear Fuel Decay (1 Metric Ton)

Combined

Fission Products

Actinides

Uranium Ore

Radioactivity in GigaBecquerels

Years After Removal

Lesson 12 continued:

12

According to the information in paragraph 1 (lines 1-16), a city of 10,000 homes would require approximately how many megawatts of electricity?
A) 10
B) 12
C) 100
D) 3,000

13

As it is used in line 29, *charge* describes
A) the importance of the item.
B) the electrical nature of UO_2.
C) the magnetic pull of a material.
D) the input to a reactor.

14

Within a nuclear reactor, initiating fission requires the achievement of a
A) supercritical state.
B) critical state.
C) subcritical state.
D) hypercritical state.

15

The word *critical*, as used in line 19, most nearly means
A) erratic.
B) aggressive.
C) steady.
D) less than ideal.

16

Choose the lines from the passage that provide the best evidence for your answer to the previous question.
A) lines 17-18 ("Uranium Oxide…use")
B) lines 20-22 ("This…neutron")
C) lines 22-24 ("The neutrons…energy")
D) lines 24-25 ("Once fission…reactor")

17

The purpose of paragraph 3 (lines 26-44) is to
A) explain how radioactive waste is classified.
B) provide evidence of the deadly nature of low-level waste.
C) refute ideas about the danger of atomic power.
D) comment on US policy regarding the disposal of nuclear waste.

18

The two main hazards associated with spent nuclear fuel are best described as
A) toxicity and weight.
B) radiation and interference.
C) heat and radioactivity.
D) transportation and heat.

19

As it is used in line 43, *proximity* most nearly means
A) sight.
B) direction.
C) vicinity.
D) realm.

20

The author of the passage would agree with which one of the following statements?
A) Nuclear power is dirty and should be replaced with traditional fossil fuel energy.
B) Radioactive waste is a problem that must be addressed in the near future.
C) Atomic energy has a long and scary track record with regards to nuclear waste incidents.
D) Using subterranean storage of high-level waste simply moves the problem without solving it permanently.

Lesson 12 continued:

21

From Figure 1, the reader can infer that
A) all uranium is consumed in a fission reactor.
B) plutonium is the most abundant byproduct of nuclear reactors.
C) fission products are the most hazardous portion of the spent fuel.
D) only a portion of the uranium is consumed in a reactor.

22

According to Figure 2, if uranium ore at its normal level of radioactivity is safe to handle, how long would it take for fission products to decay enough to safely handle them?
A) 10 years
B) 100 years
C) 1,000 years
D) 10,000 years

Lesson 12 continued:

Vocabulary: Context Answers

The following sentences contain vocabulary words used in the reading passage. Choose the answer that best completes the sentence. There may be more than one technically correct answer, but one will better exemplify the italicized vocabulary word than the others will.

1) The *depleted* runners _____.
   A. looked as fresh as when they started the race
   B. will all receive medals
   C. have slowed considerably since the eighth mile of the race
   D. had plenty of energy left to sprint up the hill at the end of the race
   E. were just getting started on the 26-mile marathon

2) While clearing out his grandmother's old house, Stan used a *repository* to _____.
   A. store assorted boxes of her personal effects
   B. distribute her belongings among his family
   C. dust off the particularly ancient chests
   D. keep an inventory of her possessions
   E. unlock containers that had missing keys

3) "Your patient is in *critical* condition," said the nurse, which made Dr. Donovan feel _____.
   A. disappointed
   B. elated
   C. sympathetic
   D. relieved
   E. worried

4) The crime scene had possibly been *compromised*; Officer Wilden _____.
   A. believed that the crime took place in a nearby hotel
   B. could not yet determine its exact location
   C. asked his team to consider distant hideaways
   D. suspected that someone had moved items around
   E. hoped that the witness had not misinterpreted the situation

5) _____ would likely *diminish* poverty in many at-risk urban areas.
   A. Closing down halfway houses
   B. Having a canned food drive
   C. Building a beautiful park
   D. Reporting on crime statistics
   E. New businesses that brought jobs

6) The *duration* _____ left Heidi feeling both exhausted and content at the end of the day.
   A. played by her basketball team
   B. of time spent at the carnival
   C. of the twisting rollercoaster
   D. that she had run that morning
   E. her students had put her through

7) Morgan appeared unnerved by the *proximity* of _____ her car.
   A. gas that remained in
   B. people in the backseat of
   C. the large pick-up truck to
   D. the long road trip on
   E. the old engine in

Lesson 12 continued:

Writing Practice

Each of the following sentences contains a modifying phrase that may or may not be clear or correct. Choose the answer that best corrects the sentence while retaining the intended meaning of the original sentence. Select NO CHANGE if the provided sentence is correct.

1) Angered by the hour-long electrical delay, the audience barely applauded when the band finally took the stage.
A. NO CHANGE
B. Angered by the hour-long electrical delay, the band was finally able to take the stage, but the people in the audience barely applauded.
C. The band was angered by the hour-long electrical delay, so when the people in the audience barely applauded, it finally took the stage.
D. The band finally took the stage and was angered by the hour-long electrical delay, but the people in the audience barely applauded.

2) Finished by the deadline, the room filled with the clacking sounds of Fiona typing vigorously on the computer keyboard.
A. NO CHANGE
B. The room filled with clacking sounds as Fiona typed vigorously, to finish by the deadline, on the computer keyboard.
C. As the room filled with clacking sounds, Fiona typed vigorously on the computer keyboard to finish by the deadline.
D. To finish by the deadline, Fiona typed vigorously on the computer keyboard and filled the room with clacking sounds.

3) Looking at the pictures of her kids, Terry's heart filled with happiness.
A. NO CHANGE
B. After looking at the pictures of her kids, Terry's heart filled with happiness.
C. Looking at the pictures of her kids, and Terry's heart filled with happiness.
D. Looking at the pictures of her kids, Terry felt her heart fill with happiness.

4) Having been repaired yesterday, Diane could use the computer without any difficulty.
A. NO CHANGE
B. The computer had been repaired yesterday, so Diane could use it without any difficulty.
C. Yesterday, having been repaired, Diane could use the computer without any difficulty.
D. Diane could use the computer without any difficulty, having been repaired yesterday.

Lesson 12 continued:

5) Remember not to ride on that bike without being completely assembled.
   A. NO CHANGE
   B. Remembering not to ride on that bike without being completely assembled, I didn't.
   C. Without being completely assembled, you should remember not to ride on that bike.
   D. Remember not to ride on that bike without it being completely assembled.

6) After winning an Academy Award, the actor's salary increased by a million dollars a picture.
   A. NO CHANGE
   B. After winning an Academy Award, the actor saw his salary increase by a million dollars a picture.
   C. The actor's salary increased by a million dollars a picture after winning an Academy Award.
   D. Winning an Academy Award, the actor's salary rose by a million dollars a picture.

7) Having just finished lunch, the thought of a cheeseburger was not on my mind until Tim mentioned it.
   A. NO CHANGE
   B. Tim mentioned having a cheeseburger, and the thought was not on my mind because I had just eaten lunch.
   C. I had just finished lunch, so the thought of a cheeseburger was not on my mind until Tim mentioned it.
   D. Having just finished lunch, until Tim mentioned it, the thought of a cheeseburger was not on my mind.

8) Moving steadily up the hill, a large glacier could be seen.
   A. NO CHANGE
   B. A large glacier could be seen as it moved steadily up the hill.
   C. Moving steadily up the hill, we observed a large glacier.
   D. Moving steadily up the hill, a larger glacier came into view.

9) The puppy looked at the chewed and ripped-apart pillow he had destroyed.
   A. NO CHANGE
   B. The puppy looked at the destroyed, chewed, and ripped-apart pillow.
   C. Chewed and ripped apart, the destroyed pillow is what the puppy looked at.
   D. Chewed and ripped apart, the puppy looked at the pillow he had destroyed.

10) When entering the doctor's office, a skeleton immediately caught my eye.
   A. NO CHANGE
   B. Entering the doctor's office, a skeleton immediately caught my eye.
   C. A skeleton immediately caught my eye when entering the doctor's office.
   D. When I entered the doctor's office, a skeleton immediately caught my eye.

Lesson 12 continued:

Vocabulary: Choosing the Right Use

The following sentences contain vocabulary words used in the reading passage. Identify the sentence or sentences that use the italicized vocabulary word properly. We have changed the form of some vocabulary words to provide new contexts; for example, some adjectives and verbs have been used as nouns.

1) A. Neither Tyler nor his sister wanted to *compromise* the dishes, so Tyler washed them tonight, and his sister will do them tomorrow.
   B. Shoppers *compromised* that the discount on all handbags in the store meant they could buy more and still save money.
   C. The hair stylist *compromised* the botched haircut by claiming it was the newest trend.
   D. The security of the information on the server was *compromised* when hackers broke through the firewall.

2) A. Mary Ellen knew that *depleting* the forests was the best way to protect the environment.
   B. Entirely *depleted*, Liam's face turned red as his classmates chuckled after his mistake.
   C. When Earth's oil is *depleted*, humankind will need to use new sources of energy.
   D. Kim could not afford the new car because her bank account was *depleted*.

3) A. The longer the flashlight was in use, the more its battery life *diminished*.
   B. Hunters readied their bows and *diminished* their spears before setting out for food.
   C. Danielle and Grace's relationship *diminished* the more Danielle began to hang out with other people.
   D. While setting up camp, the family hammered in the *diminished* stakes for the tent in order to keep it from blowing away.

4) A. After checking the patient's vital signs, the doctor declared he could be moved out of *critical* care and begin rehabilitation.
   B. As the *critical* tightrope walker moved toward the opposite end of the rope, the crowd gasped in awe.
   C. News of the child's kidnapping escalated the missing-persons case from concerning to *critical*.
   D. It was *critical* and irresponsible of the diver to leave the cage when the sharks were in a feeding frenzy.

5) A. The math test at the end of the day kept Sinclair from focusing in any of his other classes, and he spent the *duration* between lessons studying algebraic equations.
   B. The *duration* of Sandy's commute to work is forty minutes, which allows her to listen to at least two chapters from her audiobook.
   C. Monica began to increase the *duration* of her walks until she was ready to begin jogging.
   D. Because she took the red-eye flight from Los Angeles to New York, Carly slept for the *duration* of the flight.

Lesson 12 continued:

6)   A.   The binder Abby's mother keeps in the kitchen is a *repository* for all of the recipes her family has passed down for generations.

   B.   The baker combined the ingredients into a bowl before pouring the mixture into a *repository* and then into the oven to bake.

   C.   Because Will never talks badly about anyone, people trust him, and he has become a *repository* of secrets.

   D.   Our guide encouraged us to fill our *repositories* with water before continuing on our tour of the canyons.

7)   A.   Although the beach is a great place to vacation, our trip to the city was a nice *proximity* and change of pace.

   B.   In *proximity* to Perry's quick temper, his wife is patient and not easily riled.

   C.   Park rangers were notified of the forest fire's *proximity*, and they sounded an alarm that alerted all visitors to leave the area.

   D.   Kayla did not look forward to her family's road trip since she would have to sit in close *proximity* to her siblings for several hours in their small vehicle.

Lesson 12 continued:

Synonyms and Antonyms

Match the word with its *antonym*.

1) critical   **A.** full

2) fission   **B.** amplify

3) depleted   **C.** unimportant

4) diminish   **D.** fusion

Match the word with its *synonym*.

5) proximity   **E.** storehouse

6) compromise   **F.** period

7) repository   **G.** nearness

8) duration   **H.** jeopardize

END
of
LESSON 12

Lesson 13

Questions 23–32 are based on the following passage.

The following essay examines the traditional differences between literature and commercial fiction.

As one of the fastest ships in the fleet anchored in New York harbor after its **grueling** crossing of the Atlantic, a mob of New Yorkers stormed the wharf, jostling for a place as they earnestly shouted at the crew
5   for the latest news from England—specifically, "Is Nell dead?" They had been waiting to hear the news since the last installment of Nell's story and were crushed by the captain's affirmative answer, "Yes, little Nell is dead." Fortunately, little Nell didn't really exist; Nell is
10 the protagonist in Charles Dickens's *The Old Curiosity Shop*, which, in 1841, was a wildly popular **serialized** novel. Fast-forward to 2007, when thousands of readers stood in lines outside bookstores around the world, some wearing wizard hats and robes, as they eagerly waited
15 to hand cash to clerks in exchange for the final novel of J. K. Rowling's *Harry Potter* series. Both Dickens and Rowling are immensely popular writers of commercial fiction, yet in the present day, Dickens is no longer considered an author of mere **commercial** fiction; no,
20 his works are now regarded as literary fiction, which is typically perceived as more sophisticated and complex. If the content of Dickens's works remains the same, though, why has the classification of the genre changed? Does Dickens's writing really have more literary value
25 than current popular or commercial fiction?

When Dickens first published his serialized novels, there was no formal distinction between literary and commercial fiction, though **Victorian** society did promote the concept of reading for self-improvement,
30 and certain works were obviously more **didactic** than others. Commercial popularity of a novel did not inherently exclude it from being valued on literary grounds. In her journal, Queen Victoria remarks that *The Old Curiosity Shop* was "very interesting and cleverly
35 written." Its popularity was not interpreted by critics as a weakness. By the late-nineteenth century, as more works were being published, terms were created to define books into narrower categories. Most works fall into the broad category of commercial fiction, which
40 includes genre fiction like fantasy, science fiction, thrillers, and romance. Aside from fitting into specific

genres, commercial fiction is more plot- or story-driven and is typically written in understandable, entertaining prose. Most bestsellers are commercial fiction. Literary
45 fiction, in contrast, deliberately offers social commentary, political criticism, or explores the human condition. It is more character-driven, and the prose is more a product of art than entertainment, measurable in its use of writing devices such as **metaphor**, theme, and symbol.
50 Literary fiction tends to be studied as literature, while most commercial fiction is ignored by the academic community. As the re-categorizing of Dickens's works suggests, however, the division between literary and commercial fiction can be influenced by **longevity** and
55 cultural inclination.

In the current, post-modern era, the categorical distinctions are blurred. People within reading, writing, and publishing circles are beginning to recognize that many commercial fiction novels have literary value in
60 spite of, or perhaps because of, their popularity. A number of bestselling authors have been acknowledged for their literary contributions. In 2003, the National Book Awards gave Stephen King the medal for distinguished contribution to American letters. This award is usually
65 given to authors of literary fiction, not the horror fantasy that King is best known for. One literary scholar responded by writing a **scathing** opinion piece that decried King as "an immensely inadequate writer" who "shares nothing with Edgar Allan Poe." The critique
70 is ironic; Poe, who often wrote for paychecks, was a commercial author in his time and was often criticized as such. Ralph Waldo Emerson, the author of lofty **transcendentalist** essays intended to change lives, dismissed Poe as "that jingle man."

75   The publishing industry has learned to embrace the many perceived levels of literature, and eagerly catalog and sell them to their respective devotees. Book agents and publishers have created a relatively new classification: upmarket fiction. Upmarket blends the line
80 between commercial and literary fiction. It combines the more judiciously crafted prose of literary fiction with the tight plotlines of action- and drama-packed commercial fiction. A few examples of upmarket novels are *Water for Elephants* by Sara Gruen, *My Sister's Keeper* by Jodi
85 Picoult, *The Fault in Our Stars* by John Green, and *Life of Pi* by Yann Martel. They are novels rich enough in theme, complexity, and ambiguity to provide plenty of discussion for book clubs, yet commercially appealing

Lesson 13 continued:

enough to become bestsellers. Other authors have
90 blurred categorization in different ways. Kazuo Ishiguro
is known for creating works that defy classification;
his 2015 novel *The Buried Giant* uses Arthurian legend
to explore collective memory while blending fantasy
and literary fiction. This combination may seem odd
95 to modern readers and critics, who are accustomed to
distinct genres, but it's not unusual. When Dickens
included ghosts in his eternal classic *A Christmas
Carol*, literature was not thought to include elements
of **paranormal** fantasy. No one attempted to force the
100 novel into a specific genre because it wasn't thought to
be necessary: readers simply enjoyed his writing.

As Dickens illustrates, there is no definitive
boundary between literary and commercial fiction; after
all, well-written commercial fiction that withstands the
105 test of time often crosses over to become literary fiction.
If history is any indication, one day, excerpts of R. L.
Stine, Anne Rice, and Dan Brown, all powerhouses
of commercial fiction, will be studied in **anthologies**
of American classics amid the ranks of Willa Cather
110 and Nathaniel Hawthorne. Then again, the time might
already have come: There are hundreds of college
English courses focused on mainstream fiction authors,
a subject once thought unworthy of serious study. In
the future, look for doctoral theses on the psychological
115 conflicts of Harry Potter or the political symbolism of
the orcs from *The Lord of the Rings* trilogy—it's not far
away.

23

According to the passage, what is the main difference
between commercial fiction and literary fiction?
A) Authors of literary fiction tend to receive more
   praise and fame than those who write character-
   based commercial fiction.
B) There is no difference; time has blurred the
   definitions of these categories, which are typically
   based on popular trends.
C) Literary fiction provides more art and substance
   for academic study; commercial fiction focuses
   on entertaining storytelling.
D) Commercial fiction is more popular for use in
   classrooms; literary fiction is too difficult to
   understand.

24

Choose the lines that provide the best evidence for your
answer to the previous question.
A) lines 26-31 ("When Dickens…others")
B) lines 41-52 ("Aside from…community")
C) lines 56-60 ("In the…popularity")
D) lines 69-72 ("The critique…such")

25

As it is used in line 30, *didactic* most nearly means
A) educational.
B) popular.
C) expensive.
D) entertaining.

26

In paragraph 3 (lines 56-74), the critique contrasting
Edgar Allan Poe and Stephen King is described as
"ironic." Why is it ironic?
A) Poe went on to become one of the most famous
   American writers.
B) Even during Poe's career, critics were cruel in their
   comments.
C) Stephen King's award was legitimate; Poe did not
   receive one.
D) Poe, like King, was a commercial author whose
   writing was subject to criticism.

27

The best meaning for the word *inclination* as it is used
in line 55 is
A) understanding.
B) preference.
C) faith.
D) hostility.

Lesson 13 continued:

28

Choose the answer that best describes the purpose of paragraph 4 (lines 75-101).
A) It introduces the idea of paranormal fiction.
B) The paragraph concludes the main argument of the passage.
C) It defines the concept of upmarket fiction.
D) The paragraph suggests that publishers are responsible for how writing is classified.

29

The author includes *A Christmas Carol* in lines 97-98 because
A) Charles Dickens is the central figure of the passage.
B) it is an example of writing that could be classified as upmarket fiction.
C) the Victorian Era was the source of most literary fiction taught in schools today.
D) it was hailed as the best commercial writing of its day and remains so in spite of its literary value and status.

30

The author of the passage would agree with which one of the following statements?
A) The threshold between commercial and literary fiction is typically identifiable.
B) Commercial fiction of the present day might be regarded as classic literature in the future.
C) The popularity of commercial fiction is proportional to the universal decline of reading skills.
D) The best examples of literary fiction are generally confined to a single genre.

31

Choose the lines that provide the best evidence for your answer to the previous question.
A) lines 86-89 ("They are...bestsellers")
B) lines 90-94 ("Kazuo Ishiguro...fiction")
C) lines 96-99 ("When Dickens...fantasy")
D) lines 104-105 ("well-written commercial...fiction")

32

Of the choices provided, select the most appropriate title for the passage.
A) Charles Dickens: Literary Genius
B) The End of a Literary Era
C) Commercial or Literary Fiction?
D) Fiction: It's All the Same

Lesson 13 continued:

Vocabulary: Context Answers

The following sentences contain vocabulary words used in the reading passage. Choose the answer that best completes the sentence. There may be more than one technically correct answer, but one will better exemplify the italicized vocabulary word than the others will.

1) "The triathlon is *grueling*; be sure to _____," remarked Alan.
   A. get a good night's sleep
   B. remember to set your alarm
   C. avoid it at all costs
   D. ask friends to cheer you on
   E. train for the difficult tasks

2) The *scathing* review of the restaurant prompted the owner to _____.
   A. hang it near the register
   B. write the critic an angry letter
   C. expand to a second location
   D. stay open longer
   E. add items to the menu

3) "What would you say is the most popular literary *genre*—_____?" asked Suzanne.
   A. similes or metaphors
   B. cliffhangers or resolutions
   C. hard copies or audiobooks
   D. romance or science fiction
   E. Mark Twain or Harper Lee

4) Mr. Noyes, an esteemed English professor, preferred *didactic* novels over the contrasting _____ ones.
   A. light-hearted
   B. uninformative
   C. clichéd
   D. brief
   E. contemporary

5) Many educators agree that J. K. Rowling's *Harry Potter* has shown great *longevity*, _____.
   A. consisting of numerous installments
   B. featuring quite likeable characters
   C. having relevance even to adults
   D. remaining popular over time
   E. being rich with vocabulary words

6) The so-called _____ stunned the audience with displays of *paranormal* abilities all night.
   A. acrobat
   B. vocalist
   C. comedian
   D. poet
   E. psychic

7) When he finished reading, Zach decided he preferred the first _____ to the second *anthology*.
   A. author I had suggested
   B. chapter of the book
   C. series of poems
   D. title of the novel
   E. installment of the series

Lesson 13 continued:

8) Many contemporary authors choose for their works to be *serialized* _____.
   A. and devoid of censorship
   B. into several installments
   C. for children of all ages
   D. based on specific categories
   E. at readings and award ceremonies

9) "Would you consider _____ to be a *metaphor* for the joys of humanity?" posed Ms. Teekman.
   A. 'Life is a thriving garden'
   B. the elaborate imagery
   C. the author's Shakespeare reference
   D. 'You live only once'
   E. the protagonist's 'noble character'

Lesson 13 continued:

Writing Practice

Some of the following sentences are fragments, comma splices, or run-ons. Choose the answer that best corrects the sentence while retaining the intended meaning of the original sentence. Select NO CHANGE if the provided sentence is correct.

1) Mackenzie created a playlist for her trip to Cincinnati it was long but she chose good songs.
   A. NO CHANGE
   B. Mackenzie had good taste in music so she created a playlist; because her trip was long.
   C. The drive to Cincinnati to visit her sister. Mackenzie created a playlist that would last her the whole trip.
   D. Mackenzie created a long playlist for her trip to Cincinnati; she chose good songs.

2) J. R. R. Tolkien, writing that fantasy should critique and offer consolation for modernity, critic China Mieville thinks his work glorifies an enviable past.
   A. NO CHANGE
   B. Since J. R. R. Tolkien wrote that fantasy should critique and offer consolation for modernity, but critic China Mieville thinks his work glorifies an enviable past.
   C. J. R. R. Tolkien wrote that fantasy, critiquing and offering consolation for modernity, critic China Mieville thinks his work glorifies an enviable past.
   D. Because J. R. R. Tolkien wrote that fantasy should critique and offer consolation for modernity, critic China Mieville thinks his work glorifies an enviable past.

3) The five-paragraph essay is too formulaic for college writing, it teaches strong organization, so it is encouraged among high school students.
   A. NO CHANGE
   B. The five-paragraph essay is too formulaic for college writing, but it teaches strong organization, so it is encouraged among high school students.
   C. Because it teaches strong organization, the five-paragraph essay is encouraged among high school students; but it is too formulaic for college writing.
   D. Teaching strong organization, the five-paragraph essay, which is too formulaic for college writing, it is encouraged among high school students.

4) After Luke waited for the train to New York in the rain, clothing drenched.
   A. NO CHANGE
   B. Luke's clothing was drenched, he waited for the train to New York in the rain.
   C. Luke's clothing was drenched after he waited in the rain for the train to New York.
   D. Waiting in the rain with clothes drenched, Luke's train to New York.

5) The tremors from the earthquake violently shook the house scared the people who lived there.
   A. NO CHANGE
   B. The earthquake and its tremors caused damage to the house; Because it was scary.
   C. The violent tremors, the people who lived in the house were frightened by the earthquake.
   D. The tremors from the earthquake violently shook the house, scaring the people who lived there.

Lesson 13 continued:

6) Staying up hours on end to polish her résumé, write a perfect cover letter, and apply to as many jobs as possible.
    A. NO CHANGE
    B. Denise stayed up hours on end, to polish her résumé, wrote a perfect cover letter, and apply to as many jobs as possible.
    C. Denise stayed up hours on end and polishing her résumé, writing a perfect cover letter, and applying to as many jobs as possible.
    D. Staying up hours on end to polish her résumé, write a perfect cover letter, and apply to as many jobs as possible, Denise was determined to find employment after graduating from college.

7) Dividing by zero "proves" that two is equal to one. Which is why such division is not possible.
    A. NO CHANGE
    B. Dividing by zero to "prove" that two is equal to one demonstrates why such division is not possible.
    C. Divide by zero to "prove" that two is equal to one why such division is not possible.
    D. Dividing by zero to "prove" that two is equal to one, it demonstrates why such division is not possible.

8) Dr. Isaacs didn't say why painters fleeing to Venice to avoid the ransacking of Constantinople contributed to artistic movements of the Renaissance.
    A. NO CHANGE
    B. Dr. Isaacs didn't say why, painters fleeing to Venice to avoid ransacking in Constantinople, it contributed to artistic movements of the Renaissance.
    C. Dr. Isaacs didn't say why painters fleeing to Venice avoiding the ransacking. Constantinople contributing to artistic movements of the Renaissance.
    D. Dr. Isaacs didn't say why: painters fled to Venice to avoid the ransacking in Constantinople contributing to artistic movements of the Renaissance.

9) If I am lucky enough to have my name chosen out of the annual concert's raffle.
    A. NO CHANGE
    B. I am lucky enough. If I have my name chosen out of the annual concert's raffle.
    C. If I am lucky enough, my name will be chosen out of the annual concert's raffle.
    D. If I am lucky enough; to have my name chosen out of the annual concert's raffle would really help my finances.

10) Whether Mahatma Gandhi fasted to protest British imperialism and violent rebellion: his birthday is celebrated as the International Day of Nonviolence.
    A. NO CHANGE
    B. Mahatma Gandhi fasted to protest British imperialism and violent rebellion, and his birthday is celebrated as the International Day of Nonviolence.
    C. Protesting British imperialism, Mahatma Gandhi fasted his birthday is celebrated as the International Day of Nonviolence.
    D. Because Mahatma Gandhi fasted to protest British imperialism, and his birthday is celebrated as the International Day of Nonviolence.

Lesson 13 continued:

11) The volcano violently erupted, spewing lava, thousands of residents were forced to flee their homes.
   A. NO CHANGE
   B. The volcano violently erupted and spewed lava, thousands of residents were forced to flee their homes.
   C. The volcano violently erupted, spewing lava. Thousands of residents were forced to flee their homes.
   D. The volcano erupted violently, it spewed lava and thousands of residents were forced to flee their homes.

12) Emily Kngwarreye mixed traditional and modern Aboriginal and Australian styles in her painting certain Aboriginal motifs are considered communal property.
   A. NO CHANGE
   B. Emily Kngwarreye, mixing traditional and modern Aboriginal and Australian styles in her painting, certain Aboriginal motifs are considered communal property.
   C. Emily Kngwarreye mixed traditional and modern Aboriginal and Australian styles; considered communal property.
   D. Emily Kngwarreye mixed traditional and modern Aboriginal and Australian styles in her paintings, even though certain Aboriginal motifs are communal property.

13) Ashley's youngest cousin, Gene, who lives in Wisconsin but often travels east to see her in New York.
   A. NO CHANGE
   B. Ashley's youngest cousin, Gene, lives in Wisconsin, but often travels east to see her in New York.
   C. Ashley's youngest cousin often travels east to see her in New York is Gene, who lives in Wisconsin.
   D. Gene, Ashley's youngest cousin, lives in Wisconsin. Often travels east to see her in New York.

14) Olivia loves to read fantasy novels, she rarely has time for leisure reading after she finishes her homework and chores.
   A. NO CHANGE
   B. Olivia loves to read fantasy novels, unfortunately, she rarely has time for leisure reading after she finishes her homework and chores.
   C. Olivia loves to read fantasy novels she rarely has time for leisure reading after she finishes her homework and chores.
   D. Olivia loves to read fantasy novels; however, she rarely has time for leisure reading after she finishes her homework and chores.

15) I can't think of anything worse than staying up all night waiting to see the first showing of a popular movie and then hating it.
   A. NO CHANGE
   B. I can't think of anything worse than staying up all night; waiting to see the first showing of a popular movie and then hating it.
   C. I can't think of anything worse than staying up all night. Waiting to see the first showing of a popular movie and then hating it.
   D. I can't think of anything worse than: Staying up all night waiting to see the first showing of a popular movie and then hating it.

Lesson 13 continued:

Vocabulary: Choosing the Right Use

The following sentences contain vocabulary words used in the reading passage. Identify the sentence or sentences that use the italicized vocabulary word properly. We have changed the form of some vocabulary words to provide new contexts; for example, some adjectives and verbs have been used as nouns.

1) A. The poet's use of detailed and expansive *metaphor* was a technique that many aspiring writers could only dream of.
    B. Although Whitney said she was drowning in homework, her *metaphor* did not deter her teacher from assigning another worksheet.
    C. It was not a *metaphor* when Riley said that he could eat a horse; he had three burgers, two hot dogs, a plate of potato salad, and a slice of pie at the picnic.
    D. The scientists were asked if the projections of their results were *metaphorical* or based on previous tests.

2) A. Sonny's *didactic* attitude did not impress his potential employer, as it made him seem to lack a work ethic.
    B. Athletes training for the Olympics cannot develop *didactic* tendencies if they want to be taken seriously as competitors.
    C. After Christopher's mother caught him in a lie, she told him the *didactic* story about the boy who cried wolf.
    D. Mr. Clark's *didactic* teaching style not only explains information to students effectively, but improves their behavior in other classes as well.

3) A. The TV show was *serialized* into ten episodes per season before it was released on DVD.
    B. Jodi *serialized* the clothes in her closet by color and pattern.
    C. The first responders *serialized* the rations and supplies to the victims of the natural disaster based on how many people were in their family.
    D. Before it was published as a complete novel, *The Count of Monte Cristo* was originally *serialized* in a French journal.

4) A. Drew rehearsed her speech a final time before going out in front of the *anthologies* of people.
    B. Because Chelsea is taking a poetry class this semester, she needs several *anthologies* containing poems from various centuries.
    C. At the pet adoption center, the family walked past the *anthologies* of different dogs before choosing one that would be best for their lifestyle.
    D. For Phoebe's birthday, Charlie compiled an *anthology* of photos beginning at the start of their relationship.

Lesson 13 continued:

5) A. The *scathing* reports from the local news station on the unsanitary conditions of the downtown bakery caused a significant drop in customers.

B. Without flinching, the server let the *scathing* broth drip onto his hands while he carried the soup to the table.

C. *Scathing* rumors about the high school principal led to an internal investigation that resulted in the principal's dismissal.

D. Tired of eating soup that was too *scathing*, Frank bought larger bowls that helped it cool off faster.

6) A. The instructor's *grueling* workout regimen left the participants sore for the next week.

B. This past summer was so *grueling* that many people who spent too much time in the sun are still tan even though it is now February.

C. Heather's *grueling* bridesmaid is so concerned with making Heather's day perfect that she has stressed out the entire wedding party.

D. The *grueling* temperatures made it impossible to go outside this past week, and anyone who didn't have working air conditioning stayed at a friend's house.

7) A. In response to the teasing of his mother, Jacob insisted that the *genre* of his comic books was patriotism and independence, and, therefore, not just for little kids.

B. Whenever Michael is dumped by a friend, he binges on sweets and other *genres*.

C. Looking for something new to read, Olivia asked the librarian if they had any books with ghosts, suspense, and whodunits, so the librarian guided her to the section with books in the mystery *genre*.

D. If you are looking for a movie that will make you laugh, I am not sure why you are looking through the horror *genre*.

8) A. The car's tires did not have the *longevity* that was advertised, as they wore out within a few months.

B. The *longevity* of the rope bridge made Kaitlyn nervous since she is afraid of heights.

C. With the improvement of medicine, the *longevity* of human life has increased substantially.

D. Many insects' *longevity* is not determined simply by the onset of winter, and they can live for more than a few years.

9) A. Despite warnings of *paranormal* activity in the abandoned home, the family bought the house and began to restore it and make it more modern.

B. Jackie insisted there was a *paranormal* presence in her basement when the water heater continuously shut off and the breaker switches moved on their own.

C. It was *paranormal* of Brian to leave the house without telling anyone where he was going or what time he expected to return.

D. Grant insisted it is not *paranormal* for a dog to cower or run around when a thunderstorm is raging outside.

Lesson 13 continued:

Synonyms and Antonyms

Match the word with its *antonym*.

1) grueling   **A.** ordinary

2) paranormal   **B.** nonprofit

3) scathing   **C.** effortless

4) commercial   **D.** gentle

Match the word with its *synonym*.

5) longevity   **E.** collection

6) didactic   **F.** educational

7) genre   **G.** endurance

8) anthology   **H.** style

END
of
LESSON 13

Lesson 14

Questions 33–42 are based on the following passage.

This article discusses the value of geothermal energy.

The present and future of human existence and progress depend on a single resource: energy. We are lucky enough to live on a planet on which plants convert the sun's energy into chemical energy to sustain us, as
5   well as the many other animals we consume, but we are well into an age of humanity in which not even abundant food energy is enough to ensure the progress of civilization. We need to build, to travel, to farm for billions, and these activities require more energy than
10 we presently know how to harness from the sun, wind, or falling water. Fossil fuels keep us in business for the time being, but their use is both finite and dirty. It will do civilization no good if the furnace that heats our home burns the house down. What we need is an infinite supply
15 of cheap, clean energy. Luckily, we need only to look downward to find a colossal battery.

Heat from the earth is a reliable, virtually infinite energy source. While the efficiency of wind and solar power varies with the weather or time of day, **geothermal**
20 heat is constant. Of all the renewable energy sources, geothermal has by far the highest capacity factor, which is the ratio of energy produced during a given period of time to the hypothetical output of a generator operating continuously at maximum output.

25 About half of geothermal heat is generated by the decay of radioactive elements such as uranium, thorium, and potassium; the remainder is left over from the **primordial** heat of the planet's formation. This heat, starting at the 10,800° F core of molten nickel and iron,
30 conducts upward into the molten **mantle** and the solid **crust**, cooling as it approaches the surface. Geothermal **gradient** measures the rate of change of temperature with the depth of the earth. The geothermal gradient varies due to tectonic location, thermal properties of
35 rock, groundwater, and atmospheric changes. The heat in shallow ground is sufficient for heating or cooling a home, but geothermal power plants require the higher temperatures of deeper resources. Like most power plants, geothermal power plants use steam to rotate a
40 **turbine** connected to a generator to produce electricity. Geothermal energy is most readily attainable in hot spots where **seismic** activity and **magma** break up the rock

and allow water to circulate to the surface, where it often forms hot springs and **geysers**. These hot springs and
45 geysers are called hydrothermic **convection** systems. Scientists find these hot spots by measuring the ratio of helium isotopes in water samples at suspected sites; the crust contains mainly helium-4 and the mantle contains **predominantly** helium-3. Water in known geothermal
50 regions that has a higher ratio of helium-3 has been in contact with the mantle and indicates a good location to drill and build a power plant.

All geothermal power plants use hot water and steam from the ground to spin generator turbines and then
55 return the warm water to its source to prolong its heat, but there are three different designs in use: dry steam, flash steam, and **binary** cycle. Dry steam plants channel underground steam to power turbines directly; however, underground steam sources are rare. The United States
60 has only two: Yellowstone in Wyoming and The Geysers in California, which means dry steam is an uncommon **configuration**. As an open system, dry steam plants produce some emissions, including hydrogen sulfide, a toxic gas, and trace amounts of arsenic. While these
65 emissions are less harmful to the environment than emissions from fossil fuels, they are obviously not ideal. The other two systems are more environmentally viable. Flash steam, currently the most common design, uses reservoirs of water with temperatures above 360° F.
70 Water pressure drives the liquid up the wells into a tank at the surface that has significantly lower pressure. As the water depressurizes, some of it vaporizes, and that steam is separated to power the turbine. The remaining liquid and condensed steam are returned to the reservoir
75 to reheat. Binary cycle systems are used when the water source is between 225° F and 360° F. The hot water flows through a heat exchanger, where it heats another liquid, like isobutene, which has a lower boiling temperature than water. The steam from this liquid drives the turbine.
80 In binary cycle systems, the water and other liquids are contained in closed loops, so they remain isolated and uncontaminated. Most geothermal resources are below 300° F, so binary systems have the potential to provide a substantial proportion of geothermal electricity;
85 however, they are not without limitations. Less than ten percent of land hosts the conditions that cause water to circulate to the surface. Alternate methods of harnessing geothermal energy will be necessary to **optimize** the use of geothermal resources.

Lesson 14 continued:

90 Enhanced geothermal systems (EGS) are used to extract geothermal energy from hot dry rocks. In an EGS, man-made water reservoirs are created in a process similar to that of **fracking**, but without the chemicals. Cold water is injected deep into subterranean formations
95 to widen pre-existing **fissures** and increase the **permeability** of the rocks. This increased permeability allows water to penetrate the rock. The heated liquid then rises to the surface where it can be captured to generate electricity, usually in binary cycle systems.
100 EGS enables the capture of geothermal energy on a much greater scale because it is not limited to traditional hydrothermal regions. EGS is thought to cause increased seismic activity when rocks slip along fractures; however, geologists are studying fractures and seismic
105 events to determine how and where to drill responsibly.
Another alternate method is to obtain low-temperature geothermal energy through co-production with existing oil and natural gas reservoirs. In the US alone, oil and gas wells produce an average of twenty-
110 five billion barrels of hot water per year. This byproduct has traditionally been regarded as an inconvenience that must be disposed of at cost; however, it is a resource that could fulfill local electricity needs at the drilling sites or be sold to local power grids. These geothermal sites take
115 advantage of existing oil and gas field infrastructures and use binary cycle systems. Co-production, if **implemented** on a large scale, could produce thousands of megawatts of geothermal electricity at low costs.
Co-production could be the catalyst in generating
120 interest in more sustainable energy resources. Geothermal power, while presently not as easy to obtain profitably as wind or solar, will pay dividends in its superior reliability and clean environmental profile. To continue living on a massive battery that has the
125 potential to fulfill the energy needs for all of humankind, without taking advantage of it, is simply illogical.

33

From paragraph 1, a reader can infer that
A) geothermal energy will not be a viable energy source for centuries.
B) solar power is the most likely power source of the future.
C) the author thinks fossil fuels are adequate sources of power.
D) civilization requires more than just food for continued advancement.

34

According to the author, the best indicator of a location for the construction of a geothermal power facility is
A) water that has been in contact with the mantle.
B) easy access to railroad and highway transportation.
C) rock formations conducive to geysers and hot springs.
D) evidence that the water contains helium-4.

35

Choose the lines that provide the best evidence for your answer to the previous question.
A) lines 38-40 ("Like most...electricity")
B) lines 46-47 ("Scientists find...sites")
C) lines 49-52 ("Water in...plant")
D) lines 53-55 ("All geothermal...heat")

36

Of the three major types of geothermal power systems discussed, the most environmentally friendly method is
A) closed loop.
B) binary cycle.
C) flash steam.
D) dry steam.

Lesson 14 continued:

37

As it is used in line 123, *profile* most nearly means
A) scientific sketch.
B) outline.
C) dependability.
D) general properties.

38

From the tone of the passage, the author can be best described as
A) decidedly in favor of geothermal energy production.
B) having a tendency to write satirically.
C) biased against energy production other than solar.
D) indifferent to environmental concerns.

39

The enhanced geothermal system uses which material to capture and transfer the earth's energy to the surface?
A) oil
B) water
C) magma
D) isobutane

40

Choose the lines that provide the best evidence for your answer to the previous question.
A) lines 90-91 ("Enhanced geothermal…rocks")
B) lines 91-93 ("In an…chemicals")
C) lines 94-99 ("Cold water…electricity")
D) lines 100-102 ("EGS enables…regions")

41

The organizational structure of the passage is best described as
A) order of magnitude.
B) topical order.
C) pro-and-con.
D) chronological.

42

Choose the most appropriate title for the passage.
A) Binary Cycle Geothermal Energy Systems
B) The Unused Fossil Fuel: Magma
C) Geothermal Energy: Power Without End
D) The Need for an Alternative Energy Source

Lesson 14 continued:

Vocabulary: Context Answers

The following sentences contain vocabulary words used in the reading passage. Choose the answer that best completes the sentence. There may be more than one technically correct answer, but one will better exemplify the italicized vocabulary word than the others will.

1) The Mars Rover has *seismic* sensors that detect _____.

A. when it becomes dark outside
B. changes in the atmosphere
C. vibrations of the ground
D. distress beacons from other teams
E. when people tell lies

2) "How much *geothermal* _____ do the hot springs have?" wondered Aimee, as she stared in awe at the Turkish Pamukkale pools.

A. width
B. energy
C. depth
D. significance
E. toxicity

3) The Natural History Museum opened an exhibit today that featured a *primordial* _____.

A. imitation of a rain forest
B. history of the wheel
C. look into the human brain
D. exhibit on airplanes
E. set of fossils

4) Without the use of *permeable* _____, the seeds in the pot are unlikely to sprout.

A. water
B. space
C. sunlight
D. soil
E. experts

5) The *gradient* on the employee performance chart showed that _____.

A. digging below 100 feet costs more money
B. working in construction is dangerous
C. work improves as more breaks are allowed
D. the managers make too much money
E. there have been no accidents on the job

6) The components of the *binary* weed killer _____.

A. number in the hundreds
B. are green, red, yellow, and blue
C. should be piled up first
D. need more salt to be effective
E. must first be combined to work

7) The *fissure* _____, and they were lucky to escape uninjured.

A. sprang at them with bloody fangs
B. suddenly opened under their tent area
C. from the night sky just missed them
D. cut right through the water of the stream
E. was heard approaching their campsite

8) The *predominant* animal in the wilderness _____.

A. could be heard for miles
B. wandered in from the jungle
C. lived in every area
D. had just given birth
E. was the most submissive

Lesson 14 continued:

9) While conventional ovens surround cooking food with heated air, *convection* ovens _____.
   A. circulate the hot air
   B. keep the food fresh
   C. are battery-operated
   D. utilize harmless chemicals
   E. use heat from the sun

10) "Be careful near that *geyser*; it could _____," warned the park staff.
    A. spray hot water into the air
    B. give you frostbite
    C. be filled with snakes
    D. erupt molten rock
    E. break when stepped on

11) Theo planned to vote for the presidential candidate who would *optimize* _____ for youth in America.
    A. homelessness
    B. child labor
    C. educational resources
    D. money to use instead
    E. national borders

12) Courtney and her team planned to *implement* _____ crime in the neighborhood.
    A. vandalism and other
    B. nightly guards to protect against
    C. money, hoping to lessen
    D. a mysteriously unsolved
    E. a strategy to reduce

Lesson 14 continued:

Writing Practice

The underlined portion of each sentence provides two pronouns that are often used incorrectly. Choose the pronoun that completes the sentence correctly.

1) Danielle, <u>who</u> / <u>whom</u> had always had a mischievous streak, was the first student suspended for the prank.

2) The tweet for #DeadRaccoonToronto was written by <u>who</u> / <u>whom</u>?

3) It's none of his business <u>who</u> / <u>whom</u> Amanda wants to talk to.

4) Kemmie asked, "<u>Who</u> / <u>Whom</u> will read my paper?"

5) Tom wondered <u>who</u> / <u>whom</u> would have stolen his journal from his locker.

6) Isn't he that singer <u>who</u> / <u>whom</u> the police arrested for drunk driving?

7) <u>Who</u> / <u>Whom</u> do you think gave Angelina the Secret Santa gift?

8) The police department will have to respond to the victims <u>who</u> / <u>whom</u> had their reports swept under the rug.

9) <u>Who</u> / <u>Whom</u> did she tell us the present was for?

10) <u>Who</u> / <u>Whom</u> was supposed to call maintenance about the cockroaches in the bathroom?

11) Audrey seems to have fallen in love with Philip, <u>who</u> / <u>whom</u> she met last year at summer camp.

12) Why do I have to guess <u>who</u> / <u>whom</u> won the baseball game if I don't even care?

13) John knew that the freshman <u>who</u> / <u>whom</u> the bully had harassed could use some help.

14) Oliver, <u>who</u> / <u>whom</u> no one ever saw angry, shocked everyone when he lost his temper over something as trivial as there being no chips in the cafeteria.

15) Martina is the only one I know of in the entire house <u>who</u> / <u>whom</u> leaves the dirty laundry on the floor.

Lesson 14 continued:

Vocabulary: Choosing the Right Use

The following sentences contain vocabulary words used in the reading passage. Identify the sentence or sentences that use the italicized vocabulary word properly. We have changed the form of some vocabulary words to provide new contexts; for example, some adjectives and verbs have been used as nouns.

1) A. The science teacher used a *gradient* that showed changes in the time it took for salty water to freeze.
   B. Victoria increased her workout time in *gradients* so that by the end of the year she could run a marathon.
   C. The *gradient* rise of Trevor's grades influenced his grandmother's decision to buy him a bicycle.
   D. There were places on the climb to the top that were almost *gradient*, surrounded by extremely jagged rocks.

2) A. The earth and the moon have a *binary* relationship in which one orbits around the other.
   B. Computers are designed to function in a *binary* system: ones and zeros.
   C. The *binary* alliance among the three countries improved trade and international relations for all involved.
   D. Celina, Sarah, and Sierra have had a *binary* friendship since they were in elementary school.

3) A. After a *seismic* wave went through the city, inspectors were called to check the stability of the tallest buildings and structures.
   B. Rowan thought his older sister had created a *seismic* painting, but she thought it was "just OK."
   C. The local news channel warned the population to be aware of aftershocks even though the *seismic* activity had occurred hours prior.
   D. Rachel flirted with every guy at the party until she realized that a *seismic* boy really wanted to get to know her.

4) A. In order to *optimize* productivity, the boss banned all cell phones and other potentially distracting devices.
   B. Rather than have the high-calorie chocolate mousse cake for dessert, Fiona *optimized* for the fruit tart.
   C. The company decided to cut the staff in half to *optimize* efficiency.
   D. Torn between the two job opportunities, Quentin *optimized* for the position with more pay but a longer commute.

5) A. Nora liked the *permeability* of her dress because it allowed her to accessorize it with many different pieces of jewelry.
   B. The duct tape's *permeability* made it a terrible solution for the leak in the boat.
   C. Julie knew her aunt meant well, but the *permeability* of the knitted gloves Aunt May gave her made them ineffective.
   D. Jonah's family is always moving from one city to the next, which is why they appreciate the *permeability* of the dining set.

Lesson 14 continued:

6) A. Many *predominant* languages currently exist throughout the world.
    B. The *predominant* motivation that drew thousands to the gold fields of California was greed.
    C. The group was made up *predominately* of students who had skipped at least one grade.
    D. The *predominance* of one person makes dictatorship likely, which is the case in North Korea.

7) A. Brandy *implemented* her coffee maker the moment she got out of bed.
    B. In order to win the match, Kyle *implemented* a new strategy.
    C. To bring in new business, the baker *implemented* several new recipes for bread.
    D. Devin always *implemented* the television to watch the news once he arrived home from work.

8) A. The plumber poured draining solution into the pipes until the water from the sink went down in a *geyser* again.
    B. Smoke from the mansion's many fireplaces billowed out of the chimneys like *geysers*.
    C. Traffic congested on Main Street after a car hit a hydrant and sent a *geyser* of water ten feet into the air.
    D. Swimmers and boaters are warned to look out for swirling water that can form dangerous *geysers* and cause drowning.

9) A. The students watched the liquid inside a glass vial begin to boil through *convection* when their teacher placed it under an open flame.
    B. Jake's hands could not stand the *convection* that crept in while he was ice fishing.
    C. After coming inside from below zero temperatures, Travis stood in front of the fireplace until the *convection* allowed him to feel his face again.
    D. When Anna ran out of drinking water, she purified river water with the help of *convection*.

10) A. The *configuration* of every apartment in the building made the rent easy to pay.
    B. Could you please explain to me the *configuration* of how you solved the problem?
    C. One *configuration* involved a clown juggling while riding a horse around the ring.
    D. The fire destroyed more than three square miles and altered the *configuration* of the city forever.

Lesson 14 continued:

Synonyms and Antonyms

Match the word with its *antonym*.

1) predominant   **A.** impenetrable

2) primordial   **B.** last

3) optimize   **C.** weaken

4) permeable   **D.** inferior

Match the word with its *synonym*.

5) fissure   **E.** paired

6) binary   **F.** employ

7) gradient   **G.** rate

8) implement   **H.** crack

END of LESSON 14

Lesson 15

Questions 43–52 are based on the following passages.

Passage 1 is adapted from the "Economy" chapter of Henry David Thoreau's 1845 book, *Walden*. Passage 2 is adapted from Andrew Carnegie's 1889 essay, "Wealth."

Passage 1

I would fain say something, not so much concerning the Chinese and Sandwich Islanders as you who read these pages, who are said to live in New England; something about your condition, especially your outward
5 condition or circumstances in this world, in this town, what it is, whether it is necessary that it be as bad as it is, whether it cannot be improved as well as not. I have travelled a good deal in Concord; and everywhere, in shops, and offices, and fields, the inhabitants have
10 appeared to me to be doing **penance** in a thousand remarkable ways. What I have heard of Brahmins sitting exposed to four fires and looking in the face of the sun; or hanging suspended, with their heads downward, over flames; or looking at the heavens over their shoulders
15 "until it becomes impossible for them to resume their natural position, while from the twist of the neck nothing but liquids can pass into the stomach"; or dwelling, chained for life, at the foot of a tree; or measuring with their bodies, like caterpillars, the breadth of vast
20 empires; or standing on one leg on the tops of pillars— even these forms of conscious penance are hardly more incredible and astonishing than the scenes which I daily witness. The twelve labors of Hercules were trifling in comparison with those which my neighbors have
25 undertaken; for they were only twelve, and had an end; but I could never see that these men slew or captured any monster or finished any labor. They have no friend Iolaus to burn with a hot iron the root of the hydra's head, but as soon as one head is crushed, two spring up.
30 I see young men, my townsmen, whose misfortune it is to have inherited farms, houses, barns, cattle, and farming tools; for these are more easily acquired than got rid of. Better if they had been born in the open pasture and suckled by a wolf, that they might have seen with
35 clearer eyes what field they were called to labor in. Who made them **serfs** of the soil? Why should they eat their sixty acres, when man is condemned to eat only his peck of dirt? Why should they begin digging their graves as soon as they are born? They have got to live

40 a man's life, pushing all these things before them, and get on as well as they can. How many a poor immortal soul have I met well-nigh crushed and smothered under its load, creeping down the road of life, pushing before it a barn seventy-five feet by forty, its Augean
45 stables never cleansed, and one hundred acres of land, tillage, mowing, pasture, and woodlot! The portionless, who struggle with no such unnecessary inherited **encumbrances**, find it labor enough to **subdue** and **cultivate** a few cubic feet of flesh.
50 But men labor under a mistake. The better part of the man is soon plowed into the soil for compost. By a seeming fate, commonly called necessity, they are employed, as it says in an old book, laying up treasures which moth and rust will corrupt and thieves break
55 through and steal. It is a fool's life, as they will find when they get to the end of it, if not before.
Most men, even in this comparatively free country, through mere ignorance and mistake, are so occupied with the factitious cares and superfluously **coarse** labors
60 of life that its finer fruits cannot be plucked by them. Their fingers, from excessive toil, are too clumsy and tremble too much for that. Actually, the laboring man has not leisure for a true integrity day by day; he cannot afford to sustain the manliest relations to men; his labor
65 would be **depreciated** in the market. He has no time to be anything but a machine. How can he remember well his ignorance—which his growth requires—who has so often to use his knowledge? We should feed and clothe him **gratuitously** sometimes, and recruit him with our
70 cordials, before we judge of him. The finest qualities of our nature, like the bloom on fruits, can be preserved only by the most delicate handling. Yet we do not treat ourselves nor one another thus tenderly.
Some of you, we all know, are poor, find it hard
75 to live, are sometimes, as it were, gasping for breath. I have no doubt that some of you who read this book are unable to pay for all the dinners which you have actually eaten, or for the coats and shoes which are fast wearing or are already worn out, and have come to this
80 page to spend borrowed or stolen time, robbing your creditors of an hour. It is very evident what mean and sneaking lives many of you live, for my sight has been whetted by experience; always on the limits, trying to get into business and trying to get out of debt, a very
85 ancient slough, called by the Latin *æs alienum*, another's brass, for some of their coins were made of brass; still

Lesson 15 continued:

living, and dying, and buried by this other's brass;
always promising to pay, promising to pay, tomorrow,
and dying today, **insolvent**; seeking to curry favor, to
90 get custom, by how many modes, only not state-prison
offenses; lying, flattering, voting, contracting yourselves
into a nutshell of civility or dilating into an atmosphere
of thin and vaporous generosity, that you may persuade
your neighbor to let you make his shoes, or his hat, or
95 his coat, or his carriage, or import his groceries for him;
making yourselves sick, that you may lay up something
against a sick day, something to be tucked away in an old
chest, or in a stocking behind the plastering, or, more
safely, in the brick bank; no matter where, no matter
100 how much or how little.

The mass of men lead lives of quiet **desperation**.
What is called **resignation** is confirmed desperation.
From the desperate city you go into the desperate
country, and have to console yourself with the bravery
105 of minks and muskrats. A stereotyped but unconscious
despair is concealed even under what are called the
games and amusements of mankind. There is no play in
them, for this comes after work. But it is a characteristic
of wisdom not to do desperate things.

Passage 2

The problem of our age is the proper administration
of wealth, so that the ties of brotherhood may still bind
together the rich and poor in harmonious relationship.
The conditions of human life have not only been
5 changed, but revolutionized, within the past few hundred
years. In former days there was little difference between
the dwelling, dress, food, and environment of the chief
and those of his **retainers**. The Indians are today where
civilized man then was. When visiting the Sioux, I was
10 led to the wigwam of the chief. It was just like the others
in external appearance, and even within the difference
was trifling between it and those of the poorest of
his braves. The contrast between the palace of the
millionaire and the cottage of the laborer with us to-day
15 measures the change which has come with civilization.

This change, however, is not to be **deplored**, but
welcomed as highly beneficial. It is well, nay, essential
for the progress of the race, that the houses of some
should be homes for all that is highest and best in
20 literature and the arts, and for all the refinements of
civilization, rather than that none should be so. Much
better this great irregularity than universal **squalor**.
Without wealth there can be no Mycenae. The "good
old times" were not good old times. Neither master nor
25 servant was as well situated then as today. A relapse
to old conditions would be disastrous to both—not the
least so to him who serves—and would Sweep away
civilization with it. But whether the change be for good
or ill, it is upon us, beyond our power to alter, and
30 therefore to be accepted and made the best of. It is a
waste of time to criticize the inevitable.

There are but three modes in which surplus wealth
can be disposed of. It can be left to the families of the
decedents; or it can be **bequeathed** for public purposes;
35 or, finally, it can be administered during their lives by its
possessors. Under the first and second modes most of the
wealth of the world that has reached the few has hitherto
been applied. Let us in turn consider each of these
modes. The first is the most injudicious. In **monarchical**
40 countries, the estates and the greatest portion of the
wealth are left to the first son, that the vanity of the
parent may be gratified by the thought that his name
and title are to descend to succeeding generations
unimpaired. The condition of this class in Europe today
45 teaches the futility of such hopes or ambitions. The
successors have become impoverished through their
follies or from the fall in the value of land. Even in
Great Britain, the strict law of entail has been found
inadequate to maintain the status of an hereditary class.
50 Its soil is rapidly passing into the hands of the stranger.
Under republican institutions the division of property
among the children is much fairer, but the question which
forces itself upon thoughtful men in all lands is: Why
should men leave great fortunes to their children? If this
55 is done from affection, is it not misguided affection?
Observation teaches that, generally speaking, it is not
well for the children that they should be so burdened.
Neither is it well for the state. Beyond providing for the
wife and daughters moderate sources of income, and
60 very moderate allowances indeed, if any, for the sons,

men may well hesitate, for it is no longer questionable that great sums bequeathed oftener work more for the injury than for the good of the recipients. Wise men will soon conclude that, for the best interests of the members 65 of their families and of the state, such bequests are an improper use of their means.

It is not suggested that men who have failed to educate their sons to earn a livelihood shall cast them adrift in poverty. If any man has seen fit to rear his sons 70 with a view to their living idle lives, or, what is highly commendable, has instilled in them the sentiment that they are in a position to labor for public ends without reference to **pecuniary** considerations, then, of course, the duty of the parent is to see that such are provided 75 for in moderation. There are instances of millionaires' sons unspoiled by wealth, who, being rich, still perform great services in the community. Such are the very salt of the earth, as valuable as, unfortunately, they are rare; still it is not the exception, but the rule, that men must 80 regard, and, looking at the usual result of enormous sums **conferred** upon legatees, the thoughtful man must shortly say, "I would as soon leave to my son a curse as the almighty dollar," and admit to himself that it is not the welfare of the children, but family pride, which 85 inspires these enormous legacies.

As to the second mode, that of leaving wealth at death for public uses, it may be said that this is only a means for the disposal of wealth, provided a man is content to wait until he is dead before it becomes 90 of much good in the world. Knowledge of the results of legacies bequeathed is not calculated to inspire the brightest hopes of much **posthumous** good being accomplished. The cases are not few in which the real object sought by the testator is not attained, nor are 95 they few in which his real wishes are **thwarted**. In many cases the bequests are so used as to become only monuments of his **folly**. It is well to remember that it requires the exercise of not less ability than that which acquired the wealth to use it so as to be really beneficial 100 to the community. Besides this, it may fairly be said that no man is to be **extolled** for doing what he cannot help doing, nor is he to be thanked by the community to which he only leaves wealth at death. Men who leave

vast sums in this way may fairly be thought men who 105 would not have left it at all, had they been able to take it with them. The memories of such cannot be held in grateful remembrance, for there is no grace in their gifts. It is not to be wondered at that such bequests seem so generally to lack the blessing.

110 The growing disposition to tax more and more heavily large estates left at death is a cheering indication of the growth of a **salutary** change in public opinion. The State of Pennsylvania now takes—subject to some exceptions—one-tenth of the property left by its citizens. 115 The budget presented in the British Parliament the other day proposes to increase the death-duties; and, most significant of all, the new tax is to be a **graduated** one. Of all forms of taxation, this seems the wisest. Men who continue hoarding great sums all their lives, the proper 120 use of which for public ends would work good to the community, should be made to feel that the community, in the form of the state, cannot thus be deprived of its proper share. By taxing estates heavily at death the state marks its condemnation of the selfish millionaire's 125 unworthy life.

It is desirable that nations should go much further in this direction. Indeed, it is difficult to set bounds to the share of a rich man's estate which should go at his death to the public through the agency of the state, and 130 by all means such taxes should be graduated, beginning at nothing upon moderate sums to dependents, and increasing rapidly as the amounts swell, until of the millionaire's hoard, as of Shylock's, at least half "comes to the **privy coffer** of the state."

135 This policy would work powerfully to induce the rich man to attend to the administration of wealth during his life, which is the end that society should always have in view, as being that by far most fruitful for the people. Nor need it be feared that this policy would sap the root 140 of enterprise and render men less anxious to accumulate, for to the class whose ambition it is to leave great fortunes and be talked about after their death, it will attract even more attention, and, indeed, be a somewhat nobler ambition to have enormous sums paid over to the 145 state from their fortunes.

Lesson 15 continued:

43

In passage 1, paragraph 1 (lines 1-29), Thoreau equates a life of hard labor to
A) finding one's purpose.
B) traveling through life.
C) achieving spirituality.
D) atoning for sins.

44

Choose the lines that provide the best evidence for your answer to the previous question.
A) lines 1-3 ("I would…England")
B) lines 7-9 ("I have…fields")
C) lines 9-11 ("the inhabitants...remarkable ways")
D) lines 11-12 ("What I…sun")

45

In passage 1, lines 47-49, Thoreau's metaphor equates the human body to
A) a farm.
B) a temple.
C) a cow.
D) a plant.

46

In passage 2, the purpose of paragraphs 1 and 2 (lines 1-31) is to
A) refute the idea that work is pointless.
B) explain how wealth indicates progress of civilization.
C) describe the noble life of primitive societies.
D) challenge the notion that millionaires' estates should be taxed upon death.

47

As it is used in passage 2, line 48, *entail* most nearly means
A) equality.
B) merit.
C) geography.
D) birthright.

48

As it is used in passage 2, line 73, *pecuniary* most nearly means
A) housing.
B) family.
C) financial.
D) little.

49

The author of passage 2 would agree with which one of the following statements?
A) The heirs to fortunes best understand how to responsibly spend money.
B) The wealthy should be forced to provide housing to the poor.
C) The best indicator of an advanced society is the similarity of homes among the richest and poorest people.
D) The poor of the present day live much better lives than their historical counterparts did.

50

The authors of both passages would agree that wealth received from family is
A) the best way to improve.
B) a burden.
C) a blessing.
D) a necessary evil.

51

Choose the line from passage 2 that best supports your answer to the previous question.
A) lines 45-47 ("The successors…land")
B) lines 53-54 ("Why should…children")
C) lines 56-57 ("Observation teaches…burdened")
D) lines 67-69 ("It is…poverty")

52

The authors of both passages would disagree over which one of the following statements?
A) Laboring for the purpose of building wealth is pointless.
B) It is wrong for a wealthy person to hoard money.
C) Labor in the service of the public good is a noble undertaking.
D) Being in debt to others is unfortunate.

Lesson 15 continued:

Vocabulary: Context Answers

The following sentences contain vocabulary words used in the reading passages. Choose the answer that best completes the sentence. There may be more than one technically correct answer, but one will better exemplify the italicized vocabulary word than the others will.

1) The Thatcher family donut shop finally _____ after slowing customer traffic caused them to become *insolvent*.
   A. was featured in a blog
   B. expanded the building
   C. changed its menu
   D. closed permanently
   E. teamed up with a competitor

2) Mallory's _____ revealed to the audience her great *desperation*.
   A. clear voice
   B. forgetting the lyrics
   C. witty banter
   D. shaking hands
   E. supportive staff

3) Couples who attend counseling do so in order to *cultivate* _____.
   A. further conflict
   B. each other's differing perspectives
   C. each other in a healthy manner
   D. advice from an outside expert
   E. feelings of love and respect

4) "There was honestly nothing about your film that _____," admitted Nina *coarsely*.
   A. I enjoyed
   B. I understood
   C. seemed confusing
   D. felt unrealistic
   E. bothered me

5) In Louie's final testament, he *bequeathed* _____ his daughter.
   A. everyone who had inspired him, especially
   B. that the neighborhood look out for
   C. his savings to a charity run by
   D. upon the beautiful times spent with
   E. a short story that he had written with

6) _____ clearly *depreciated* the usefulness of laptops.
   A. Successful computer companies
   B. Cell phones with Internet access
   C. The ability to share music
   D. A pro-technology movement
   E. Some investigative reporters

Lesson 15 continued:

7) Archaeologists found large *coffers* _____.
   A. that were probably poisonous
   B. of hidden pottery and tools
   C. that amounted to a fortune
   D. that led to a smaller area of the house
   E. of ancient bones in a common grave

8) The king's *retainers* _____ while he sat upon his majestic throne.
   A. shared a drink with him
   B. fed him grapes and kiwi
   C. kept his hands warm
   D. gave him a boost of energy
   E. were always to be obeyed

9) Sally's *penance* _____ included baking the family a delicious cake.
   A. for breaking the window
   B. to generously offer her time
   C. to the upcoming birthday party
   D. for making elaborate desserts
   E. of things she could not do

10) A *posthumous* analysis revealed _____.
   A. what time of day it was
   B. how the person had died
   C. where the party would be
   D. when the butler stole the crown
   E. our favorite decorations

11) The soldier's _____ *thwarted* his troop's surprise attack on its enemy.
   A. sharp commands
   B. perfect camouflage
   C. magnificent strategizing
   D. quiet footsteps
   E. accidental noise

12) The police officer used _____ to *subdue* Jaclyn at the scene of the crime.
   A. a cup of coffee
   B. interrogation
   C. a taser
   D. sympathy
   E. video evidence

13) The university's *graduated* set of rules _____.
   A. summarized each policy to alleviate stress on new members
   B. specified expulsion for more serious violations
   C. caused the association to begin to use ancient law
   D. seemed too long to discuss within a span of two hours
   E. never seemed to have changed throughout the years

14) When George _____, he could hardly believe the *squalor* he observed.
   A. traveled to poor areas of Asia
   B. left the confines of the airport
   C. spoke to the United Nations
   D. told a story about space travel
   E. argued about political issues

Lesson 15 continued:

15) With a look of *resignation*, Denise _____.
   A. increased her speed to pass her opponent
   B. watched the previews before the movie
   C. opened her umbrella and ran to her car
   D. jumped for joy over her birthday present
   E. waited for the judges to rate her chili

16) After a summer of travel and relaxation, Tiana *deplored* _____.
   A. the idea of going back to school
   B. to have just as much fun in autumn
   C. her extra two weeks' vacation
   D. her parents, whom she hadn't seen
   E. a book about her adventures

17) The buying of Alaska from Russia was called "Seward's *Folly*" because _____.
   A. it was a brilliant plan
   B. Alaska is freezing cold
   C. Seward worked at it for years
   D. people felt it was a foolish purchase
   E. Alaska is close to Russia

Lesson 15 continued:

Writing Practice

The underlined portion of each sentence possibly contains a flaw related to the construction of the sentence. Select the answer that best corrects the flaw. Select NO CHANGE if the underlined portion is correct.

1) Brynn assured me that she would take good care of my pet cats and would be able to water my houseplants, <u>feed my fish, turn lights on and off, and call me</u> if any problems arose.
   A. NO CHANGE
   B. feed my fish, would turn lights on and off, and would call me
   C. feed my fish, as well as turning lights on and off, and would call me
   D. feed my fish, turned lights on and off, and would call me

2) Tanya had driven recklessly that morning, rushing to work, ignoring three red lights, <u>and</u> two stop signs.
   A. NO CHANGE
   B. and even
   C. and overlooking
   D. and overlooked

3) "Mr. Kingsfield needs to be better organized; he never arrives on time, always mixes up his notes, <u>and his students' names</u>," complained Monica.
   A. NO CHANGE
   B. and our names get forgotten
   C. also, his students' names
   D. and often forgets his students' names

4) The goals of the meeting are to evaluate sales for the year, <u>delegating</u> tasks for the new project, and discuss budget limitations.
   A. NO CHANGE
   B. delegate
   C. delegation of
   D. we will delegate

5) I hope that Marco recovers from his knee injury <u>quick</u>, smoothly, and painlessly; we really need him back on the soccer team.
   A. NO CHANGE
   B. to be quick
   C. with quickness
   D. quickly

Lesson 15 continued:

6) "You should come to the music festival; you can listen to cool music, eat from food trucks, and <u>souvenirs can be purchased</u>," persuaded Mika.
   A. NO CHANGE
   B. purchasing souvenirs
   C. purchase souvenirs
   D. souvenirs are available

7) Even in the summertime, <u>families still come</u> and enjoy their time at this Californian vacation spot.
   A. NO CHANGE
   B. families still come to
   C. families are still coming
   D. the influx of families comes

8) While reading and <u>she edited</u> her best student's research paper, Ms. Tayck noticed very few errors.
   A. NO CHANGE
   B. editing
   C. edited
   D. to edit

9) "Please don't forget to clean your room, vacuum the den, and <u>to take out the trash</u> before our guests arrive," reminded Mom.
   A. NO CHANGE
   B. the trash should be taken out
   C. take out the trash
   D. taking out the trash

10) The student body nominated Luis for president of student government because of his intelligence, his sense of humor, and <u>he was kind to others</u>.
    A. NO CHANGE
    B. treating others kindly
    C. his kindness to others
    D. others were treated kindly by him

11) <u>Speedily</u> and gracefully, Monica reached the end of the pool lane, winning the swim meet for her team.
    A. NO CHANGE
    B. Speeding
    C. With great speed
    D. Speedy

Lesson 15 continued:

Vocabulary: Choosing the Right Use

The following sentences contain vocabulary words used in the reading passages. Identify the sentence or sentences that use the italicized vocabulary word properly. We have changed the form of some vocabulary words to provide new contexts; for example, some adjectives and verbs have been used as nouns.

1) A. *Thwarted* by the baker's design for her wedding cake, the bride-to-be demanded a new one.
    B. Beckett's plans to sneak out were *thwarted* when he realized his father had installed motion detector lights around the house.
    C. Students were *thwarted* with the grades they received that their teacher blamed on poor study habits and lack of ambition.
    D. The villain cursed the meddling kids and their dog when they *thwarted* his evil plans.

2) A. After years of working with lumber, the carpenter's hands were calloused and *coarse*.
    B. Alec forgot to shave this morning, and his daughter complained that his face was too *coarse* when he kissed her good-bye.
    C. The praise the tennis team received from their coach when they won the championship match was short, happy, and *coarse*.
    D. Most of the reviews for the new television series were positive, with the exception of a few *coarse* critics.

3) A. The longer Francis waited to trade in his car, the more the value of it *depreciated*.
    B. Delilah *depreciated* Ivan's efforts to make up after he embarrassed her in front of the class.
    C. The jeweler said the ring Seth had inherited from his great aunt had *depreciated* significantly because the stone was cracked.
    D. Unfortunately for the firefighter, the kitten *depreciated* his attempt to get it down from the tree.

4) A. Gavin and his brothers volunteer at the college every other weekend to help tutor the *insolvent* students.
    B. No one was surprised when the company declared it was *insolvent* after it gave huge bonuses to its top employees.
    C. After political leaders unwisely spent the nation's budget, the country became *insolvent*.
    D. When the storm finally passed, many families were left *insolvent* and had to live in a shelter for weeks afterwards.

5) A. When the chimpanzee escaped its enclosure, zookeepers had to come up with a plan to *subdue* it.
    B. In order to *subdue* his mother after he admitted he had been suspended, Nick brought her flowers and offered to clean the pool for a week.
    C. The doctor tried to *subdue* the wound by applying pressure to the gash on the patient's knee before stitching it up.
    D. Madison hoped her hasty paint job would *subdue* the mark she had accidentally made when taking down the shelves in her dorm room.

Lesson 15 continued:

6) A. As *penance* for sneaking out the night before, Tyler was grounded: no videogames or hanging out with friends.
   B. Because Natalia felt terrible for failing her science test, she refused her allowance for a month as *penance*.
   C. The king's proclamation said, "Those who obey the newly enacted laws will receive a *penance* for their actions."
   D. For failing to defend his client, the lawyer continued to find ways to clear his client's name as *penance*.

7) A. Unless she pays a fee, Stacy's *retainer* with her landlord keeps her from being able to move somewhere else until the end of the year.
   B. According to the *retainer* Bret signed with the contractor, he has to pay the workers only once the renovation is completed, not for every hour that is spent on the project.
   C. The defendant's lawyer, having won the *retainer*, did not last long once she received the bill.
   D. Perfume and makeup companies keep actresses and musicians as *retainers* to promote some products.

8) A. Lucy continued to play softball *posthumous* of her elbow surgery.
   B. Since the novel was published *posthumously*, all of the royalties will go to the author's favorite charity.
   C. Barbara accepted the *posthumous* award on her grandfather's behalf and encouraged the audience to continue what he had begun.
   D. Whatever *posthumous* material came from the quarry was unnecessary, as enough metal had already been dug up.

9) A. My aunt would love a greenhouse so she could *cultivate* her favorite seasonal flowers year-round.
   B. Nadia had *cultivated* Latin and, consequently, understood it better when she attended college.
   C. Sometimes when his roommate is away, Isaac will steal from his roommate's *cultivated* stash of candy bars.
   D. Some new mothers insist on listening to classical music because they believe it will *cultivate* a love of learning in their children.

10) A. Lisa sighed in *resignation* as she handed the TV remote to her brother at her mother's request.
    B. When they came into the office on Monday, many workers were surprised to see the *resignation* stating that there would be an employee evaluation later in the day.
    C. Bonnie posted a *resignation* on her desk stating she would be away on vacation for the next week.
    D. The Daily Star opened its editorial by saying, "With great *resignation*, Senator Howard announced that he would not support the bill."

11) A. Greg *deplored* his mother's decision to sell his car, even though it was not ecofriendly or always reliable.
    B. Mordecai receives low grades in his English class even though he *deplores* reading and would rather solve equations.
    C. In the middle of the race, Tiffany *deplored* her decision to wear new shoes that she had not had time to break in.
    D. Until Ruby tried her grandmother's recipe, she *deplored* coleslaw.

Lesson 15 continued:

12) A. After running the marathon, Tristen wanted to wash off the *squalor* of the number that had been inked on his shoulder.
   B. Potential buyers noticed the stains on the carpet and the smell of mold and determined that the previous owner had lived in *squalor*.
   C. Owen spent the day taking the *squalor* off the back of the new refrigerator.
   D. With his styled hair and expensive suit, none of Anthony's associates would guess that he had come from a life of *squalor* and poverty.

13) A. Knowing his computer was *folly*, Gabriel traded it in for a sleeker and lighter laptop with the latest programs.
   B. Peter's *folly* got him into serious trouble when he tried to surf big waves after only a few lessons.
   C. The store clerk moved all of the *folly* merchandise to the clearance section.
   D. Even though Miguel had spent months writing the play, it was *folly* to think it would be ready for a performance without a month's rehearsal.

14) A. The fundraiser's *coffers* were steadily filled by the people who came out to the bake sale.
   B. Lucas suggested that the *coffers* be used to buy school supplies for children from disadvantaged homes.
   C. The flyer read that all donated hats, coats, and *coffers* would go the local women's shelter.
   D. Isabella is the treasurer for the club and keeps the *coffers* locked in the filing cabinet.

15) A. When Timothy fell into the well, he called up in *desperation* and hoped someone would help get him out.
   B. At the news of the approaching tornado, the cattle rancher acted out of *desperation* and ran to herd his livestock into the safety of the barn.
   C. In *desperation* and not really knowing what to do, Blake suggested using a tourniquet over the snakebite.
   D. In order to increase his friend's *desperation*, Victor suggested they go home for a while.

16) A. As construction of the skyscraper moved ahead, the *graduated* building became progressively wider.
   B. The flight arriving in Hawaii *graduated* toward its destination twenty minutes ahead of schedule.
   C. Erin poured the water into the *graduated* measuring cup until she had exactly 6 ounces.
   D. Harley's tower of cards *graduated* when her mom opened a window and a breeze blew inside.

17) A. Ron knew that he was not *privy* to his sister's inner thoughts, but that did not stop him from trying to read her diary.
   B. Alana made sure that no one was *privy* to the fact that she had a new boyfriend, especially since they had been "just friends" for years, and it would be embarrassing.
   C. The room did not have a *privy*, as it was missing a door, and three of the walls had massive windows.
   D. Tracy waited until she was in *privy* before opening the note her friend had slipped her during class.

Lesson 15 continued:

18) A. In her will, Jackson's grandmother *bequeathed* half of her estate to him.
    B. The king *bequeathed* the sword that was prophesized to be able to slay the dragon to his best knight.
    C. Unable to lift the fallen tree on his own, Adam called his niece over and they *bequeathed* the weight together.
    D. Over dinner, Aria *bequeathed* the events of her day to her family.

19) A. Citizens hope that the people within the *monarchy* will be able to reach an agreement on the issue of healthcare before the year is over.
    B. The country's *monarchy* is beloved by many people, but it is the prime minister who approves the laws.
    C. Those who become part of the *monarchy* are expected to uphold certain traditions that have been in place since the birth of the country.
    D. Leaving their regal robes behind, members of the *monarchy* set out in the attire of the working class in order to blend in and tour the city.

Lesson 15 continued:

Synonyms and Antonyms

Match the word with its *antonym*.

1) cultivate
2) extol
3) coarse
4) desperation
5) deplore
6) squalor
7) thwart
8) folly

A. refined
B. wealth
C. hopefulness
D. wisdom
E. kill
F. criticize
G. approve
H. assist

Match the word with its *synonym*.

9) penance
10) subdue
11) depreciate
12) insolvent
13) graduated
14) gratuitous
15) salutary
16) confer
17) resignation
18) encumbrance
19) privy

I. healthful
J. bankrupt
K. devalue
L. graded
M. secret
N. atonement
O. hopelessness
P. conquer
Q. award
R. complimentary
S. hindrance

END
of
LESSON 15

Lesson 16

Writing and Language Test

A set of questions accompanies each passage. The questions will ask you to make editorial decisions that improve or correct language, grammar, and construction errors in the paragraphs, including any accompanying graphics. Read the passage and then choose the best answer to each of the questions. In some instances, no change will be necessary.

Questions 1–11 are based on the following passage.

— 1 —

It is possible that { **1** } **<u>literally</u>** all science fiction is not wrong in its **prognostication** of future fashion; someday, the ultimate daily wear for men and women might, in fact, be featureless spandex unitards. Before you shake off the chill that just went down your spine, consider how popular sports activewear has become during the last decade or so. It's one of the leading trends, and { **2** } <u>it's</u> popularity increases every year. Once available only in specialty sports stores such as { **3** } <u>Nike and Lululemon,</u> activewear can now be found in any big box store or mall **clothier**, including Forever 21, Old Navy, and Walmart. Because they go where the money goes, and the global sports apparel market is expected to top $178 billion before the end of the { **4** } <u>decade. The retailers</u> will, without doubt, be increasing their stockpiles of the so-called "athleisure" products as they **relegate** their old-fashioned cotton T-shirts to the clearance aisles.

1
A) NO CHANGE
B) exceptionally
C) virtually
D) actually

2
A) NO CHANGE
B) it is
C) its'
D) its

3
A) NO CHANGE
B) Nike, and Lululemon
C) Nike, Lululemon, and
D) Nike and, Lululemon,

4
Choose the best revision to connect the sentences at the underlined portion.
A) decade, the retailers
B) decade; the retailers
C) decade the retailers
D) decade: The retailers

Lesson 16 continued:

— 2 —

Four major trends contributed to the sudden boom in athletic clothing sales. { 5 } <u>More breathable and sweat-wicking textiles than ever have been improved upon by advancements in technology.</u> The new fashion component of activewear—often **exemplified** by legions of weekenders modeling simple logos against **minimalist**, solid backgrounds of synthetic fibers—has contributed to the wildly successful brand focus of sportswear companies. Finally, among the reasons people are buying more activewear { 6 } <u>are, oddly enough,</u> the fact that Americans are exercising more. Gyms have **augmented** their programs with more and more specialty exercise classes; yoga classes alone, for example, are up in attendance from 15 million in 2008 to 20 million in 2012. Gyms around the country have incorporated additional boutique fitness classes such as SoulCycle, CrossFit, Pilates, and dance-inspired programs, creating several options to appeal to everyone's personal favorite form of exercise.

— 3 —

With everyone exercising perpetually, it's a terrible time to be someone who doesn't exercise, or at least { 7 } <u>looking like someone</u> who doesn't exercise. Luckily, activewear solves that problem, too. Increasingly, people are combining traditional workout gear with daywear fashions, a style that connotes an active life, whether the wearer plans to go for a jog after work or grow roots on a sofa for the rest of the night, eating cheese puffs and playing video games. On the street, however, the wearers look like they might lead healthy lifestyles; after all, why else would they spend { 8 } <u>$60 dollars</u> on a sweat-wicking T-shirt? Activewear, just like steel-studded leather motorcycle jackets or hemp-woven Baja hoodies, are very much a type of lifestyle fashion.

5

Choose the best revision to replace the underlined sentence.

A) Athletic fabrics have been improved by advancements made in textiles, which has made them more breathable and sweat-wicking than ever before.

B) Textiles are better than they have been in the past, due to advancements because of technology.

C) Advancements in textiles have improved athletic fabrics, rendering them more breathable and sweat-wicking than ever.

D) More sweat-wicking and breathable textiles, improvements on the old ones, have been made possible by technology.

6

A) NO CHANGE
B) is, oddly enough,
C) are, oddly, enough
D) is oddly, enough

7

A) NO CHANGE
B) to look like people
C) looking like a person
D) look like someone

8

A) NO CHANGE
B) $sixty dollars
C) $60
D) Sixty Dollars

Lesson 16 continued:

— 4 —

Because lifestyle clothing is so definitive of personality and values, and tends to sell itself as such, everyone is trying to get a share of the market. Gap Inc., the parent company of Gap, Banana Republic, and Old Navy, recently turned around **waning** sales with a foray into activewear through its Athleta brand. Athleta's success has prompted Gap to expand the brand into youth clothing and begin selling activewear in its other stores. { **9** }

— 5 —

[1] No doubt annoyed by the obtrusion of discount athleisure wear, some fashion executives remark that those looking for high-performance workout gear should continue shopping at specialty sports stores instead of traditional { **10** } <u>retailers, they cite</u> the differences in quality and engineering between high-end athletic clothes and what is typically found in discount retail chains. [2] The materials of high-end clothes are designed to exceed the most basic requirements of exercise clothing. [3] Some fabrics are designed to **inhibit** bacterial growth. [4] Others keep water out but allow perspiration to escape. [5] Some fabrics are plain, while others are stylish. [6] Marathoners, yoga masters, and Olympic cross-trainers might not be fooled by the cheaper activewear, but others might be willing to overlook some sub-**par** materials that should last long enough to be seen walking the dog or standing in line for ice cream. { **11** }

9

The author would like to insert the following sentence at this point in the passage:

> Typical activewear is made of polyester, spandex, or nylon, but higher-end clothing often contains silver, bamboo, or wool.

Should the writer make the addition here?
A) No, because the paragraph is about the psychology of clothing choices and sales strategy.
B) Yes, because it is an appropriate transition between paragraphs 4 and 5.
C) No, because the content of the sentence is better suited to paragraph 3.
D) Yes, because the paragraph should contain more details related to the psychology of clothing choice.

10

Select the revision that best corrects the two sentences at the underlined portion.
A) retailers: They cite
B) retailers. They cite
C) retailers and they cite
D) retailers; however, they cite

11

If the writer wanted to delete an unnecessary sentence from paragraph 5, which sentence would be the best candidate?
A) sentence [1]
B) sentence [2]
C) sentence [3]
D) sentence [5]

Lesson 16 continued:

Vocabulary: Context Answers

The following sentences contain vocabulary words used in the reading passage. Choose the answer that best completes the sentence. There may be more than one technically correct answer, but one will better exemplify the italicized vocabulary word than the others will.

1) The three friends decided to patronize a nearby location of a *clothier* to buy _____.
   A. new cell phones cases
   B. closet organizers
   C. summer dresses
   D. sports equipment
   E. concert tickets

2) A tennis player who performed below *par* would _____ fans.
   A. likely excite his
   B. probably disappoint
   C. be playing close to
   D. hardly surprise the
   E. definitely confuse

3) *Waning* support of the arts in education resulted in _____.
   A. the introduction of new painting classes
   B. a push for improved teaching methods
   C. a decrease in music programs
   D. an increase in the number of courses
   E. increased funding for music class

4) Though Henrietta said she had had a "cool" night out, Betsy's had been *literally* cool, as she had _____.
   A. wandered around a new city
   B. stood outside in the brisk cold
   C. gotten help from a stranger
   D. seen a popular band perform
   E. controlled her temper all night

5) According to Ms. DiAnton's research, _____ *inhibits* a normal sleep schedule.
   A. turning in at 10:00 pm nightly
   B. drinking too much coffee
   C. nine hours of sleep per night
   D. feeling refreshed in the morning
   E. taking naps once in a while

6) _____ *exemplified* Sanjay's tendency to forget important events.
   A. Arriving at his sister's graduation
   B. Buying a new calendar to use as a reminder
   C. Reminding others not to miss Layla's recital
   D. Being an incredibly busy individual
   E. Not showing up at the wedding

Lesson 16 continued:

7) Typically, _____ *connotes* feelings of joy and approval.
   A. sadness
   B. an insult
   C. applause
   D. music
   E. motivation

8) Alyssa wanted to pay off all her bills quickly, so she *augmented* her income by _____.
   A. telling no one about her increase in salary
   B. giving more money to charity
   C. borrowing money from the bank
   D. telling her boss that she is quitting
   E. taking a second job delivering pizzas

9) Emily's *prognostication* that our flight was cancelled _____.
   A. ruined our carefully planned family vacation
   B. was due to her extreme fear of flying over water
   C. prompted the airline staff to ask her to calm down
   D. was based on one weather report and a few snowflakes
   E. turned out to be a lie she told as a practical joke

10) Because Laura didn't show up to the prom committee meeting, Trevor *relegated* _____.
   A. her to the cleanup crew as punishment
   B. someone else to be co-chairman of the event
   C. her on the importance of responsibility
   D. loudly to everyone about her thoughtlessness
   E. the meeting and rescheduled it for another day

11) Because of her *minimalist* taste, Beatrice chose the _____ curtains to hang in her living room.
   A. iridescent
   B. striped
   C. beige
   D. old-fashioned
   E. satin

Lesson 16 continued:

Writing Practice

Each of the following sentences contains a modifying phrase that may or may not be clear or correct. Choose the answer that best corrects the sentence while retaining the intended meaning of the original sentence. Select NO CHANGE if the provided sentence is correct.

1) The scientists who live and work in Antarctica endure wind chills of frequently greater than 150 degrees below zero.
   A. NO CHANGE
   B. The scientists who live and frequently work in Antarctica endure wind chills of greater than 150 degrees below zero.
   C. The frequent scientists who live and work in Antarctica endure wind chills of greater than 150 degrees below zero.
   D. The scientists who live and work in Antarctica frequently endure wind chills of greater than 150 degrees below zero.

2) The bread my dad baked expertly went missing from the windowsill.
   A. NO CHANGE
   B. From the windowsill, the bread my dad baked expertly went missing.
   C. The bread my dad expertly baked from the windowsill went missing.
   D. The bread my dad expertly baked went missing from the windowsill.

3) The star high school athlete being recruited eagerly felt he had his choice of colleges.
   A. NO CHANGE
   B. The star high school athlete, who was being recruited eagerly, felt he had his choice of colleges.
   C. Being recruited, the eager star high school athlete felt he had his choice of colleges.
   D. The star high school athlete felt he had his choice of colleges, being recruited eagerly.

4) Though she wanted to be more involved in the performance, just Audrey was picked to play a minor part.
   A. NO CHANGE
   B. Though she wanted to be more involved in the performance, Audrey was just picked to play a minor part.
   C. Though she wanted to be more involved in the performance, Audrey was picked to play just a minor part.
   D. Though she just wanted to be more involved in the performance, Audrey was picked to play a minor part.

5) The painter almost sold all her portraits at the art show.
   A. NO CHANGE
   B. The painter sold all her portraits, almost, at the art show.
   C. Almost, the painter sold all her portraits at the art show.
   D. The painter sold almost all her portraits at the art show.

6) My grandmother told me, whispering quietly, bothers some people.
   A. NO CHANGE
   B. My grandmother told me that whispering quietly bothers some people.
   C. Some people are quietly bothered by whispering, my grandmother told me.
   D. My grandmother told me whispering bothers some people quietly.

Lesson 16 continued:

7) Fans of the old band waited in line for two hours to buy tickets to the reunion concert.
   A. NO CHANGE
   B. Fans of the old band waited in line to buy tickets, to the reunion concert, for two hours.
   C. The old band's fans waited in line for two hours to the reunion concert to buy tickets.
   D. Fans of the old band waited in line to buy tickets for two hours to the reunion concert.

8) Frank, the owner of the restaurant down the street, asks tourists to sign up for a drawing for a free dinner every time they eat there.
   A. NO CHANGE
   B. For a free dinner, Frank, the owner of the restaurant down the street, asks tourists to sign up for a drawing every time they eat there.
   C. The owner of the restaurant down the street, Frank, asks tourists to, every time they eat there, sign up for a drawing for a free dinner.
   D. Every time tourists eat there, Frank, the owner of the restaurant down the street, asks them to sign up for a drawing for a free dinner.

9) Hurrying to the movie theater after I worked late, my boss called my phone to tell me to return to the office.
   A. NO CHANGE
   B. Having worked late, my boss called my phone to tell me to return to the office, hurrying to the movie theater.
   C. My boss called my phone to tell me to return to the office, hurrying to the movie theater after I worked late.
   D. While I was hurrying to the movie theater after I had worked late, my boss called my phone to tell me to return to the office.

10) Vincent looked at the dark gray cloud with a scowl when it started to rain.
   A. NO CHANGE
   B. Vincent scowled at the dark gray cloud when it started to rain.
   C. When it started to rain, Vincent looked at the dark gray cloud with a scowl.
   D. Vincent looked, with a scowl, at the dark gray cloud, when it started to rain.

Lesson 16 continued:

Vocabulary: Choosing the Right Use

The following sentences contain vocabulary words used in the reading passage. Identify the sentence or sentences that use the italicized vocabulary word properly. We have changed the form of some vocabulary words to provide new contexts; for example, some adjectives and verbs have been used as nouns.

1) A. Scott's dedication to the campaign was *exemplified* when he stayed up all night designing potential logos.
   B. Gwen *exemplified* her collection of salt and pepper shakers to Ned.
   C. A lightning bolt split a tree in two in an instant, *exemplifying* the power of nature.
   D. Hoping to impress his girlfriend, Les *exemplified* his latest trick on the surfboard.

2) A. The stylist was almost sold on the dress, but was still unsure about the pattern of the *clothier*.
   B. Thinking it would be the perfect *clothier* for her kids' Halloween costumes, Sharon ordered fifteen yards of the material.
   C. Megan does not understand why parents of small children would buy them outfits from a designer *clothier* when they will outgrow them in a few months.
   D. The sales clerk at Randy's favorite *clothier* suggested that he pair a navy blazer with gray pants.

3) A. After there was an increase in wads of gum found under the desks, the principal put an *inhibition* on bubblegum.
   B. The fence *inhibits* trespassing, but does not completely prevent it.
   C. The scientists *inhibited* mold growth on their samples by spraying them with a chemical preservative.
   D. Pool rules *inhibit* on glass bottles in order to prevent cuts and other injuries.

4) A. In the long run, whether Carla chooses to take night classes or buy a new car, her debts will be on *par* with each other, but a car will provide more fun.
   B. Eliza's grades were above *par* this semester since she stopped playing videogames when she got home and focused on her homework first.
   C. The realtor made sure the framed pictures were *par* with each other and the magazines were fanned neatly on the coffee table before opening the house to the first potential buyer.
   D. Lucas kept his headphones on for the entirety of the flight because he was sitting *par* to a screaming child.

5) A. The pilot-in-training was named a hero after having landed the plane with *minimalist* knowledge of flying.
   B. Brad's parents were not impressed by their son's *minimalist* effort in school when they saw his report card.
   C. Environmental activists were surprised when Chase's *minimalist* approach to conserving water was so effective.
   D. Jerry kept his apartment primarily *minimalist* by owning only the bare essentials and not having anything on the simple white walls.

Lesson 16 continued:

6) A. The so-called psychic's inability to *prognosticate* even the simplest things correctly, such as the winner of the election, caused her followers to doubt her claims.
    B. One recent *prognostication* cost Mr. Kendall over a thousand dollars because the seller valued it that highly.
    C. "*Prognosticate* all you want, Jimmy; you're still not going to be allowed to stay up until midnight," said the babysitter.
    D. We called my grandfather "The Great *Prognosticator*" because, in 1928, he claimed that the stock market would crash the next year.

7) A. The Millers' basement was *literally* flooded when a pipe burst in their kitchen upstairs.
    B. Colette *literally* died when she saw how many "likes" her photo received.
    C. When Ethan came home, he complained he was *literally* buried in homework and that it would take forever to finish.
    D. The announcer *literally* could not be heard over the crowd's screaming after the team scored the winning touchdown.

8) A. The fact that Kelsey began sneezing once my pet kitten entered the room *connotes* that she is allergic to cats.
    B. While Richard appears willing to manage the entire project, his suggestion that his group members take on the majority of the work *connotes* the opposite.
    C. The quick response to the alarm *connotes* that the firefighters are in a hurry to put out a blaze.
    D. The "No Trespassing" sign on Mr. Wright's lawn *connotes* either that he is not friendly or that he has had problems with people in the past.

9) A. No matter what skills the ten-year-olds had, nobody was *relegated* to sitting on the bench in Little League games; everybody played the field and had chances to bat.
    B. Since I already had an A average in geometry, I *relegated* studying for the math final to the back of my mind, after English and American History.
    C. If you *relegate* me to playing the old man again simply because my hair is gray, I'm going to quit the theater group. I want some different roles.
    D. The king's ministers realized the monarch had gone mad and wondered how it would be possible to *relegate* his enormous power before he did something destructive.

10) A. The debate over T-shirt designs for the theater club was *augmented* as soon as the president made the decision to use a rose.
    B. Greek myth states that if a head of the Hydra is cut off, more will be *augmented* from the wound.
    C. Randall, stranded on the island, *augmented* his stash of food with whatever edible nuts or roots he found.
    D. Snowplows could not keep up with the flakes that came down heavily and *augmented* a foot every hour.

Lesson 16 continued:

11) A. Although initially confident, Sally's *waning* self-assurance was brought on by the increasing difficulty of the test questions.

B. With the *waning* of August, Paige went to the store to buy new school supplies and dug out her uniform from the back of her closet.

C. The night had been peaceful until Oliver began *waning*, and the babysitter had to pause her movie until he was asleep again.

D. Parents often tell *waning* children that they will not get dessert if they continue their behavior.

Lesson 16 continued:

Synonyms and Antonyms

Match the word with its _antonym_.

1) literally   **A.** fact

2) augment   **B.** increase

3) prognostication   **C.** figuratively

4) wane   **D.** aid

5) inhibit   **E.** reduce

Match the word with its _synonym_.

6) exemplify   **F.** basic

7) connote   **G.** suggest

8) relegate   **H.** demonstrate

9) minimal   **I.** demote

10) par   **J.** standard

END
of
LESSON 16

Lesson 17

Questions 12–22 are based on the following passage.

— 1 —

Fantasy and science fiction { 12 } <u>is an example of genre that allows</u> readers to escape reality. Readers can forget about { 13 } <u>there own</u> real problems temporarily, while they journey with Frodo to destroy the ring in Mount Doom or watch Katniss battle the **repressive** Capitol. The typical elements of these two genres, such as dragons, magic, and faster-than-light travel, are so far removed from reality that a reader must **disengage** from his or her own in order to enjoy { 14 } <u>them, there</u> are, of course, other fiction genres, but most of the others portray **realism** or the details of the real world.

— 2 —

[1] Fantasy and science fiction writers and readers sometimes take offense at the idea that the works they create and { 15 } <u>are enjoyed by them</u> are simply **escapist** fiction that has no greater purpose than to provide an escape from reality; escapism, however, should not have the negative connotation that literary critics and other adults assign to it. [2] In his essay "On Fairy Stories," J. R. R. Tolkien argues, "Why should a man be scorned if, finding himself in prison, he tries to get out and go home?" [3] Escapist fiction removes readers from their weariness-induced prisons. [4] Tolkien equates the weariness of real life to living in prison. { 16 }

12

A) NO CHANGE
B) are examples of genres that allow
C) is an example of a genre which allows
D) are an example of genre that allows

13

A) NO CHANGE
B) they're own
C) their own
D) one's own

14

A) NO CHANGE
B) them: there
C) them there
D) them; there

15

A) NO CHANGE
B) enjoy
C) are enjoyed
D) to enjoy

16

Choose the sentence that should be deleted from paragraph 2 because it does not contribute to the topic.
A) sentence [1]
B) sentence [2]
C) sentence [3]
D) sentence [4]

Lesson 17 continued:

— 3 —

Fantasy is less an escape from reality than it is a tool for understanding it. In its portrayal of unfamiliar worlds, fantasy makes the real world more understandable; the alternate realities of fiction { **17** } <u>forces consideration</u> of the good and bad qualities of reality. Escapism allows people to test their values and assess the direction society is, or might be, headed. This important aspect of escapism is especially true in science fiction, which often attempts to **extrapolate** a future based on the present state of civilization. *The Lord of the Rings* emphasizes the importance of bravery and friendship while **decrying** warfare and the destruction of the earth; *The Hunger Games* trilogy shows how oppressed people can rise up against a { **18** } <u>**totalitarian regime**</u>, but cautions how violent rebellion is not a solution without its own new problems. These themes in fantasy novels clearly offer commentaries on real world values and issues. The metaphorical or **allegorical** nature of fantasy also allows authors to address social and ethical issues without singling out the real people who inspired the commentary. { **19** }

17

A) NO CHANGE
B) forces the consideration
C) force consideration
D) forces considerations

18

A) NO CHANGE
B) Totalitarian regime
C) Totalitarian Regime
D) totalitarian Regime

19

The author would like to insert the following sentence at this point in the passage:

> Perhaps fantasy is not so much an escape from reality as it is a means to understand it.

Should the writer make the addition here?
A) Yes, because it effectively emphasizes the argument of the paragraph.
B) No, because the sentence is too obviously redundant; it simply restates the first sentence.
C) Yes, because the paragraph needs a conclusion that revisits the example titles included in the paragraph.
D) No, because the sentence is in no way related to the subtopic of the paragraph.

Lesson 17 continued:

— 4 —

[1] In addition, fantasy and science { **20** } <u>fiction also serve</u> other important functions in society. [2] They teach readers, especially young ones, how to find meaning by making connections between seemingly unrelated things or concepts. [3] This **cognitive** ability is crucial in understanding the complexity of the world. [4] Fantasy and science fiction also **foster** imagination, which should not be disregarded as **trite** daydreaming. [5] In 2007, having realized that imagination is critical for innovation and technology, even the Chinese Communist Party reversed its negative stance toward science fiction and approved a fantasy and science fiction { **21** } <u>convention, that was meant to</u> encourage citizens to innovate and invent. [6] Escapist fiction opens the possibilities of new inventions, advancements, and ways of life. [7] As literature, it also allows us to explore our identities as individuals and as a culture. [8] It is no wonder that ancient myths, such as *The Odyssey*, *Beowulf*, and even some of Shakespeare's plays, contain elements of escapist fiction; it has been a necessity from the beginning. { **22** }

20

A) NO CHANGE
B) fiction additionally serve
C) fiction, also serve
D) fiction serve

21

A) NO CHANGE
B) convention meant to
C) convention, which means to
D) convention; that was meant to

22

The writer is considering dividing paragraph 4 into two paragraphs. Choose the sentence that should begin the new paragraph.
A) sentence [3]
B) sentence [5]
C) sentence [6]
D) sentence [7]

Lesson 17 continued:

Vocabulary: Context Answers

The following sentences contain vocabulary words used in the reading passage. Choose the answer that best completes the sentence. There may be more than one technically correct answer, but one will better exemplify the italicized vocabulary word than the others will.

1) The virtual reality video game *disengaged* _____ actual life.
   A. special effects to mimic
   B. users to stop playing and to live
   C. children from the joys of
   D. in technology to improve on
   E. visuals to appear different from

2) Art displayed at the annual gallery reflected *realism*: The artists _____.
   A. used lines, shapes, and strange colors
   B. depicted daily life and average people
   C. painted from a child's perspective
   D. created work using only charcoal
   E. cleverly distorted the human figure

3) Most people would consider the poem *trite*, but Mack _____.
   A. dislikes the way it doesn't rhyme
   B. read it last year in English class
   C. thinks it is easier than they do
   D. considers it charming and refreshing
   E. is worried that he'll never understand it

4) Alex Travis, known for _____, fits squarely into the category of "*escapist* author."
   A. basing most of her work on the material of others
   B. her ability to report on current events in an unbiased way
   C. refusing to meet with the press or her fans
   D. her tendency to state her opinion on divisive issues
   E. writing novels about captivating, imaginary lands

5) The ruler of Wayward Island insisted upon _____ and engaging in other types of *repressive* actions.
   A. maintaining freedom of speech
   B. letting the poor live in his castle
   C. having a national anthem
   D. using corporal punishment
   E. being waited on by his staff

6) Under the *totalitarian* leadership, citizens _____.
   A. often complained to the king
   B. enjoyed total freedom
   C. could be imprisoned for any tiny offense
   D. learned to love their leader, in spite of his ineffective policies and unfair rule
   E. controlled the government

Lesson 17 continued:

7) Professor Tetrault *extrapolated* _____ the experiment by examining the results of previous studies.
   A. interns to learn about
   B. the basic process of
   C. necessary equipment for
   D. public protests about
   E. the likely outcome of

8) The incident in the novel in which the protagonist becomes trapped in a cave is meant to be *allegorical* because it_____.
   A. represents humanity's limited understanding
   B. is a scene from a classic short story
   C. is taken from something written previously
   D. attacks societies that are oppressive
   E. shows how past civilizations lived

9) The advocacy group spent the majority of the human rights conference *decrying* _____.
   A. the liberty to practice religion in America
   B. its message, policies, and long-term goals
   C. attendees about the rising poverty rates
   D. other similar-minded, successful organizations
   E. politicians for reducing funds for education

10) Robert sought to *foster* a sense of teamwork between his coworkers because he knew that _____ would be beneficial in the long run.
    A. disallowing it
    B. pointing it out
    C. hard work
    D. natural development
    E. helping to develop it

11) _____ negatively affected Leon's *cognitive* abilities.
    A. Breaking his leg
    B. Forgetting his hearing aid
    C. Falling on his head
    D. Contracting laryngitis
    E. Losing his glasses

Lesson 17 continued:

Writing Practice

The underlined portion of each sentence possibly contains an error related to the use of restrictive and nonrestrictive clauses. Select the answer that best corrects the flaw. Select NO CHANGE if the underlined portion is correct.

1) Many countries restrict the Internet usage and travel <u>of citizens, who are suspected of participating in anti-government activities.</u>
   A. NO CHANGE
   B. of citizens, which are suspected of participating in anti-government activities.
   C. of citizens who are suspected of participating in anti-government activities.
   D. of citizens, who are suspected of participating in anti-government activities.

2) <u>Some people in my neighborhood don't care that playing their loud music disturbs others.</u>
   A. NO CHANGE
   B. Some people, in my neighborhood, don't care that playing their loud music disturbs others.
   C. Some people, who live in my neighborhood don't care that playing their loud music disturbs others.
   D. Some people in my neighborhood, don't care that playing their loud music disturbs others.

3) Picasso painted for <u>himself, not for people, who thought his style was incomprehensible.</u>
   A. NO CHANGE
   B. himself, not for people, who thought his style, was incomprehensible.
   C. himself, not for people who thought, that his style was incomprehensible.
   D. himself, not for people who thought his style was incomprehensible.

4) <u>A large door often opening into a magnificent library and den was only one of the attractions of the mansions built in previous centuries.</u>
   A. NO CHANGE
   B. A large door, often opening into a magnificent library and den, was only one of the attractions of the mansions built in previous centuries.
   C. A large door often opening into a magnificent library and den was only one of the attractions of the mansions, built in previous centuries.
   D. A large door, often opening into a magnificent library, and den, was only one of the attractions of the mansions built in previous centuries.

Lesson 17 continued:

5) Only linguists who are fluent in both Arabic and Farsi should apply for the translator job which would involve moving to New York City.
   A. NO CHANGE
   B. Only linguists, who are fluent in both Arabic and Farsi, should apply for the translator job, which would involve moving to New York City.
   C. Only linguists who are fluent in both Arabic and Farsi should apply for the translator job, which would involve moving to New York City.
   D. Only linguists who are fluent in both Arabic and Farsi, should apply for the translator job, which would involve moving to New York City.

6) Dr. Simons who lectured at the hall that was named after him repeatedly warned about the dangers of prejudice.
   A. NO CHANGE
   B. Dr. Simons, who lectured at the hall that was named after him, repeatedly
   C. Dr. Simons, who lectured at the hall, that was named after him, repeatedly
   D. Dr. Simons who lectured at the hall, that was named after him, repeatedly

7) *Adventures of Huckleberry Finn* that had been written by Mark Twain was on the summer required reading list.
   A. NO CHANGE
   B. *Adventures of Huckleberry Finn*, that had been written by Mark Twain, was
   C. *Adventures of Huckleberry Finn* which had been written by Mark Twain was
   D. *Adventures of Huckleberry Finn*, which had been written by Mark Twain, was

8) Martin Luther King who won the Nobel Peace Prize in 1964 for his efforts to end racial segregation in the US will always be remembered as a leader of people seeking equality.
   A. NO CHANGE
   B. Martin Luther King, who won the Nobel Peace Prize in 1964, for his efforts to end racial segregation in the US will always be remembered
   C. Martin Luther King who won the Nobel Peace Prize in 1964 for his efforts to end racial segregation in the US will always be remembered,
   D. Martin Luther King, who won the Nobel Peace Prize in 1964 for his efforts to end racial segregation in the US, will always be remembered

9) Adult students who are enrolled in night classes and have young children are encouraged to take advantage of the child-care facility in Room 109A.
   A. NO CHANGE
   B. Adult students who are enrolled in night classes and have young children, are encouraged to take advantage of
   C. Adult students who are enrolled in night classes, and have young children, are encouraged to take advantage of
   D. Adult students, who are enrolled in night classes, and have young children, are encouraged to take advantage of

Lesson 17 continued:

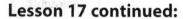

10) Edgar Allan Poe once wrote, "Those who dream by day are cognizant of many things, which escape those, who dream only by night."
   A. NO CHANGE
   B. Those who dream, by day are cognizant of many things which escape those, who dream only by night.
   C. Those who dream by day are cognizant of many things that escape those who dream only by night.
   D. Those, who dream by day, are cognizant of many things, which escape those, who dream only by night.

11) The only suspect, in the police lineup, who has blond hair, and a moustache, matches the witnesses' descriptions perfectly.
   A. NO CHANGE
   B. The only suspect, in the police lineup who has blond hair, and a moustache matches the witnesses' descriptions perfectly.
   C. The only suspect in the police lineup, who has blond hair and a moustache matches the witnesses' descriptions perfectly.
   D. The only suspect in the police lineup who has blond hair and a moustache matches the witnesses' descriptions perfectly.

Lesson 17 continued:

Vocabulary: Choosing the Right Use

The following sentences contain vocabulary words used in the reading passage. Identify the sentence or sentences that use the italicized vocabulary word properly. We have changed the form of some vocabulary words to provide new contexts; for example, some adjectives and verbs have been used as nouns.

1) A. From the test data collected from fossilized plants, scientists were able to *extrapolate* when the first ice age began.
   B. Using the "Jaws of Life," first responders were able to *extrapolate* the accident victim from the wreckage.
   C. The children cheered when their aunt *extrapolated* a stuffed animal from the claw machine on her first try.
   D. Because we've had a quiz every two weeks since the start of the semester, I can *extrapolate* that we'll have another one in two weeks.

2) A. Critics praised the author of the bestseller for having captured readers with the story's *realism* and relatable, original characters.
   B. Guests within the *realism* section of the art museum saw works that depicted life as it was when the artist painted it.
   C. Wilma's mother has often told her that she can daydream after she practices the piano, but until then she must remain in *realism*.
   D. Unaware of the events taking place in *realism*, Carrie was too preoccupied with her thoughts to realize she had a huge fish on the end of her line.

3) A. On his way home from work, Todd's car *disengaged*, and he had to call a tow truck.
   B. Seeing his girlfriend arrive, Steve *disengaged* himself from the conversation with his friends and went to meet her.
   C. At eleven o'clock at night, Jordan decided it was past her bedtime and *disengaged* from the Internet.
   D. The plane's engines *disengaged* for a moment as it was flying over the ocean, but started again much to the relief of the passengers.

4) A. When the principal learned the guest speaker had suddenly cancelled, she and the other administrators scrambled to find someone to *foster*.
   B. Despite their differing opinions about how the budget should be spent, the board members tried not to *foster* any ill feelings toward one another during the meetings.
   C. Even after going through what little remained of their house after the storm, the Grant family still *fostered* hope of rebuilding.
   D. After accidentally breaking her brother's action figure, Caroline found one to *foster* it and hoped he would not notice the difference.

Lesson 17 continued:

5)   A. In the *allegorical* poem, the caged bird is a representation of the wife's entrapment within her loveless marriage.

        B. Francine did not realize the story was *allegorical* and, therefore, had deeper meaning.

        C. To her surprise, Nancy's boyfriend had sent her flowers with the *allegorical* meaning of love.

        D. Penny thought that painting her home a cheerful yellow would be *allegorical* of her happy and welcoming nature.

6)   A. Having successfully robbed the bank, the *escapists* met their driver in the getaway car and outran the authorities.

        B. Jack's mother saw the glazed look in her son's eyes and realized he was lost, as usual, in some sort of *escapist* fantasy world instead of listening to her.

        C. Hoping to end on a good note, the magician attempted an *escapist* trick by submerging himself in a tank of water while bound in handcuffs.

        D. The action film is the perfect movie for *escapists* looking to imagine that they live in a world of superheroes and villains.

7)   A. Usually *trite* and mean, the school bully seemed to have had a change of heart over the summer.

        B. While the novel received excellent reviews, I thought the plot was *trite* and that the characters were uninteresting.

        C. Ruby's aunt did not appreciate her niece's *trite* attitude when she was told she could not have the doll in the shop window.

        D. At the risk of sounding *trite*, Ralph repeated the comment that you "should let sleeping dogs lie."

8)   A. The *totalitarian* government decided to place a dusk-to-dawn curfew on all teenagers.

        B. The club decided it would no longer tolerate Brandon's *totalitarian* ways of running the meetings and elected a new leader who would hear out the opinions of others.

        C. Realizing she could not do it on her own, Marian dropped her *totalitarian* pretense and asked her family to help her set up the tent.

        D. The majority of the *totalitarian* participants agreed that the membership fee should be cut in half and that profits from fundraisers would make up the difference.

9)   A. Studies have shown that a parent who reads to a child at an early age is likely to improve the child's *cognitive* development.

        B. Instead of making decisions solely on what your feelings tell you, it would be best to be *cognitive* as well.

        C. Contractors must be careful around sites that may contain hazardous gases, as inhaling the fumes could have negative effects on *cognitive* functioning.

        D. Penny hoped the long hours of practicing for the play would benefit her ability to be *cognitive*.

Lesson 17 continued:

10) A. Students protested the *repressive* rules put in place by the new officials on the School Board.
    B. The *repressive* waves made it difficult for surfers to stay on their boards, and the lifeguards soon closed the beach.
    C. The Senate's policies were vetoed by the president because she believed they were too *repressive* for small businesses.
    D. *Repressive* winds cut the hot air balloon ride short, and the clients argued with the owner for a refund.

11) A. Members of the historical society *decried* the city's decision to demolish the old theater.
    B. Abigail missed practice because she was *decrying* the loss of her pet gerbil with her siblings.
    C. The scientist *decried* the use of her research to build a new type of weapon.
    D. Even though they could not attend the funeral, the Wilsons still sent flowers and their condolences to the *decrying* family.

Lesson 17 continued:

Synonyms and Antonyms

Match the word with its *antonym*.

1) repressive   **A.** endorse

2) realism   **B.** original

3) decry   **C.** connect

4) disengage   **D.** destroy

5) foster   **E.** unrestrictive

6) trite   **F.** fantasy

Match the word with its *synonym*.

7) cognitive   **G.** tyrannical

8) escapist   **H.** mental

9) extrapolate   **I.** deduce

10) totalitarian   **J.** imaginative

END
of
LESSON 17

Lesson 18

Questions 23–33 are based on the following passage.

Look out, broadcast TV; it seems as though the Internet is taking over. According to recent statistics, the total amount of TV viewed on the { 23 } <u>Internet went up by</u> a whopping 400% between 2013 and 2014. This figure is unrelated to the amount of time a user spends on the Internet in general; in one year, the number of unique viewers of Internet-based television more than doubled, increasing by almost { 24 } <u>150% percent</u>.

The increase is most **conspicuous** in the category of **episodic** television. Generally, people enjoy watching a television series, or even multiple seasons, in quick succession, or through "**binge**-watching," more than they enjoy watching shows the traditional way of waiting for one episode to air in its designated time slot once each week. Internet streaming easily **circumvents** inconveniences that accompany traditional TV viewing, including time overlaps between a person's schedule and a { 25 } <u>TV networks'</u> schedule, interruptions in the form of commercial breaks, and the inability to pause a program. Convenience, it seems, is { 26 } <u>key; therefore,</u> the demand for content does not **deviate**. People seem willing to **appropriate** whichever technology allows them to consume the content conveniently.

In the modern world, in which a "hello" from a friend or directions to a favorite restaurant are but one click away, how exactly does the media industry { 27 } <u>keep up. Bigger</u> screens, of course, and easier access to programming. These **imperatives** are visible in the evolution of smartphones. With each upgrade comes a larger, sleeker screen better suited to watching media content—watching the media content anywhere, that is. Success in media now requires people to be **enamored** by it, but it also must be fast and portable for people who { 28 } <u>wish to consume the media content</u> on the go.

23
A) NO CHANGE
B) Internet increased by
C) Internet amplified by
D) Internet rose up by

24
A) NO CHANGE
B) 150 per cent
C) 150 Percent
D) 150%

25
A) NO CHANGE
B) TV networks
C) TV Network's
D) TV network's

26
A) NO CHANGE
B) key, though
C) key; however,
D) key, subsequently,

27
A) NO CHANGE
B) continue. They make bigger
C) keep up? They make bigger
D) press on; they make bigger

28
A) NO CHANGE
B) wish for the consumption of it
C) wish for consuming the media content
D) wish to consume it

Lesson 18 continued:

[1] There are reasons for the recent shift. [2] First, the number of apps and sites available for watching content has dramatically increased. [3] Viewers do not have to commit to just one avenue, due in part to gaming consoles like the Nintendo Wii, Sony Playstation, and Microsoft Xbox, as well as devices like Apple TV and Chromecast that provide TV and movie content without the need for traditional TV cable. [4] The **sheer** amount of content also contributes to the growth of Internet TV streaming. [5] Approximately 400 scripted television shows aired in 2015, many of them admittedly **abhorrent**. [6] If a person wants to watch two or three shows that air on different channels but at the same time, Internet streaming allows for it, and more and more people continue to take advantage of it. { 29 }

Though it may seem as though the change is a fully positive one for viewers, there are actually some negatives for streaming audiences. With the combination of lightning-speed media consumption and outlets for the instantaneous spread of information, spoilers—critical information about the plot of a series or movie that may ruin the surprise or suspense—are becoming difficult, if not impossible, to avoid. Any person with access to a computer can exclaim into the virtual megaphone that is social media, "Here is my opinion of this crazy thing that just happened on this popular show!" These types of **proclamations** can easily ruin someone's television experience { 30 } if they are faced with the misfortune of having prior **obligations** that day while the show aired the first time.

The risk of spoilers multiplies when companies like Netflix or Amazon release entire seasons of new shows. { 31 } Spraying spoilers all over the Internet almost immediately after bingeing on the latest releases, companies have been forced to try creative solutions to the problem of **overzealous** fans. In 2014, when Netflix released the second season of its original show, *House of Cards*, it simultaneously issued another product called a "Twitter Spoiler Foiler," which allowed *House of Cards* fans to purge their Twitter feeds of any possible spoilers. Netflix even went as far as to try to profit from spoilers by creating a mini-website with the purpose of sharing, celebrating, and discovering TV spoilers. By embracing the trend, Netflix acknowledged that TV consumption is not just as simple as watching a show anymore.

29

The writer wants to combine two sentences in the paragraph. Choose the two that would be logical to combine.
A) sentences [1] and [2]
B) sentences [2] and [3]
C) sentences [4] and [5]
D) sentences [5] and [6]

30

A) NO CHANGE
B) if he or she is
C) if each are
D) if they happen to be

31

Choose the best revision of the underlined sentence.
A) Fans who are overzealous are forced to try creative solutions against bingeing companies' latest releases, spraying spoilers all over the Internet.
B) Companies are forced to try creative solutions to overzealous fans, having binged on the latest releases and sprayed spoilers all over the Internet.
C) Companies, having sprayed spoilers all over the Internet, are forced to try creative solutions against overzealous fans, having binged on the latest releases.
D) Overzealous fans almost immediately spray spoilers all over the Internet, forcing companies to try creative solutions to the problem.

Lesson 18 continued:

The shift from traditional to Internet TV viewing affects industries beyond TV providers and their viewership. Advertising has been doing virtual gymnastics in order to keep up with the changes in media delivery. Thanks to the ability to fast-forward 30-second commercial spots, on which companies spend many millions of dollars, especially for slots amid popular shows or specials, are becoming obsolete, and the companies must find other ways to spread the word about their products. Businesses that once relied on TV spots have now taken to social media, mobile apps, and website banners. Essentially, advertisers have come to understand that an individual is more likely to pay attention to an ad that appears in the palm of his or her hand than to a time-specific commercial in a time-specific televised broadcast. { 32 } { 33 }

32

The writer wants to make the passage more relevant to the chart data. This would best be accomplished by

A) discussing why streaming movies and TV shows increased more than sports did.

B) adding another year of data to the chart.

C) re-titling the chart to say, "Average Number of Programs Watched per Month."

D) including chart data about the amount of money spent on increasing the amount of movie viewers.

33

The central topic of the passage puts traditional TV watching in opposition to Internet streaming. Which data, central to the argument, does the writer fail to provide?

A) changes in Internet/streaming viewership

B) types of devices used by viewers

C) changes in traditional TV viewership

D) the challenges presented to Internet TV viewing

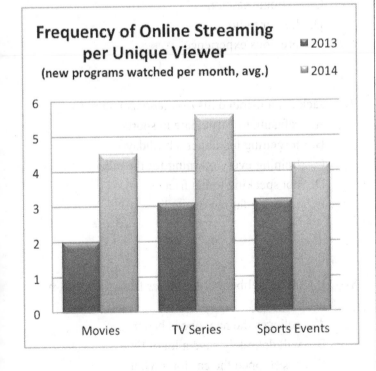

Frequency of Online Streaming per Unique Viewer
(new programs watched per month, avg.)
■ 2013
■ 2014

Lesson 18 continued:

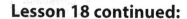

Vocabulary: Context Answers

The following sentences contain vocabulary words used in the reading passage. Choose the answer that best completes the sentence. There may be more than one technically correct answer, but one will better exemplify the italicized vocabulary word than the others will.

1) Mackenzie _____ the prank on Principal Simmons because the door to his room was *conspicuously* left open.
   A. forgot the details of
   B. finally confessed to
   C. recruited friends for
   D. successfully pulled
   E. failed to execute

2) Most people would consider _____ to be a rather *abhorrent* activity.
   A. kidnapping
   B. donating to charity
   C. running a marathon
   D. riding a bike
   E. dieting

3) The *sheer* amount of data everyone receives in modern society _____.
   A. can be overwhelming to absorb
   B. makes finding the truth much easier
   C. is minimal compared to the 19th century
   D. allows us to pursue daily life without worries
   E. causes panic among those who do not read

4) The pirate captain _____ in order to *appropriate* the treasure map.
   A. followed his superb nautical instincts
   B. sailed for days to the designated island
   C. attacked a rival captain's ship
   D. copied what he remembered from it
   E. ordered an immediate retreat from the battle

5) "Do you prefer *episodic* television, or would you rather _____?" asked Dad.
   A. hear about current events
   B. spend time watching comedies
   C. just watch a movie
   D. watch the installments weekly
   E. access reruns on the Internet

6) Officer Buller used _____ to *circumvent* sections of the highway experiencing traffic jams.
   A. his car's siren
   B. back roads
   C. extreme caution
   D. his car radio
   E. previous experience

7) Jack demonstrated his *overzealous* nature by _____.
   A. refusing to participate in sports
   B. forgetting his father's birthday
   C. training every morning for the race
   D. not speaking to his friends
   E. cheering far too excitedly

8) If a driver deliberately *deviates* from the route, he or she _____.
   A. believes the new one is better
   B. will definitely save a lot of time
   C. has stopped the car for a while
   D. will probably run out of gas
   E. must think something is wrong

Lesson 18 continued:

9) Mom avoided *obligations* as a parent by _____.
   A. running for a Board of Education position
   B. skipping parent-teacher conferences
   C. providing all meals for her children
   D. asking a parenting group for advice
   E. agreeing to coach her daughter's soccer team

11) From the _____ way Jerome speaks, I can tell just how *enamored* he is of his farm animals.
   A. hateful
   B. worried
   C. proud
   D. loving
   E. skeptical

10) Phylicia's *binge* on cake resulted in _____.
   A. her losing ten pounds
   B. a massive stomachache
   C. protests from her children
   D. her winning the baking contest
   E. a large mess in the kitchen

12) For a novice, one *imperative* in figure skating is _____.
   A. watching a professional fall down
   B. selecting the right music
   C. studying how to perform double axels
   D. knowing how to enjoy the experience
   E. putting the skates on securely

Lesson 18 continued:

Writing Practice

The following sentences contain words that are often misused. Choose the correct word in each sentence.

1) If you had to <u>imply</u> / <u>infer</u> something from his remarks, what would it be?

2) Sneaking around the neighborhood in the middle of the night carries certain <u>inferences</u> / <u>implications</u>, whether what you are doing is innocent or not.

3) Spend <u>fewer</u> / <u>less</u> time arguing and more time studying.

4) Marcy's great-grandfather <u>emigrated</u> / <u>immigrated</u> from Nazi Germany just a few months before Hitler came to power.

5) Before the presidential candidate chose Rosa Maguire as a running mate, the campaign looked at her entire resume and noted a years-old arrest for <u>elicit</u> / <u>illicit</u> conduct.

6) Hank received an A on his final, which <u>assured</u> / <u>ensured</u> his rank as valedictorian of his class.

7) Ted had <u>fewer</u> / <u>less</u> than eight coins in his pocket, and they totaled <u>less</u> / <u>fewer</u> money than he needed for the magazine.

8) Most <u>emigrants</u> / <u>immigrants</u> to foreign countries bring part of their culture with them.

9) He glanced at the girl out of the corner of his eye and <u>elicited</u> / <u>illicited</u> a smile from her.

10) The doctor <u>assured</u> / <u>ensured</u> Frieda that she would live to see her great grandchildren.

11) Let's not spread the rumor; we'll just keep it <u>among</u> /<u>between</u> you, me, and Kyle.

12) If I had to choose <u>among</u> / <u>between</u> the Stones and the Beatles, I'd say the Beatles were the better recording band, but the Stones certainly performed better live.

Lesson 18 continued:

Vocabulary: Choosing the Right Use

The following sentences contain vocabulary words used in the reading passage. Identify the sentence or sentences that use the italicized vocabulary word properly. We have changed the form of some vocabulary words to provide new contexts; for example, some adjectives and verbs have been used as nouns.

1) A. The only *deviation* in the game that the coach allowed was to play as hard as possible.
   B. An hour after we *deviated* from the directions on the map, everyone realized we were lost.
   C. Henry has not *deviated* from his daily routine of sit-ups and weightlifting in more than two years.
   D. One *deviation* that Leon cannot stand is his having to pay rent by check rather than online.

2) A. People who have succeeded say that it is *sheer* lunacy to attempt to canoe through those rapids.
   B. It took courage and *sheer* determination to board the airplane in order to overcome her fear of flying.
   C. Donald wanted to decorate his apartment with see-through curtains, but his wife objected in a *sheer* voice.
   D. During the debate, Arnold confronted his opponent with a clear example of how *sheer* her answer about nuclear power was.

3) A. Harvey thought he had hid his brother's present in a safe place, but it was too *conspicuous* a spot to stay hidden for long.
   B. The officer received a medal for having exhibited *conspicuous* courage in the line of duty.
   C. John's *conspicuous* behavior led his boss to believe that he was not telling the truth about who took the last donut.
   D. Mike brought his dog to the vet when he saw that she was acting *conspicuous*.

4) A. I took credit for the idea of completely eliminating cubicles, but I actually *appropriated* the concept from my previous job.
   B. Once Karl had *appropriated* the key to the car and filled the tank, we were able to leave the gas station.
   C. In the middle of the spy's belt was a hidden area, in which he could conceal the pictures he had *appropriated* on his own.
   D. The Clarkson family *appropriated* their vacation in Hawaii for two weeks.

5) A. As much as Heather wanted to go to the county fair, she had other *obligations* she had to see to first.
   B. After he was caught sneaking out of the house, Tom had to serve his *obligations* by whitewashing the fence.
   C. In response to the robbery, Mr. Kent threatened the unknown robber with *obligations* of charges that would lead to imprisonment.
   D. Rose is the treasurer of the honor society, so her *obligations* include taking and keeping track of who has paid their dues.

Lesson 18 continued:

6) A. From the way they looked on their trip to Hollywood, it was clear that the students had become *enamored* of the lifestyle of the stars.
    B. The starving boa constrictor saw the mouse and immediately felt *enamored* at the thought of a meal.
    C. I sent my girlfriend an anniversary card telling her how *enamored* I am with her.
    D. No one could have been more *enamored* by a simple test on geometry than I was yesterday.

7) A. The committee appreciates enthusiasm, but has warned some members not to become *overzealous* during protests in order to prevent chaos.
    B. Aaron's mom began collecting salt shakers as a hobby, but soon became a little *overzealous* and now has more than a thousand of them.
    C. Marty was *overzealous* with worry when his cat went missing, so the neighbors offered to help him look for her.
    D. Ginny dislikes *overzealous* police who seem to love giving out tickets.

8) A. Zane thought the scene where there aliens' ship blew up was *episodic* and he talked about it the whole ride home from the theater.
    B. Trish worries that certain videogames are too *episodic*, so she always reads the parental warning before buying one for her kids.
    C. Felicity prefers movies to the *episodic* nature of television series that make viewers wait a week for every new show.
    D. Doctors will prescribe medication for people trying to control their *episodic* mood swings.

9) A. Hillary *circumvented* to Lane that she needed his help immediately in order to move the large wardrobe.
    B. In order to *circumvent* that everything is going well, many cultures use a thumbs-up gesture.
    C. In order to *circumvent* any complications during the procedure, doctors decided to use a bypass machine for Adelaide's heart surgery.
    D. Fran *circumvented* Richard's success by throwing his test in the garbage before Ms. Phillips had graded it.

10) A. Professor Watkins posted a list of *imperatives* for students to follow in her class.
    B. The employees did not like the demanding and *imperative* manners of their new boss.
    C. Nothing is more important than being aware of your *imperatives* when hiking through the forest.
    D. The server nearly lost her patience with her *imperative* table of customers.

Lesson 18 continued:

11) A. Isaac immediately regretted *bingeing* on potato chips before dinner because he lost his appetite for the pizza his father brought home.

   B. Percy hoped his *binge* of swimming would help him win the tournament the following week.

   C. Even after telling herself she would not overeat, Heather could not help *bingeing* on the all-you-can-eat buffet.

   D. Rhonda's husband dropped the receipt when he saw how much she had spent on her *binge* of flowers at the market.

12) A. Hazel was *abhorrent* to the suggestion that she make dinner for the third time in a row.

   B. As punishment for the *abhorrent* crime, the prisoner was sentenced to life in prison without the chance of parole.

   C. Despite what happened last week with the other team, you cannot respond to their *abhorrent* treatment in the same way.

   D. Although pleased that he passed the class, Josh was still *abhorrent* by his overall grade.

Lesson 18 continued:

Synonyms and Antonyms

Match the word with its *antonym*.

1) conspicuous   **A.** lovable

2) enamored   **B.** rule

3) abhorrent   **C.** unnoticeable

4) imperative   **D.** repulsed

Match the word with its *synonym*.

5) circumvent   **E.** commitment

6) overzealous   **F.** spree

7) sheer   **G.** announcement

8) obligation   **H.** take

9) deviate   **I.** excitable

10) binge   **J.** stray

11) proclamation   **K.** bypass

12) appropriate   **L.** total

END
of
LESSON 18

Lesson 19

Questions 34–44 are based on the following passage.

— 1 —

[1] Daylight Saving Time (DST) has been part of human timekeeping { **34** } <u>to some degree, more or less, since</u> a man in New Zealand, George Hudson, proposed it. [2] Hudson collected insects and wanted an extra two hours of light to do so. [3] His collection of insects from all over the world is currently the largest in all of New Zealand. [4] His suggestion grew into the almost-worldwide acceptance of DST, but it was not until 1916 that two countries, Germany and Austria, actually implemented the idea. { **35** }

— 2 —

[1] During WWII, President Roosevelt **instituted** what was called "War Time," another name for DST, that lasted all year long. [2] Roosevelt's measure was intended to help save energy that was needed for the war effort. [3] In 1974, in another effort to save energy, President Nixon signed into law the Emergency Daylight Saving Time Energy Conservation Act. [4] Nixon's action was a result of an **embargo** of Middle Eastern oil. [5] In 1966, President Johnson signed the Uniform Time Act that standardized the practice of losing/gaining an hour in spring and fall, but if a state didn't want to participate in this national **uniformity**, it could back out of the Act simply by passing a state law. { **36** }

— 3 —

{ **37** } <u>Daylight Saving Time is begun by most of the United States at 2:00 am</u> on the second Sunday in March and stops on the first Sunday in November. The reason that two in the morning was chosen is that doing it at midnight, which is when laws go into effect and other changes happen, would mean Sunday would revert to Saturday for an hour. Long after DST was **initiated**, many parts of society use those specific dates for reasons unrelated to the time shift; for example, fire departments urge citizens to check fire alarm batteries when changing the time.

34

Select the best revision of the underlined portion of the sentence.
A) to some degree since
B) to more or less some degree since
C) to some degree—more or less—since
D) to some degree; more or less, since

35

Choose the sentence that is not necessary to paragraph 1 and could, therefore, be deleted without affecting the passage negatively.
A) sentence [1]
B) sentence [2]
C) sentence [3]
D) sentence [4]

36

Sentence 5 does not fit the logical flow of information in paragraph 2. Choose the best place in the paragraph to relocate the sentence.
A) before sentence [1]
B) before sentence [2]
C) before sentence [3]
D) before sentence [4]

37

Choose the best revision of the underlined portion of the sentence.
A) Daylight Saving Time, to most of the United States, is begun at 2:00 AM
B) Most of the United States begins Daylight Saving Time at 2:00 am
C) At 2:00 am, Daylight Saving Time is begun by most of the United States
D) Most of the United States begins Daylight Saving Time at two o'clock in the am

Lesson 19 continued:

— 4 —

[1] Many **rationales** have been used to explain how DST helps society, though some of these { **38** } <u>so-called</u> benefits have been shown to have no value. [2] Retail stores can sell more products if they stay open { **39** } <u>later, however</u> while the sun is still shining and people are still shopping. [3] Using less nighttime lighting saves on electric costs; modern electrical consumption, however, which uses power more efficiently, has generally negated that argument. [4] DST causes many problems with individual sleep patterns, with farming techniques, and with countries or states that do not conform to the switching of clocks back and forth. [5] Arizona and Hawaii do not use DST, while the other 48 states do. [6] If a person lives in Kingman, Arizona, and visits a relative in Needles, California, he or she takes an hour to drive there, but must remember that there is a one-hour time **differential**. [7] If that person returns home the next day, it involves an additional time change. [8] What will the person's smartphone or computer do about it? [9] Probably nothing, which would be the best thing; however, imagine if a woman were to give birth to twins just as the time changes in the fall. [10] One baby is born at 1:58 in the morning and the other one is born ten minutes later, at 1:08. [11] Therefore, the first one born is "younger" than the second. { **40** }

— 5 —

On the positive side, those arguing for the continuation of DST point to the fact that people will have an extra hour of daylight after work that they can use for leisure, spending time with the family, or doing things they couldn't do at night. People living in the North, South, or near the equator, aren't as { **41** } <u>effected</u> by DST as the middle **latitude** societies are because their workday is distorted either by the lack of sunlight in the North and South or because there is very little variation in the length of the day in countries near the equator. Researchers point out that there is great economic savings in Daylight Saving Time: In 1984, *Fortune* magazine estimated that an extension of DST would give convenience stores an estimated extra $30 million. A golf organization predicted that a seven-week extension would raise revenues $200 to $300 million. These financial gains would also apply to other leisure activities such as travel: The European Union's leisure **sector** estimates that such an extension would mean a 3% increase in revenues.

38

A) NO CHANGE
B) explicit
C) mentioned
D) included

39

A) NO CHANGE
B) later; but
C) later, especially
D) later, if

40

One of the sentences in paragraph 4 should be moved to paragraph 5. Identify the sentence that should be moved.

A) sentence 2, because it describes a benefit of DST
B) sentence 4, because it is written in the general style of paragraph 5
C) sentence 5, because it supports the argument of paragraph 5
D) sentence 8, because it provides the best conclusion to the pros and cons of DST

41

A) NO CHANGE
B) effective
C) impacted
D) affected

Lesson 19 continued:

— 6 —

By some measures, DST helps in the manufacturing of { 42 } Vitamin D which is a beneficial vitamin that may help circumvent depression or Seasonal Affective Disorder. On the other hand, National Geographic reported that heart attacks increase by 10% in the weeks after DST begins because of **disrupted** sleep patterns. A 2008 study found that suicide in men increased during that same time interval and then fell later, after the DST time adjustment. There is no disagreement, though, in the fact that traffic deaths are decreased by DST. A research paper on the topic showed that total fatalities would drop by 13% and fatalities among people inside their cars would be reduced by 3% during rush hours. These figures may seem **pedestrian**, but not if you are the one involved.

— 5 —

The greatest **discrepancy** in the debate over DST is energy consumption. A United States Department of Energy study found that DST could reduce the country's use of fossil fuel for energy by 1%. That may seem small, but in 2014, the country consumed over four quadrillion, one-hundred billion kilowatt hours (4,100,000,000,000 kWh), so the savings really would be significant. One year later, the US Bureau of Standards studied the issue and { 43 } concluded the contrary, there would be no savings. In Japan and Great Britain, similar sets of studies also produced different, contradictory results. A 2008 Department of Energy report concluded that DST saves fuel, but this, too, has been shown to be false. { 44 }

42

A) NO CHANGE
B) Vitamin D, which is
C) vitamin D, that is
D) vitamin D, which is

43

A) NO CHANGE
B) concluded the contrary, because there
C) concluded that there
D) came to the conclusion to the contrary; therefore, there

44

The writer wants to add a concluding sentence at the end of the passage. Select the most appropriate sentence for that purpose.
A) Truly, no one knows whether DST is a good idea or a bad idea.
B) With such inconsistent findings, it seems that the inconvenience of "spring forward; fall backward" is no longer justifiable.
C) In spite of so much proof that DST is not as beneficial as it is hoped to be, DST will last as long as people enjoy daylight.
D) There was not a good reason to institute DST in the past, and there is no good reason to keep it.

Lesson 19 continued:

Vocabulary: Context Answers

The following sentences contain vocabulary words used in the reading passage. Choose the answer that best completes the sentence. There may be more than one technically correct answer, but one will better exemplify the italicized vocabulary word than the others will.

1) "Which *sector* _____?" asked the freshman.
   A. of campus do you live in
   B. of college provides the best memories
   C. offers the most helpful guidance
   D. should I choose as a major
   E. is the primary biology building

2) After her graduate work, Francesca *instituted* _____ shelters for the homeless population.
   A. to a foreign country to construct
   B. friends to work with her in
   C. an organization that built
   D. about a man who maintained
   E. to an area that was full of

3) One *discrepancy* between Flora and Joe was that _____.
   A. they both took a yoga class
   B. one enjoyed jazz, and one hated it
   C. Flora once stole Joe's lawnmower
   D. Joe often bought Flora presents
   E. Joe's mother disliked Flora

4) Congress announced an *embargo* that _____.
   A. altered the boundaries of the country
   B. changed the way the US runs elections
   C. justified his role as president
   D. banned trade with Communist countries
   E. created numerous new trading opportunities

5) What could possibly be your *rationale* _____?
   A. about how great your favorite team played
   B. for accidentally getting there late
   C. while you were at the movies
   D. if you have a great deal of work to do.
   E. for having wasted all this time

6) Countries in the far southern *latitudes* are quite _____, according to the world traveler who visited our class.
   A. humid
   B. tropical
   C. frigid
   D. dangerous
   E. lush

7) The cult issued a decree for all members to _____ in order to promote *uniformity*.
   A. openly express themselves
   B. live in separate houses
   C. earn a living wage
   D. vote in an election
   E. wear the same outfit

8) Jim, a great soccer player, watched the *pedestrian* _____.
   A. as she taped up his ankle
   B. stadium during the snow storm
   C. amateurs handle the ball
   D. fans take their seats
   E. rain, which might cancel the game

Lesson 19 continued:

9) "Did you see any *differential* between the two experimental trials, or _____?" asked the scientist.
   A. did you work on them alone
   B. were the trials successful
   C. did all go as planned
   D. were the reactions dissimilar
   E. were they exactly the same

11) After *initiating* karate classes, Mr. Kuo _____.
   A. first taught young students the basics
   B. sold the studio where they had been held
   C. felt that he had truly mastered the art
   D. told his students not to practice at home
   E. believed a returning student was excellent

10) The only thing that *disrupted* my lunch _____.
   A. occurred when I was done
   B. was that the food was cold
   C. didn't bother me at all
   D. was a loud noise from outside
   E. was an extra hour of free time

Lesson 9 continued:

Writing Practice

The following sentences contain words that are often misused. Choose the correct word in each sentence.

1) I allow my dog to walk off leash because I have explicit / implicit trust that when I whistle, she'll stop what she's doing and run back to me.

2) Which object is farther / further from the sun, Jupiter or Neptune? I always get the two confused.

3) The city couldn't expand much more, so, instead, it began raising / rising the heights of its tallest buildings little by little every year.

4) Charlotte exclaimed, "What an obedient puppy! You've had him only a month, and he'll already set / sit on command."

5) "Lay / Lie your head down, and mommy will tell you a bedtime story." I swear that was what she'd say every night, up until I was about eight.

6) Jess could have been more explicit / implicit about her family's money if she had simply said, "We're rich," but that type of bragging isn't her style.

7) During their argument, the wife pleaded, "Please don't push me any farther / further, or I'll probably start to scream at you and say things I'll regret."

8) At three in the morning, the sergeant entered the barracks, and the soldiers had to raise / rise out of their bunks immediately for a five-mile run.

9) After trying four different places, Jane finally asked the movers, "Could you please set / sit the piano over there in the corner?"

10) I know it's not true, but Larry has laid / lain in that same position for so long that I'm beginning to think he died there.

11) I couldn't really tell much difference between the way the plot was developed in the book and it's / its development in the movie, but it's / its a shame that the acting was so poor.

12) Jason wanted to spend sometimes / some time / sometime with his kids, but work kept him away; sometimes / some time / sometime next year, he'll take a vacation.

13) Most self-help books advice / advise you to leave time for everyday / every day things like spending time just sitting and relaxing.

Lesson 19 continued:

Vocabulary: Choosing the Right Use

The following sentences contain vocabulary words used in the reading passage. Identify the sentence or sentences that use the italicized vocabulary word properly. We have changed the form of some vocabulary words to provide new contexts; for example, some adjectives and verbs have been used as nouns.

1) A. The fire alarm *disrupted* the convention, and everyone was forced to evacuate.
   B. Despite being interrupted by her siblings while studying, Angela did well on her test, *disrupting* her already flawless grade point average.
   C. Kelsey *disrupted* her dogs' eating pattern by ensuring that she fed them at the same time every day.
   D. Ms. Greene would not tolerate any student who *disrupted* her class: She sent obnoxious students straight to the main office.

2) A. If Allison could develop a plan for concluding the conversation, she felt sure that *initiating* the discussion would be easy.
   B. Andre *initiated* the information by mistyping his password into the computer.
   C. Debbie *initiated* a debate between Hiro and Logan by asking a controversial question that sparked a heated conversation.
   D. Using her key, Zoey *initiated* her car and pulled out her open duffel bag carefully in order to avoid spilling its contents.

3) A. The principal gave the students unprecedented *latitude*, even banning trips to the restroom.
   B. In the 16th century, many sailing ships became trapped in southern *latitudes* because there was no wind.
   C. Will was given strict *latitude* by his parents when they left for vacation: he could not even have friends come over.
   D. Mr. Fredricks's *latitude* meant that his students would have extra homework on Thursday.

4) A. Kevin, Haley's manager, noticed the *discrepancies* between Haley's scheduled hours and her time card.
   B. Quan immediately reported *discrepancies* on his bill to the credit card company so that he would not be charged for fraudulent purchases.
   C. No one considered cheating in class a serious *discrepancy*.
   D. *Discrepancies* in their stories ensured George and Michael's release because the alibis were exactly the same.

Lesson 19 continued:

5) A. *Uniformity* was important to Imogene as she created signs for her new business; she wanted them to be as consistent as possible.

B. Janine's opinions were very different than those of her classmates, but she refused *uniformity*.

C. Citizens were annoyed by the complete *uniformity* of the candidates' viewpoints on complicated issues.

D. *Uniformity* ensures that no superior solutions will be heard, so those who think differently should speak out.

6) A. Wally's paper, though well-organized, focused on *pedestrian* intricacies rather than the larger consequences of economic recessions.

B. Critics said that the new art exhibit was *pedestrian*, but its visitors thought it was lively and original.

C. Pierre drew on too many sources, restating their opinions, resulting in a *pedestrian*, repetitive speech.

D. While her friends often found Henrietta's *pedestrian* attitude annoying, her detail-oriented organizational skills could be helpful.

7) A. Because of the *embargo*, products like coffee and chocolate were very difficult to find.

B. When the rope snapped, the bucket fell into the deep, dark *embargo* of the well.

C. The school choir placed an *embargo* on any food from the rival bake sale in the chorus room.

D. Though the Neave family knew that the cave was safe, they could not help feeling as if they were traveling farther and farther into an endless *embargo*.

8) A. The state legislature *instituted* a new ban on e-cigarette use in public places, like stores and restaurants.

B. In the students' eyes, Mr. Jameson *institutes* Isabel and Esther's arguments by letting them sit together during class.

C. Beverly unknowingly *instituted* a fight between her other two siblings over who could use the computer.

D. Emma *instituted* a new club at school, dedicated to raising money for victims of natural disasters overseas.

9) A. Lab reports in chemistry class required a section explaining students' *rationale* for conducting the experiment in the way that they did.

B. The tsunami was cited as a *rationale* for the sudden famine in Pacific island nations.

C. The *rationale* of students' failing grades was clearly their reluctance to complete their homework on time.

D. After Evelyn explained the *rationale* behind her controversial decision, her parents accepted her seemingly illogical plan.

Lesson 19 continued:

10) A. The *sector* nearest to the post office had a cemetery and a large bell tower.

B. The local politician was praised for his outstanding work in the public *sector*, while the opposing candidate was criticized for his career in business.

C. One *sector* of the neighborhood was protected by a gate, while the rest of the town was easily accessible.

D. Since they were young, the Gallagher children had always attended the local *sector* on Sunday mornings.

11) A. Josephine disliked that her father gave her and her siblings *differential* chores based on their age and gender.

B. Cassidy would not tolerate *differential* treatment simply because her grades were not as high as her classmates' grades.

C. When Rei threatened to quit her job, her employers gave her a raise because she is *differential* to the company.

D. *Differential* information was missing from the files that the detective needed to continue working on the case.

Lesson 19 continued:

Synonyms and Antonyms

Match the word with its *antonym*.

1) disrupt   **A.** similarity

2) uniformity   **B.** sustain

3) initiate   **C.** inconsistency

4) differential   **D.** terminate

Match the word with its *synonym*.

5) latitude   **E.** reasoning

6) institute   **F.** boring

7) embargo   **G.** mistake

8) sector   **H.** division

9) pedestrian   **I.** ban

10) rationale   **J.** establish

11) discrepancy   **K.** line

END of LESSON 19

Lesson 20

Essay

The optional essay portion of the 2016 SAT allocates 50 minutes to read a short passage and respond with a well-organized analytical essay based on observations of the passage (no opinions or personal experiences—all the information needed to write the essay will be contained within the passage).

Three criteria of the essay will be scored: reading, analysis, and writing. After completing an essay, evaluate your writing using the scoring guide provided on pages 196-197.

Prompt

Choose one of the two passages from **Lesson 15** and reread it.

As you read the passage, consider how the author uses the following elements:

- **evidence** – the use of facts, examples, data, research, etc., to support claims

- **reasoning** – the development of ideas and the connection of evidence in support of the argument

- **style** – persuasive language, word choice, emotional appeals, and figurative language that add power to ideas

Write an essay in which you explain how the author builds an argument to persuade his audience of his point about work or wealth. In your essay, analyze how the author uses one or more of the elements listed above to strengthen the logic and persuasiveness of his argument. Be sure that your analysis focuses on the most relevant features of the passage.

Your essay should not explain whether you agree with the author's claims, but rather how the author builds an argument to persuade his audience.

SAT Power Prep: Summit
Essay Scoring Guide*

Points	Reading	Analysis	Writing
4	- demonstrates thorough comprehension of the source text - shows an understanding of the text's central idea(s) and of most important details and how they interrelate, demonstrating a comprehensive understanding of the text - free of errors of fact or interpretation with regard to the text - skillful use of textual evidence (quotations, paraphrases, or both), demonstrating a complete understanding of the source text	- offers an insightful analysis of the source text and demonstrates a sophisticated understanding of the analytical task - offers a thorough, well-considered evaluation of the author's use of evidence, reasoning, stylistic and persuasive elements, and feature(s) of the student's own choosing - contains relevant, sufficient, and strategically chosen support for claim(s) or point(s) made - focuses consistently on those features of the text that are most relevant to addressing the task	- cohesive and demonstrates a highly effective use and command of language - includes a precise central claim - includes a skillful introduction and conclusion - demonstrates a deliberate and highly effective progression of ideas both within paragraphs and throughout the essay - has a wide variety in sentence structures - demonstrates a consistent use of precise word choice; the response maintains a formal style and objective tone. - shows a strong command of the conventions of standard written English and is free or virtually free of errors
3	- demonstrates effective comprehension of the source text - shows an understanding of the text's central idea(s) and important details - free of substantive errors of fact and interpretation with regard to the text - makes appropriate use of textual evidence (quotations, paraphrases, or both), demonstrating an understanding of the source text	- offers an effective analysis of the source text and demonstrates an understanding of the analytical task - competently evaluates the author's use of evidence, reasoning, and/or stylistic and persuasive elements, and/or feature(s) of the student's own choosing - contains relevant and sufficient support for claim(s) or point(s) made - focuses primarily on those features of the text that are most relevant to addressing the task	- is mostly cohesive and demonstrates effective use and control of language - includes a central claim or implicit controlling idea - includes an effective introduction and conclusion; demonstrates a clear progression of ideas both within paragraphs and throughout the essay - includes variety in sentence structures; demonstrates some precise word choice; maintains a formal style and objective tone - shows a good control of the conventions of standard written English and is free of significant errors that detract from the quality of writing

*Adapted from materials appearing on www.collegeboard.com, the official website of the College Board

SAT Power Prep: Summit

Essay Scoring Guide continued:

Points	Reading	Analysis	Writing
2	- demonstrates some comprehension of the source text - shows an understanding of the text's central idea(s) but not of important details - may contain errors of fact and/or interpretation with regard to the text - makes limited and/or haphazard use of textual evidence (quotations, paraphrases, or both), demonstrating some understanding of the source text	- offers limited analysis of the source text and demonstrates only partial understanding of the analytical task - identifies and attempts to describe the author's use of evidence, reasoning, and/or stylistic and persuasive elements, and/or feature(s) of the student's own choosing, but merely asserts rather than explains their importance, or one or more aspects of the response's analysis are unwarranted based on the text - contains little or no support for claim(s) or point(s) made - may lack a clear focus on those features of the text that are most relevant to addressing the task	- demonstrates little or no cohesion and limited skill in the use and control of language - may lack a clear central claim or controlling idea, or may deviate from the claim or idea over the course of the response - may include an ineffective introduction and/or conclusion; may demonstrate some progression of ideas within paragraphs but not throughout the response - has limited variety in sentence structures; sentence structures may be repetitive. - demonstrates general or vague word choice; word choice may be repetitive; may deviate noticeably from a formal style and objective tone - shows a limited control of the conventions of standard written English and contains errors that detract from the quality of writing and may impede understanding
1	- demonstrates little or no comprehension of the source text - fails to show an understanding of the text's central idea(s), and may include only details without reference to central idea(s) - may contain numerous errors of fact and/or interpretation with regard to the text - makes little or no use of textual evidence (quotations, paraphrases, or both), demonstrating little or no understanding of the source text	- offers little or no analysis or ineffective analysis of the source text and demonstrates little or no understanding of the analytic task - identifies without explanation some aspects of the author's use of evidence, reasoning, and/or stylistic and persuasive elements, and/or feature(s) of the student's choosing, or numerous aspects of the response's analysis are unwarranted based on the text - contains little or no support for claim(s) or point(s) made, or support is largely irrelevant - may not focus on features of the text that are relevant to addressing the task - offers no discernible analysis (e.g., is largely or exclusively a summary)	- demonstrates little or no cohesion and inadequate skill in the use and control of language - may lack a clear central claim or controlling idea - lacks a recognizable introduction and conclusion; does not have a discernible progression of ideas - lacks variety in sentence structures; sentence structures may be repetitive; demonstrates general and vague word choice; word choice may be poor or inaccurate; may lack a formal style and objective tone - shows a weak control of the conventions of standard written English and may contain numerous errors that undermine the quality of writing

Vocabulary Terms

Vocabulary Note: Especially archaic words or technical terms such as "metabolite," "mole," and "half-life," appear in the glossary to facilitate reading; however, they do not appear in lesson exercises.

Lesson 1

antagonistic	*adj.*	hostile; working against
circumlocution	*n.*	the use of evasive and unnecessary language to explain something
concoct	*v.*	to make up; to create
consummation	*n.*	the completion or fulfillment of something
curt	*adj.*	rudely brief and to the point
deprecate	*v.*	to belittle; to find fault with
engender	*v.*	to cause; to bring about
faculty	*n.*	a capability of the body or mind
fathom	*v.*	to understand
gradation	*n.*	a stage or phase of development
impel	*v.*	to drive something or someone to action
impetuous	*adj.*	with little thought
impulse	*n.*	a compelling drive to act or feel a certain way
innate	*adj.*	belonging to the basic nature of; arising from within
laconic	*adj.*	using few words to communicate
meditate	*v.*	to consider thoughtfully or reflect deeply
mortification	*n.*	humiliation
obtrude	*v.*	to intrude or interfere
paradoxical	*adj.*	contradictory
petulance	*n.*	impatience and irritability
precipice	*n.*	the peak of a dangerous situation
propensity	*n.*	a natural inclination or feeling
prostrate	*v.*	to throw oneself down on the ground
sentiment	*n.*	a feeling or attitude toward something
sophistry	*n.*	a deliberately false or misleading argument
swoon	*n.*	a fainting spell
thoroughfare	*n.*	a street

Lesson 2

abrasion	*n.*	the rubbing off or scraping
advocate	*n.*	a supporter
capacitor	*n.*	a device that builds up and temporarily stores an electrical charge
composite	*n.*	something, especially a material, made up of two or more distinct parts
comprise	*v.*	to be made up of; to contain

Usage Note: Traditionally, the whole comprises the parts, e.g., the United States comprises fifty states.

conductivity	*n.*	the ability of a substance to conduct or transmit electrical or heat energy
conduit	*n.*	a channel or way of transmitting
copious	*adj.*	large in quantity; plentiful
electron	*n.*	a negatively charged particle that orbits the nucleus of an atom
geodesic	*adj.*	using interlocking shapes to form a curved dome structure

Lesson 2 continued

geostationary	*adj.*	orbiting Earth at the same direction and speed at which Earth rotates, so as to always be over the same spot on Earth
hypothetical	*adj.*	existing as an idea only; supposed
infuse	*v.*	to put into or fill with something
lattice	*n.*	a structure made of crisscross strips of material
nanotube	*n.*	a cylinder-shaped structure made from connected carbon molecules
nuclear	*adj.*	(1) pertaining to the nucleus of an atom (2) pertaining to the use of atomic energy
practical	*adj.*	useful; easy to understand
resiliency	*n.*	the ability to recover or return to the original form
tensile	*adj.*	pertaining to the capability of being stretched out under stress
transistor	*n.*	a device that controls the flow of electric current by either switching or amplifying the current
ubiquitous	*adj.*	existing everywhere
valence	*n.*	the potential to combine with something, especially another atom or chemical element

Lesson 3

amicability	*n.*	friendliness and goodwill
appeal	*n.*	a request for a court's decision to be reconsidered
blight	*n.*	disease; decay
capricious	*adj.*	changing unpredictably
convent	*n.*	a building that houses a community of women, usually nuns, devoted to religious life
court martial	*n.*	a trial conducted by a court of military personnel
defector	*n.*	a person who abandons his or her allegiance to something
disaffected	*adj.*	angry and disloyal
exorbitant	*adj.*	excessive
expatriate	*n.*	a person who has withdrawn allegiance from his or her native country
gallows	*n.*	a wooden apparatus used to execute people by hanging
obscurity	*n.*	a state of being unknown or forgotten
prospect	*n.*	the expectation of something advantageous
rampant	*adj.*	moving quickly through a population unchecked
regiment	*n.*	a large unit of soldiers, usually containing multiple battalions

Lesson 4

biochemical	*adj.*	pertaining to the chemistry of living organisms
compound	*n.*	a substance consisting of two or more parts or ingredients
	v.	to make worse by adding something
derivative	*adj.*	copied or adapted from a different source; not original
	n.	something taken from an original source; a copy of something else
metabolite	*n.*	a substance produced chemically during an organism's living processes, such as producing energy from food and creating substances needed for life
myriad	*n.*	a great number; things that are nearly uncountable
	adj.	innumerable
pathogen	*n.*	an agent that produces disease, especially a virus or bacterium
pharmaceutical	*adj.*	pertaining to the production or manufacture of drugs and medicine
phylum	*n.*	a collection of organisms with certain shared characteristics, more specific than kingdom, but not as specific as order
retrovirus	*n.*	a virus which, unlike a typical virus that injects DNA into host cells, injects RNA into host cells to create new DNA, which then creates clones of the retrovirus
shingles	*n.*	a disease causing painful rashes on the skin
solvent	*n.*	a substance that can dissolve another substance
symbiosis	*n.*	a mutually beneficial relationship between two people or things
synthesize	*v.*	to create something new by combining smaller parts or elements
systemic	*adj.*	affecting the whole body
virus	*n.*	a pathogen that infects a living host by inserting its genetic material (usually DNA) into host cells, causing them to produce clones of the virus

Lesson 5

aggressor	*n.*	someone who initiates hostility
belligerent	*n.*	a participant in war
caste	*n.*	a social group determined by rank, job, wealth, or any other distinction
elite	*n.*	(1) a group of people who are powerful, influential, or have superior abilities (2) superior, of high quality
enunciate	*v.*	to announce or declare clearly
furor	*n.*	an outburst of rage
holocaust	*n.*	an act of complete destruction or death
ideology	*n.*	a body of beliefs
imperial	*adj.*	pertaining to empires or the rule of an emperor
implication	*n.*	something that is suggested without directly having been said

Lesson 5 continued

indulge	*v.*	to surrender to one's desire
insidious	*adj.*	deceitful in a subtle way; gradually harmful
manifestation	*n.*	the materialization of something
plowshare	*n.*	the cutting edge of a plow
plutocracy	*n.*	a government in which the wealthy rule
posture	*n.*	a position or attitude
predecessor	*n.*	someone or something that came before another
provocation	*n.*	something that instigates or causes anger
régime	*n.*	a particular governing administration
republic	*n.*	a form of government in which the people hold the power and elect officials to rule within the limits of law or a constitution
statesmanship	*n.*	skill in managing public affairs, nationally or internationally

Lesson 6

caucus	*n.*	a meeting of a group of members from a specific political party
jockey	*v.*	to seek an advantage
herald	*v.*	to announce, especially the arrival of something
inconspicuous	*adj.*	not easily noticed
inflation	*n.*	a loss in the value of currency, which causes prices to increase
primary	*n.*	an election in which voters choose the candidates who will run for office
protracted	*adj.*	lengthened in time; drawn-out
pundit	*n.*	a person who offers opinions or criticism about a subject, often politics
speculate	*v.*	to guess the results based on incomplete facts

Lesson 7

ambiguous	*adj.*	having more than one possible meaning
albeit	*conj.*	although; even though
auditory	*adj.*	pertaining to the ear or the sense of hearing
dominant	*adj.*	having the most power or control
gaping	*adj.*	open wide
inclination	*n.*	a tendency to do a certain thing or act in a certain way
millennium	*n.*	a thousand years
phenomenon	*n.*	a strange, extraordinary occurrence
posit	*v.*	to present a fact or assumption, often as the basis for an argument
	n.	a fact or assumption offered for the basis for an argument
psychosis	*n.*	a mental disorder in which the victim distorts or loses contact with reality
subliminal	*adj.*	existing or occurring without the awareness of the conscious mind

Lesson 8

adept	*adj.*	skilled
clinical	*adj.*	(1) concerning the treatment of patients
		(2) direct and impersonal; unemotional
competence	*n.*	the ability or skill to complete a task
comprehensive	*adj.*	including everything; broad in scope
cortex	*n.*	the outer region of an organ or body part
diagnosis	*n.*	an analysis of a condition or situation that requires a solution, such as illness
doctorate	*n.*	the highest attainable academic degree
fellow	*n.*	(1) an associate having a similar job or background
		(2) a person in an advanced study or training program
gene	*n.*	the basic unit of heredity made up of DNA that determines a physical characteristic of a living organism
impediment	*n.*	(1) an obstruction
		(2) a defect or disorder
natal	*adj.*	pertaining to birth
neurology	*n.*	the study of nerves and the nervous system
pathology	*n.*	the study of disease and its causes
prerequisite	*adj.*	needed before moving on; required beforehand
relapse	*v.*	to return to a previous condition or habit
	n.	a return to a previous condition or habit

Lesson 9

abnormality	*n.*	an irregularity
affliction	*n.*	a state or cause of suffering or distress
anomaly	*n.*	a thing or event that is out of the ordinary; an irregularity
calamitous	*adj.*	causing sudden damage and distress; disastrous
cognizance	*n.*	awareness; knowledge of
deteriorate	*v.*	to weaken and wear away
neuron	*n.*	a cell in the nervous system that transfers electrical impulses
plaque	*n.*	a built-up or deposited unwanted substance, often on teeth, skin, or other body parts
prevalence	*n.*	the state of being widespread and common
prone	*adj.*	having a tendency to; inclined

Lesson 11

battery	*n.*	a fortified structure, usually for the placement of defensive artillery
cataract	*n.*	a waterfall
consign	*v.*	(1) to set aside for a special purpose
		(2) to place in the care of another
dale	*n.*	a valley
decoction	*n.*	a medicine or flavoring created by extracting a substance by boiling it
flourish	*n.*	a stylish or fancy gesture or embellishment
idolatrous	*adj.*	showing excessive admiration
indignity	*n.*	a humiliating insult or injury
infliction	*n.*	a punishment; suffering
insular	*adj.*	closed to new ideas; narrow-minded
Manhattoes	*n.*	the Native American people who inhabited what is now Manhattan, the center of New York City
metaphysical	*adj.*	pertaining to unprovable theories and ideas about reality, existence, and imagination
mole	*n.*	a stone wall built to protect a harbor
plumb	*adv.*	(1) completely; utterly
		(2) perfectly vertical
reverie	*n.*	a reflection or meditation, usually pleasant
salt	*n.*	an old, experienced person, especially a sailor
spar	*n.*	a wooden pole from which a ship's sail hangs
Stoics	*n.*	ancient Greeks who believed in abstaining from emotion and worldly pains and pleasures
urbane	*adj.*	elegant and polite

Lesson 12

compromise	*v.*	(1) to weaken or reduce in value
		(2) to expose to a hazard or risk; to make vulnerable
		(3) to settle a dispute by giving up something (on both sides)
critical	*adj.*	(1) important; crucial
		(2) the point at which a sudden change occurs
depleted	*adj.*	worn-out; reduced in supply or number
diminish	*v.*	to make or to become less; to reduce
duration	*n.*	a length of time
fission	*n.*	the act of splitting into parts, especially heavy elements into two lighter elements accompanied by a release of energy
half-life	*n.*	the time required for half the atoms of a radioactive substance to disintegrate
neutron	*n.*	one of the three basic particles that make up an atom (electron, proton, neutron), and has no electrical charge
radioactive	*adj.*	emitting energy and particles from an atomically unstable source
reactor	*n.*	a device in which nuclear fission is sustained to produce power

Lesson 12 continued

repository	*n.*	a place where things are deposited for safekeeping
proximity	*n.*	nearness in relation to something else

Lesson 13

anthology	*n.*	a collection of selected writings
commercial	*adj.*	pertaining to goods produced for profit, usually in large quantity
didactic	*adj.*	having educational or moral value
genre	*n.*	a category of art or literature based on its style, physical form, or type of content
grueling	*adj.*	exhaustingly difficult
longevity	*n.*	a long life
metaphor	*n.*	a figure of speech in which one thing is used to represent something else
paranormal	*adj.*	pertaining to things or events that defy scientific explanation, especially psychic or supernatural activity
scathing	*adj.*	severe; harmful
serialize	*v.*	to publish in installments
transcendentalist	*adj.*	valuing intuitive and imaginative independence over tradition or scientific knowledge
Victorian	*adj.*	pertaining to life and ideas during the time around Queen Victoria's reign of England, roughly 1840 to 1900

Lesson 14

binary	*adj.*	having two parts; pertaining to a two-part system
configuration	*n.*	the arrangement of parts
convection	*n.*	the transfer of heat through the movement of heated molecules
crust	*n.*	the outermost layer of the earth
fissure	*n.*	a long, narrow crack
fracking	*n.*	the process of releasing oil or natural gas from underground rocks by injecting the rocks with liquid, causing the rock to fracture
geothermal	*adj.*	pertaining to the internal heat of the earth
geyser	*n.*	a hot spring that emits water and steam
gradient	*n.*	(1) the rate at which a quantity changes in response to changes made upon it (2) a regular rate of change in color, temperature, etc.
implement	*v.*	to put into action; to make use of
magma	*n.*	molten rock within the earth's crust
mantle	*n.*	the layer of the earth between the (outermost) crust and the (innermost) core
optimize	*v.*	to make the best use of something
permeable	*adj.*	capable of being passed through or penetrated

Lesson 14 continued

predominant	*adj.*	main; paramount
primordial	*adj.*	existing from the earliest stage
seismic	*adj.*	pertaining to earthquakes or vibrations of the earth
turbine	*n.*	a machine with a rotor driven by a moving fluid (gas or liquid), for the purpose of converting energy to mechanical power

Lesson 15

bequeath	*v.*	to pass on one's wealth or possessions
coarse	*adj.*	harsh; rough
coffer	*n.*	a supply or store of money
confer	*v.*	to bestow; to grant
cultivate	*v.*	to grow or promote the growth of something
deplore	*v.*	to disapprove of strongly; to condemn
depreciate	*v.*	(1) to reduce the value of something (2) to decrease in value
desperation	*n.*	total hopelessness and defeat
encumbrance	*n.*	a burden
extol	*v.*	to praise
folly	*n.*	a foolish action
graduated	*adj.*	increasing by levels of measurement
gratuitous	*adj.*	given for nothing in return; free
insolvent	*adj.*	unable to pay one's debts
monarchy	*n.*	a government ruled by inherited position, usually by a king or queen
pecuniary	*adj.*	pertaining to money
penance	*n.*	a punishment undertaken to atone for one's sins
posthumous	*adj.*	occurring after death
privy	*adj.*	(1) private; hidden (2) sharing in the knowledge of something secret or private
resignation	*n.*	unresisting acceptance; submission
retainer	*n.*	(1) a servant or devoted employee (2) a fee paid in advance for a service, especially that of a lawyer
salutary	*adj.*	wholesome; beneficial to health
serf	*n.*	a person bound to serve a nobleman, usually as a farmer or servant
squalor	*n.*	filth and misery
subdue	*v.*	to win control of; to overcome
thwart	*v.*	to prevent from happening

Lesson 16

augment	v.	to increase or make larger in size or quantity, usually by adding to
clothier	n.	a store or person that sells clothing
connote	v.	to suggest or imply a second, or less obvious, meaning for something
exemplify	v.	to show as an example
inhibit	v.	to hold back; to restrain
literally	adv.	actually; without exaggeration
minimalist	adj.	characterized by simplicity or the bare minimum
par	adj.	average
	n.	an equality with something or someone
prognostication	n.	prediction based on signs or clues
relegate	v.	to assign to an inferior rank or status
wane	v.	to decrease

Lesson 17

allegorical	adj.	using characters or events in fiction to represent certain ideas or values
cognitive	adj.	pertaining to the mental processes involved in awareness and thinking
decry	v.	to denounce openly; to condemn
disengage	v.	to free oneself from a connection
escapist	adj.	avoiding reality by focusing on imagination or entertainment
extrapolate	v.	to guess by reasoning further about what is already known
foster	v.	to nurture; to help grow or develop
realism	n.	the portrayal of things as they actually are in the physical world
repressive	adj.	maintaining total control through use of fear or force
totalitarian	adj.	ruling with absolute control, often through use of fear and force
trite	adj.	overused; banal

Lesson 18

abhorrent	adj.	detestable; terrible
appropriate	v.	(1) to take for one's own use, especially without permission
		(2) to set aside for a specific purpose
binge	n.	a period of excessive indulgence
	v.	to consume without restraint
circumvent	v.	to avoid by maneuvering around; to bypass
conspicuous	adj.	noticeable; obvious
deviate	v.	to depart from the expected direction, course of action, or behavior
enamored	adj.	filled with love for
episodic	adj.	divided into a series of connected parts
imperative	n.	a rule that requires certain action
	adj.	extremely important
overzealous	adj.	showing excessive devotion or enthusiasm
obligation	n.	a duty or responsibility
proclamation	n.	a public announcement
sheer	adj.	(1) completely so; total
		(2) so steep as to be perpendicular

Lesson 19

differential	n.	the difference between two similar things
discrepancy	n.	a conflict between expectation and result; an obvious error or oversight
disrupt	v.	to cause a stop in progress
embargo	n.	a restriction on trade or commerce
initiate	v.	to begin; to start
institute	v.	to establish officially
latitude	n.	(1) the distance, on Earth, measured north or south of the equator, represented by horizontal lines on a map
		(2) freedom from restriction
pedestrian	adj.	dull and common
	n.	a person walking
rationale	n.	the reasoning or logic behind a decision or a belief
sector	n.	a specialized division or part
uniformity	n.	a state of overall sameness; consistency